Progress to Proficiency

New Edition

Teacher's Book

Progress to Proficiency

New Edition
Teacher's Book

Leo Jones

CAMBRIDGE
UNIVERSITY PRESS

Published by the Press Syndicate of the University of Cambridge
The Pitt Building, Trumpington Street, Cambridge CB2 1RP
40 West 20th Street, New York, NY 10011-4211, USA
10 Stamford Road, Oakleigh, Melbourne 3166, Australia

© Cambridge University Press 1986, 1993

First published 1986
Eighth printing 1992
Second edition 1993

Printed in Great Britain
at the University Printing House, Cambridge

ISBN 0 521 42574 3 Teacher's Book
ISBN 0 521 42575 1 Student's Book
ISBN 0 521 42542 5 Set of 3 cassettes

Contents

Contents

Thanks

I'd like to thank everyone who generously gave their advice and made comments and suggestions which have helped to shape this New Edition of *Progress to Proficiency*.

Heartfelt thanks to Jeanne McCarten, who started the ball rolling and kept the project moving along. Her discerning ideas and wise advice encouraged me to incorporate countless improvements.

Thanks to the teachers who provided feedback on the first edition:
Craig Andrew, C.A.R.E.L., Royan   Liz Charbit, Geos Academy, Hove
Anne Cosker, MPT Harteloire, Brest   Marina Donald & Margery Sanderson,
Stevenson College, Edinburgh   Shirley Downs, British Institute, Rome
Brian Edmonds, British Institute, Paris   Hilary Glasscock &
Jenny Henderson, Cambridge Centre for Advanced English   Cecilia Holcomb,
Scanbrit School of English, Bournemouth   Ian Jasper, British Council,
Bilbao   Anne Koulourioti & Ourania Petrakis, Asimenia Featham School of
English, Rethymnon, Crete   Sheila Levy, Cambridge Academy of English
Vicki Lynwoodlast, English Language Centre, Hove   P.L. Nelson-Xarhoulakou,
Athens   Steve Norman, Cambridge School, Barcelona   Bruce Pye, VHS
Spracheninstitut, Nuremberg   Michael Roche, Academia de Idiomas Modernas,
Valladolid   Cristina Sanjuan Alvarez, Escuela Oficial de Idiomas, Zaragoza
Jennie Weldon, The English Centre, Eastbourne

I'm particularly grateful to everyone who wrote detailed reports on the first edition, and recommended particular improvements and changes:
Margaret Bell, International House, London   Jennie Henderson, Cambridge
Centre for Advanced English   Ruth Jimack, British Council, Athens   Jill
Mountain, British Institute, Rome   Clare West, English Language Centre, Hove

The New Edition was greatly enriched with ideas, criticisms and suggestions from:
Ruth Jimack   Jenny Johnson   Rosie McAndrew   Laura Matthews
Pam Murphy   Jill Neville   Madeline Oliphant   Alison Silver
Bertha Weighill   Clare West

And thanks to the following people for their contributions and assistance:

Peter Taylor, who devoted so much time and effort to collecting the authentic interviews, who produced the studio recordings and edited all the recorded material, with the help of Peter, Leon, Andy and Di at Studio AVP.

Thanks

The actors who took part in the studio recordings, and who talked about their own experiences and attitudes:
    Ishia Bennison   Tim Bentinck   Amanda Carlton   Elaine Claxton
    Charles Collingwood   Karen Craig   Rupert Farley
    Michael Fitzpatrick   Gordon Griffin   Tim Monro   Jacqui Reddin
    Anne Rosenfeld   Chris Scott   Kerry Shale   Ken Shanley
    Coralyn Sheldon   Steve Tomkinson

The people who generously agreed to be interviewed:
    Steve Abbott   Fiona Bristow   Vince Cross   Ray Gambell
    Kate Gooch   Abdulrazak Gurnah   Stephen and Susan Hill
    Amanda Hooper   Karen Lewis   Christine Massey   Alastair Miller
    Jilly Pearson   David Reindorp   Sarah Springman   Lisa Wood

Lindsay White who coordinated the production of the book with friendly aplomb, tact and skill

Amanda Ogden for her impeccable, resourceful work on researching the photographs, cartoons and reading texts

Ruth Carim for proof-reading the material so carefully

Nick Newton for his tasteful ideas for the design of the book

Peter Ducker for his stylish, meticulous work on the design and layout of each page of the book

Alison Silver guided the project smoothly, efficiently and cheerfully towards its publication. Her eye for detail, thoroughness and discernment enhanced the book enormously. Working with her was, as always, such a pleasure.

Finally, thanks to Sue, Zoë and Thomas for everything.

From the first edition

My special thanks to Christine Cairns and Alison Silver for all their hard work, friendly encouragement and editorial expertise.

Thanks also to all the teachers and students at the following schools and institutes who used the pilot edition of this book and made so many helpful comments and suggestions: The Bell School in Cambridge, the British Council Institute in Barcelona, The British School in Florence, the College of Arts and Technology in Newcastle upon Tyne, the Eurocentre in Cambridge, Godmer House in Oxford, the Hampstead Garden Suburb Institute in London, Inlingua Brighton & Hove, International House in Arezzo, Klubschule Migros in St Gallen, The Moraitis School in Athens, the Moustakis School of English in Athens, the Newnham Language Centre in Cambridge, VHS Aachen, VHS Heidelberg, VHS Karlsruhe, the Wimbledon School of English in London and Ray Thomson in Switzerland. Without their help and reassurance this book could not have taken shape.

Introduction

Progress to Proficiency is for any group of students preparing for the University of Cambridge Local Examinations Syndicate Certificate of Proficiency in English – the 'Proficiency' exam or CPE, for short. It is also suitable for students preparing for an exam of similar level and scope, such as a university examination. It contains a wide variety of practice activities and exercises which increase in difficulty and complexity unit by unit until, towards the end, students are tackling tasks of exam standard.

Students using this course will have passed the Cambridge First Certificate (FCE) exam – or reached an equivalent level – and may also have taken the Cambridge Certificate in Advanced English (CAE) exam, perhaps using *Cambridge Advanced English* by Leo Jones.

This book has two main aims:
– to help students to improve and refine their language skills so that they can do their very best in the Proficiency exam
– to help students to improve the language skills that they will need in real life: in social situations and in their work or studies

Its varied and interesting activities and exercises increase students' confidence and flexibility and also allow them to discover what aspects of their English they still need to learn to improve in order to become more accurate and fluent users of English.

Why a New Edition?

Since its first publication, *Progress to Proficiency* has been an outstandingly popular and effective coursebook, used with great success in Proficiency classes all over the world. But, in the meantime, some of the original texts seemed to be getting rather dated, amendments have been made to the exam syllabus, and new ideas have come along. So we asked teachers to suggest how the original edition could be improved, and they sent their 'wish lists' for their ideal Proficiency coursebook.

What might have simply been an updating of the original edition has become a completely new edition, containing about 90% new or extensively revised material. There are four completely new units as well as many new or revised sections, incorporating new reading passages, new recordings, new communicative activities and new exercises. At the same time, those features of the original edition of *Progress to Proficiency* which teachers and students appreciated, and which led to so many successful exam results, have been retained.

1

Some unit titles from the original edition no longer appear in the New Edition, but the most popular material from the lost units has been included elsewhere in the New Edition. For example, in the New Edition, **How things work** includes material from 'The future' as well as 'Science and technology', and **The past** includes material from 'War and peace' as well as 'History'.

The revisions and improvements in the New Edition are based on comments and reports from teachers who had been using the first edition successfully for many years. The New Edition prepares students for the latest version of the exam, including all the amendments made to the syllabus and the exam papers since 1984. The format of each unit has been changed to provide a more balanced lesson structure and much greater flexibility.

There are completely new sections in every unit, covering:
– grammar review, including the main problems which advanced students have
– advanced grammar, including revision sections
– vocabulary development
– writing skills
And exercises on idioms and phrasal verbs in even-numbered units.

There is considerably more help for students preparing for each paper of the examination:
– abundant examination advice with tips on how to approach each paper
– annotated exam-style exercises to help students to approach the exam with confidence
– development of summary writing skills
– development of writing skills and composition writing

There are many new reading texts, with pre- and post-reading tasks and discussion questions. Around twenty of the reading passages from the original edition have been retained, but they all have new or revised tasks, and discussion activities.

Those listening sections which have been retained from the original edition have been completely re-recorded with new tasks and discussion activities. There are also many new recordings, including authentic interviews in most units.

If you've used *Progress to Proficiency* before, you'll recognise plenty of 'old friends' here, but you'll also find that a great deal has changed – it's a completely new course based on the original edition, rather than a 'revised edition'. You'll be pleased that the New Edition is much more thorough, more flexible, more stimulating and enjoyable, and easier to use.

STUDY TOURS '94

New York
Portugal
French Alps
Rome

THE QUEEN'S UNIVERSITY OF BELFAST

New York Art

A 6 day Study Tour, 24 - 30 March 1994

Cost ex Belfast: £687 plus insurance (including £50 returnable emergency fee)

Leaders: Nicole Mezey, Geoffrey McNab

This trip provides an opportunity to examine some of the great Art collections of the World, assembled in some of its most distinctive galleries. After a half-day guided tour of the city by coach, we will visit the Old Masters of the Metropolitan Museum, the Medieval treasures of the Cloisters, the exquisite variety of the Frick, and the 20th century works in the Guggenheim Gallery and the Museum of Modern Art.

The fee covers flights by scheduled airline, 5 nights accommodation in a 1st class hotel, city tour, transfers by private coach, and guided visits to the art collections.

Students may opt for a longer stay on payment of an additional charge, for changing dates, of £25 plus insurance, if arranged when booking.

Birds of Southern Portugal

An 8 day Study Tour: 8 - 15 May 1994

Cost ex Belfast: £645 (including £50 returnable emergency fee)

Leaders: Ian Forsyth, John Measures

The coastline of the Algarve, from the cliffs of Cape St Vincent to the dunes and lagoons of Vila Real , along with the grassy plains of Baixo Alentejo offer an interesting variety of birds in a range of habitats. Our visit ties in with the return of the winter migrants to their breeding areas.

Amongst the birds we expect to see are Marbled Teal, Great Bustard, Little Bustard, Crested Coot, Purple Gallinule, Pratincole, Black Tern, Nightjar, Wryneck, Thekla Lark, a range of warblers and buntings, and Azure-winged Magpies. There is also the possibility of seeing some of the 11 species of raptor which occur in the area.

The price includes flights ex Belfast, one week's accommodation in a self-catering apartment, use of a minibus, and the services for 4 days of John Measures, an experienced ornithologist and botanist resident in the Algarve since 1968.

As a small party is required for a trip of this nature, **places are very limited and you are advised to apply early to avoid disappointment.**

Flowers of the French Alps

A 15 day Study Tour: 25 June - 9 July 1994

Cost ex Belfast: £1164 (including £50 returnable emergency fee)

Leader: Dr Ralph S. Forbes

The French Alps comprise an area of high mountains comparable in size to the whole of Switzerland and offer as much variety of flowers and scenery as anywhere in the Swiss Alps. This will be a 2-centre trip, split equally between a ' high ' village - the well-known ski resort of Val d' Isere at 1840 m in the Graian Alps, and the ' low ' centre of Briancon (1321 m), further south in the Cottian Alps. Both areas are justly famous for their flowers, which in addition to choice Alpines should also include an admixture of Mediterranean species. The 2 venues have been chosen to allow easy access to the alpine levels by means of numerous cable cars and a series of high mountain Passes.

The party size will be limited to 20 plus the leader. **While most walking is downhill, all participants must be fit enough for all-day walks at their own pace.** The fee includes scheduled flights to Lyon via Heathrow, coach transfers, half-board accommodation , plus the use of a coach on 3 days per week, insurance and the services of the botanical leader. The cost of additional local travel such as cable-cars or chair-lifts is not included. Lunches will normally be picnics and should be inexpensive.

This is the 12th Alpine Flowers Study Tour led by Ralph Forbes, who has wide experience of mountain flowers throughout the Alps and Pyrenees, and extensive knowledge about the flora of the region.

Study Tour Rome

September 1994

Leader: Nicole Mezey

There will be an art study tour to Rome in September 1994. We will concentrate on the Classical and Renaissance monuments, such as the Colosseum and the work of Michelangelo and Raphael in the Vatican but will also visit the great galleries of art and some of the baroque masterpieces of this historic city. For further information contact Nicole Mezey on (0232) 245133 Ext 3810/3323

Separate leaflets describing each tour in more detail and including an application form are available from: **The Institute of Continuing Education, Queen's University, Belfast, BT7 1NN, Tel (0232) 245133 Ext 3323/4/6.**

Progress to Proficiency – New Edition

The eighteen topics in *Progress to Proficiency New Edition* have been selected not just because they 'come up' in the Proficiency exam but because they are important for advanced learners and include themes which any educated person should be confident enough to read about, hear about and discuss – not as an expert or a professional, but as an informed lay person.

Teachers familiar with *Progress to First Certificate* or *Cambridge Advanced English* will notice that this book includes many of their more effective and enjoyable features. However, thanks to the higher level of the Proficiency exam, students are set free to explore topics and ideas that are more intellectually demanding, and go into greater depth.

As you work through the book, you will become aware of a progression from unit to unit:
- from exercises and activities where the questions can be discussed
    to exam-style questions
- from exercises and activities with problems to be solved with a partner
    to exercises which have to be done alone
- from exercises and activities where guidance is given
-     to exercises where students have to use the knowledge and skills they
        have acquired
- from exercises and activities which help students to learn
    to exercises which, like the exam, test their knowledge
- from exercises and activities where students work at their own speed
    to exercises which have to be done within exam-style constraints of
        time and length

Hence the title: ***Progress to Proficiency***.

To do all the sections in one unit will take about 5 or 6 hours – longer if a lot of time is devoted to discussion. The whole course thus requires 90 to 110 hours to complete, though students who spend time preparing exercises at home may not need so long. Any substantial pieces of written work (i.e. compositions, written tasks and summaries), as well as reading the longer passages through for the first time will, it is assumed, be done as homework in any case.

It is advisable to **select** certain parts of each unit to concentrate on with your class, which means that some parts may be omitted. This is left to your discretion, as it is dependent on each class's strengths and weaknesses, as well as on their interests.

For example, if there isn't enough time to do one of the reading passages in a unit, it can be set for homework. Or if a particular grammar point is easy for your students it can be left out altogether. Or if your class find listening comprehension fairly easy, then it may be a good idea to omit one of the listening sections in a unit. The material in this book is designed to be used selectively, though some sections in a unit do depend on previous sections.

The Proficiency exam

The Proficiency exam consists of five papers:

Paper 1 Reading comprehension (1 hour)   Part A consists of 25 multiple-choice questions which test candidates' knowledge of vocabulary. Part B consists of 15 multiple-choice questions (each worth 2 marks) on three or more reading passages.   Total marks: 40

Paper 2 Composition (2 hours)   This paper tests candidates' ability to write extended pieces of prose. Candidates write two compositions of 300 to 350 words from a choice of five questions, one of which is based on the prescribed books. An impression mark is given.   Total marks: 40

Paper 3 Use of English (2 hours)   Part A of this paper contains four exercises which test candidates' command of English grammar and usage. Part B contains a reading passage with comprehension and vocabulary questions to answer and a summary writing question. The total score of about 80 is scaled down to give a total of 40 marks. Part B carries just under half of the marks for the paper.

Paper 4 Listening comprehension (about 30 to 40 minutes)   This paper consists of three or more recorded listening passages (interviews, broadcasts, messages, announcements, etc.) with comprehension tasks.   Total marks: 20

Paper 5 Interview (15 to 20 minutes)   This paper is done with candidates working one-to-one with an examiner, or in groups of three with the examiner prompting and assessing. To encourage them to speak, candidates are given one or more photos to talk about and one or more short passages to comment on, before they take part in a discussion or communication activity. Total marks: 40

The complete examination carries a total of 180 marks. There are no fixed, definitive pass marks, but successful candidates score at least 24 marks on Papers 1, 3 and 5, 16 marks on Paper 2 and 12 marks on Paper 4.

➡ For comprehensive details of the format of the exam, together with marking schemes and sample candidates' compositions, you should consult *Cambridge Proficiency Examination Practice Books* – STUDENT'S BOOK and TEACHER'S BOOK (Cambridge University Press).

If you have not taught a Proficiency class before, besides looking at *Cambridge Proficiency Examination Practice Books*, you should also study the current Examination Regulations, obtainable free of charge from your Local Examinations Secretary, which also includes the list of books for **Prescribed reading** (see page 12).

Exam preparation and exam practice

Examination practice tests, though they are certainly helpful to accustom students to the kinds of tasks they will encounter in the exam, should not be overused in class for a number of reasons:

- the questions in tests are based on a random selection of different language points, which is confusing for students
- many of the questions in tests seem impossibly hard (only the best candidates will get them right) while others seem very easy (even the weakest candidates will get a few marks on these), and this is frustrating for students
- in tests the reading passages and the recordings are chosen because they are suitable for testing purposes, not because they are intrinsically interesting or enjoyable, and not because they provoke discussion
- no help whatsoever is given to help students to improve their performance, since the purpose of the test is only to assess candidates' proficiency, not to help them

By contrast, *Progress to Proficiency* provides comprehensive and, above all, systematic coverage of the wide range of language skills required in the Proficiency exam. Some of the exercises are simply designed to help students to learn, some provide a challenge so that they will 'stretch' their English, some provide opportunities for discussion. The texts have been chosen because they are likely to interest, entertain, inform, provoke or intrigue students. The entire course is designed to help students to progressively improve their skills in the different areas tested in the exam.

In a Proficiency course there has to be a realistic balance between exam preparation (after all, everyone wants to do well in the exam!) and improving language skills that will be useful in the real world. Using the material in this book will help you to make sure that this balance is maintained throughout the course.

The teacher and the students

The role of the teacher in a Proficiency class cannot be overstressed. The best source of explanations and advice on grammar, usage, style and writing skills is not a book but the teacher. The teacher is the person who knows the students personally: only the teacher knows what their strengths and weaknesses are, what they know already and what their interests and enthusiasms are. Only the teacher knows what kind of action to take when difficulties arise – perhaps action as straightforward as suggesting better ways of saying or writing things, or more complex such as introducing suitable supplementary material.

No textbook can replace the teacher because the problems of any particular group of students are individual and unpredictable. Lengthy explanations of grammar points, detailed advice on how to write a good essay or exhaustive analyses of appropriate style which are general enough to be relevant to every student would be unwieldy and time-consuming in a textbook – but the teacher can tailor such explanations and advice to the needs of each class.

The teacher therefore has an essential creative contribution to make – not just by regulating the pace and intensity of each lesson and deciding which sections to concentrate on, but by adapting the material to the students' needs and interests, by giving the right kind of advice and by maintaining a friendly, cooperative working atmosphere in class.

Proficiency students cannot expect to sit back and be 'taught', they have to 'learn' – by asking questions, by finding things out for themselves, by reading widely, by drawing on each other's knowledge, by discovering what they can do well and what they are weak at, but above all by improving their ability to use the English they already know in a flexible, confident way to perform a wide range of tasks.

It's a sad fact that students at this level find it difficult to appreciate that they are making progress: you can give them encouragement by keeping a permanent record of their work throughout the course. Each student's work can be sub-categorised into the different skills that will be assessed in the exam: vocabulary, reading comprehension, composition writing, use of English, listening comprehension and speaking skills (communicative ability, grammatical accuracy and pronunciation). These individual 'profiles' can be kept up-to-date and shown to students from time to time, so that they can see what improvements they have made and also what aspects of their English they still need to work on. Make sure they realise that the purpose of this is to help, not intimidate them!

Working in pairs or groups

Many of the exercises in *Progress to Proficiency* are designed to be done by students working together in pairs or in small groups of three or four, and not 'round the class' with each student answering one question. There are several advantages to this approach:

- Students get an opportunity to communicate their ideas to each other while they are discussing each exercise.
- Students are more likely to remember answers they have discovered or worked out by themselves than answers other students give – or answers the teacher announces to the class.
- Students working in groups are more active than if they are working as a class: they talk more and do more thinking too. If a class of, say, 20 were doing a 10-question exercise 'round the class' half of them wouldn't get the chance to answer a single question.

- Weaker students can be lulled into a false sense of security by writing down all the correct answers and kidding themselves that they have 'done' the exercise.

One drawback of doing exercises in pairs or groups is that it does take time. However, as many of the exercises can be done as homework, time can be saved by setting some exercises to be done at home. Then, back in class next time, students can begin the session by comparing their answers in pairs or groups, and discussing as a class any problems they encountered.

Another possible problem is that errors may go uncorrected and that students might even learn 'bad habits' from each other. This can be dealt with by vigilant monitoring of students as they are working together and encouraging students to correct each other's mistakes – which they should be able to do quite efficiently at this level. (See also **Mistakes: marking and correction** on page 17.)

What's in each unit?

A typical unit starts with a warm-up discussion activity, followed by work on Topic vocabulary and a Reading passage to introduce the topic of the unit. In most units these are followed by Grammar review, further Reading passages (one with an accompanying Questions and summary exercise), Vocabulary development, Advanced grammar, Writing skills, Listening and Composition writing. Even-numbered units end with a Verbs and idioms exercise.

But there is no fixed sequence of sections: each unit looks and feels rather different from the one before. For students and teachers it is reassuringly easy to find your way round each unit, but each unit contains some surprises so that there are unpredictable elements.

Topic vocabulary

Each unit has a section covering some of the vocabulary connected with the topic of the unit. There are various types of exercises and activities in these sections, including warm-up discussion questions and a follow-up activity. Some of these are open-ended discussion activities (e.g. 1.1) where discussion among the students leads them to discover the gaps in their vocabulary and encourages them to ask questions or use a dictionary. Some are activities which encourage students to explore and exploit vocabulary in intriguing ways (e.g. 5.1 and 9.1).Some of these sections contain exercises with gaps to fill (e.g. 4.1). An exercise of this type is to some extent a test, if only because no two students share the same knowledge of English. However, different students will benefit from different parts of each exercise: learning new words, being reminded of words they don't actively use, finding words with similar meanings and determining how they are used. Such exercises cover the skills required for the first part of Paper 1 in the exam, with discussion activities which foster the kind of communication skills tested in Paper 5.

There is a progression in the book:

from   activities which introduce and practise vocabulary without reference
        to the exam
to   exercises where students have to choose three words that are ....
        appropriate ✓ correct ✓ suitable ✓ good authentic
to   exercises with exam-style multiple-choice questions where only
        .... alternative is correct
        one ✓ two three four
to   exercises where there are also questions on grammar and usage, as in
        the exam

Besides the sections dedicated to Topic vocabulary, students will encounter
relevant vocabulary in other sections in a unit, particularly in the Reading
sections, many of which contain special vocabulary exercises.

For the teacher, there are two big problems about helping students to learn
new vocabulary:

One is the difficulty of helping students to remember vocabulary items –
giving them a large amount of controlled oral practice in class is no
guarantee that they will remember everything a week later!

The other is helping students to develop a sensitivity towards the kinds of
contexts and situations in which each vocabulary item can be used: which
words are formal or informal, which are used jokingly or seriously, which are
used in a derogatory or complimentary sense, and what collocations the
words are used in. Students also need to develop an awareness of the
connotations or associations of different vocabulary items, since many
broadly synonymous expressions may have quite different connotations.

Unfortunately, there are no easy solutions. What will certainly help is:

- DISCUSSION of the meanings, connotations and usage of vocabulary
  introduced or encountered in class.
- Encouraging students to use a DICTIONARY intelligently, particularly by
  studying the EXAMPLES given after the definitions.
- Encouraging students to highlight unfamiliar vocabulary items which
  they want to remember.
- Making sure that students get plenty of EXPERIENCE in reading English,
  not just reading the texts in this book, but through wider reading in
  English for pleasure and information.
- A REALISTIC approach to the problems: it's the students who have to do
  the remembering – all the teacher can be expected to do is encourage
  students to experiment with new vocabulary and not play safe by using
  simple words.
- Systematic use of NOTEBOOKS to store useful new vocabulary items,
  preferably devoting separate pages to each topic. Students should be

encouraged to discuss which systems of vocabulary storage they consider most effective. (See 1.2E in the Student's Book and **Vocabulary development** below.)

Vocabulary development

Each unit contains a section on Vocabulary development, which is designed to help students to expand their vocabulary in various ways. The following aspects are covered in these sections:

1.5 Adjective + noun collocations
2.5 Words easily confused
3.8 Opposites
4.5 Forming adjectives
5.5 Position of adjectives & participles
6.5 Collocations: adverbs of degree
7.5 Compound nouns
8.5 Prefixes
9.6 Abstract nouns
10.5 Different styles
11.5 Collocations: idioms
12.5 Suffixes
13.5 Underlying meanings
14.5 Collocations: verb phrases
15.6 Exam practice
16.7 Synonyms
17.8 Modifying adjectives & participles
18.1 Examination practice

Vocabulary exercises can't 'teach' students new vocabulary, they can only introduce them to new words and phrases, and remind them of what they have come across before. The students themselves are the only people who are fully aware of what they already know, and of what they need to learn. The exercises in *Progress to Proficiency* should be viewed as a SOURCE of new vocabulary and revision of vocabulary they may have encountered previously. It should not be assumed that doing the exercises in this book will magically 'teach you everything you need to know'. Learning new vocabulary is not such a simple process.

Whenever students come across a potentially useful new word or phrase in this book (or in their reading generally), they should use a dictionary to look it up, paying particular attention to the example sentences and any information given about collocations. Next time they come across the word, they should notice the collocation.

If a word or phrase seems unusual or specialised, they shouldn't necessarily try to remember it – often they can guess its meaning from the context anyway.

Using a dictionary is best done in private and in their own time outside class. This means that it is essential for students to prepare work before each class and spend time alone following it up afterwards. Just 'doing their homework' is not enough – they should make time for this sort of preparation and follow-up work.

Students should highlight useful new words (using a fluorescent highlighter) so that the words stand out whenever they flip through the book. It is advisable to flip through the units they have covered so far regularly – this could easily be done on the bus on their way to or from class, for example. This will help them to assimilate the words so that eventually they can incorporate them into their own active vocabulary, and use them in their writing and conversation. As the weeks go by, if the highlighting fades, they should re-highlight the words they still want to be reminded of.

Writing new words in a notebook is another good way of memorising new words, particularly their spelling. It usually helps to store words in categories (e.g. under topic headings), or alphabetically, rather than make a chronological list. The best kind of notebook for this is a loose-leaf personal organiser or Filofax, into which new pages can easily be inserted.

Every student must also possess a good English-English dictionary, such as the *Longman Dictionary of Contemporary English*, the *Oxford Advanced Learner's Dictionary of Current English*, the *BBC English Dictionary* or the *Collins COBUILD English Language Dictionary*, so that they can look up the meanings of words and find other examples of their uses. A bilingual dictionary is NOT sufficient for Proficiency students.

The Teacher's Book contains answer keys and suggestions for handling the exercises.

Reading

Progress to Proficiency contains a wide variety of authentic texts taken from newspapers and magazines and from fiction and non-fiction books. The questions focus on different reading skills: reading for gist or reading to extract specific information, as well as recognising and appreciating the style of the passage and the writer's attitude or intention. The passages are all chosen as springboards for discussion.

Before many of the reading comprehension tasks there are pre-reading tasks, preliminary discussion questions or questions about the theme that students may be able to answer from their own previous knowledge. These tasks help students to approach the text with more interest and curiosity than if they merely had to 'Read the text and answer the questions'.

It is essential for students to realise that they don't have to be able to understand every single word in a passage to perform the tasks in this book, or even to answer the questions in the exam. They should concentrate on what the writers are trying to say and the information they are communicating. Unfamiliar words in a reading text may be distracting but students should not assume that every single one is important and 'worth learning'.

There are many exercises where students have to highlight certain vocabulary items in a passage. This encourages them to deduce meanings from the context and also to notice the contexts in which particular words are used. The reading passages have numbered paragraphs, or numbered lines, to help students to search for words and to make it easier to refer to parts of the text in discussion or follow-up work.

After the reading comprehension questions there are usually further discussion questions, to encourage students to use some of the new words they have encountered in the text and share their reactions to its content with each other. In some cases there is a Communication activity or a writing task, arising from the content of the passage.

There is a progression unit by unit:

from	exercises where students are asked questions like this:
	Who made the first move? **Harry**
or	The person who made the first move was ....**Harry**....
or	true/false questions: It was Holly who made the first move. **False**
to	exam-style multiple-choice questions:
	The one who made the first move was . . .
	Harry ✓ Henry Holly Hetty

In the exam candidates' understanding is 'sampled' only, so there are fewer questions to answer than in this book. To save time in class, students should be asked to prepare the reading passages by reading them through at home beforehand.

The Teacher's Book contains background information on the writers whose work is reproduced. Most of the texts from works of fiction are the opening paragraphs of a book – this is intended to whet the reader's appetite and encourage further reading.

Students also need to be encouraged to read widely for pleasure and information, selecting material that suits their own interests and tastes – fiction and non-fiction, books, newspapers and magazines in English. Weekly news magazines like *The Economist*, *The Guardian Weekly*, *Newsweek* or *Time* are particularly recommended.

Prescribed reading

Progress to Proficiency does not contain questions on particular books, as these change each year. However, in Unit 11 students are given an opportunity to discuss one of the prescribed books and write about it.

Choosing one of these books not only gives students an extra topic to choose from in Paper 2 and to talk about in the Interview, but also gives them a good chance to improve their reading skills and enrich their vocabulary. Provided that one of the books suits your students' interests and tastes, it should be recommended and discussed regularly in class. One of the others might also be recommended as reading for pleasure. A wide range of tastes is catered for in the selection of texts, as this list for 1993 shows:

Heat and Dust by Ruth Prawer Jhabvala
Lord of the Flies by William Golding
Sour Sweet by Timothy Mo

Written work should be set on the particular book chosen: the kind of questions that might be asked would relate to the characters, plot, style and relevance of the particular book. For examples of typical questions, see *Cambridge Proficiency Examination Practice 4* and other volumes in the same series.

The latest Examination Regulations booklet obtainable from your Local Examinations Secretary contains each year's list of prescribed books.

Grammar review and Advanced grammar

The Grammar review sections are designed to cover the main problem areas of English grammar that cause difficulties for advanced students. The Advanced grammar sections cover areas of grammar which students may not have dealt with before, though they are likely to have encountered them in their reading. Particular attention is given in the Advanced grammar sections to points that 'come up' in the Proficiency exam, and to structures which students will find useful in their composition writing.

Both types of section contain a variety of exercises: contrasted sentences where students have to discuss the differences in meaning, error correction exercises, cloze exercises, transformation exercises, gap–filling exercises and sentence–completion exercises, together with other more open–ended tasks. Many of these exercises reflect the kinds of questions that students will encounter in the Use of English paper.

Towards the end of the book more emphasis is placed on the techniques students will require in Part A of the Use of English paper, with annotated exam-style exercises and hints for dealing with different kinds of test items.

The points covered in these sections are as follows:

Grammar review		Advanced grammar	
1.3	Comparing and contrasting	1.8	Using participles
2.2	Articles and determiners	2.7	Position of adverbs
3.2	Reporting – 1	3.7	Using inversion for emphasis
4.3	*–ing* and *to* __	4.8	*Wh–* clauses
5.4	The passive – 1	5.8	*Should* and *be*
6.3	The future	6.7	Revision and exam practice
7.3	Past and present	7.7	Further uses of *–ing*
8.3	Modal verbs	8.7	*There* . . .
9.3	Question tags & negative questions	9.8	Reporting – 2
10.3	Conditional sentences – 1	10.7	Uses of the past
11.3	Conjunctions & connectors – 1	11.7	*It* . . . constructions
12.3	Verbs + prepositions	12.7	The passive – 2
13.3	Revision: As the saying goes . . .	13.7	Conditional sentences – 2
14.3	Word order: phrasal verbs	14.7	Revision and exam practice
15.4	Prepositions	15.8	Conjunctions & connectors – 2
16.3	Relative clauses	16.9	Exam techniques: Use of English
17.4	Adjectives + prepositions		
18.4	Examination practice		

If you feel that a particular Grammar review section covers points which present no difficulties for your students, you should leave out that section, or maybe recommend that it is done as homework with a short follow-up discussion in class.

Students should realise that if they require more detailed rules or guidelines and further examples they should refer to a reference grammar book, such as *Practical English Usage* by Michael Swan (OUP). They should be encouraged to ask questions if they are unsure about any points in the grammar sections.

Questions & summary

In most units there is a section where the comprehension questions on a passage have to be answered in complete written sentences and a summary has to be written, in preparation for Section B of the Use of English paper. The questions focus attention on explaining the meaning of certain words used in the passage, explaining the reference of cataphoric and anaphoric devices (such as *it* or *this*), as well as selecting relevant information and writing a summary.

Many students find this part of the exam particularly difficult, as it often requires skills they haven't used before. Special attention is given to these skills in *Progress to Proficiency* and students are given ample practice in rephrasing quotations from texts in their own words and in summarising passages within a fixed word limit.

Often these exercises are done orally by students working together before they write their answers down, probably for homework.

There is a progression unit by unit:

from   exercises where only a few questions have to be answered and a short summary is required

to   exercises requiring a summary of a certain length (e.g. 80 words)

to   exam-style exercises with a variety of questions requiring written answers

The Teacher's Book contains Model summaries which you may photocopy, if you wish, for your students to compare with their own.

Listening

The cassettes contain a wide variety of recordings, including many broadcasts, authentic interviews and discussions. The exercises and tasks are designed to help students to develop their skills in finding the important information in the recording, listening for gist, note-taking, interpreting a speaker's attitude, etc. Some of the longer recordings are split into shorter sections, with different tasks to be done on each section.

The listening comprehension tasks are often preceded by pre-listening tasks, preliminary discussion questions or questions about the theme which students may be able to answer from their own previous knowledge. These tasks help students to approach the recording with more interest than if they merely had to 'Listen to the cassette and answer the questions'.

As the exam may include a variety of question types, the tasks include exercises with true/false questions, exercises with open-ended questions, exercises where the answers have to be shown graphically, exercises where a form or chart has to be completed and exercises with multiple-choice questions.

There is a progression unit by unit:

from   recordings that are relatively easy to understand, with straightforward questions on the content, or questions for discussion

to   recordings that are more difficult to understand, with more demanding exam-style questions that may catch out the unwary student

It may be helpful to 'set the scene' for students before they hear the recording by explaining where the speakers are and what their relationship is (colleagues, good friends, etc.). Remember that students will be trying to understand disembodied voices coming out of a loudspeaker without the aid of a transcript, and this is much more difficult than being in the same room as a real person who is speaking to you, and who can adapt what they are saying according to your reactions.

In some of the listening exercises, students may need help with vocabulary. It is a good idea to read through the transcript in your copy of the Teacher's Book before the lesson, and **highlight** any vocabulary that you wish to draw your students' attention to.

Most students will need to hear each recording at least twice to extract all the required information. In some classes, where students are weak at listening, you may need to pause the tape frequently and play certain sections again to help them to understand more easily. The transcripts for some of the longer recordings contain suggested 'places for pausing' indicated with ★★★.

However, it is essential for students to realise that they don't have to be able to understand every single word to answer the questions. Generally, they should concentrate on what the speakers are trying to say and the information they are communicating, NOT the actual words they are using. Occasionally, however, there are questions where students are required to write down the exact words used.

Generally, there is a difference between the recordings in which authentic interviews are used, and the ones based on broadcasts. In the former, where people are talking about their experiences, it is usually easier to absorb the information they give, thanks to the naturally occurring repetition, emphasis and redundancy that happens in conversations. In the latter, a lot of information is sometimes given in a short time, and students may need to hear the recording more than twice to pick up all the information. This means that although some of the authentic interviews last over ten minutes, they will actually take less time to do in class than some of the shorter passages.

After the listening comprehension task there are often further discussion questions, to encourage students to share their reactions with each other and discuss the implications of what they have heard. In some cases there is a Communication Activity, related to the theme of the listening text.

In some units there is a listening activity which leads in to a discussion, providing students with an opportunity to hear native speakers giving their views on the topic before they take part in their own discussion.

Frequently the last Listening section in a unit is linked to a Composition which the students have to write, where the information given in the recording provides information or ideas which will stimulate students to put their own ideas in writing.

The Teacher's Book contains a complete transcript of the recordings and answers.

Writing skills & Composition

The Writing skills sections are designed to develop students' writing skills by focusing on various aspects of writing compositions, and encouraging students to develop their own personal repertoire of styles.

The following points are covered in the Writing skills sections:

Many of the Composition tasks are linked to listening or reading input, where students will already have heard or read related ideas and information and had an opportunity to discuss them. This means that they don't have to approach the composition tasks 'cold', searching for inspiration, nor do they need to spend too long working out their ideas or finding out information before writing. Instead they can concentrate on the main task of actually planning and writing their composition.

These exercises cover all the types of composition and essay required in the Proficiency exam: descriptive, narrative, discursive – as well as shorter more specific tasks where students are expected to write a report or a letter, based on specific information. The composition tasks are designed to be discussed beforehand and afterwards – not just written in isolation and handed in for the teacher to evaluate.

In the Composition sections there is a progression from unit to unit towards exam-style exercises where students write compositions of exam length and against the clock.

Make sure you do allow your students time to read each other's written work. This is particularly important if composition writing is to be considered as more than 'just an exercise'. Any piece of writing should be an attempt to communicate ideas to a reader. If students know that their partners as well as you, are going to read their work, they are more likely to try to make it interesting, informative and entertaining! If you, their teacher, are the only reader, the process of writing seems less realistic. Students can learn a great deal by reading each other's work – and from each other's comments on their own work. A piece of written work should be regarded as a piece of communication, not simply an opportunity to spot the grammatical errors that students make.

You may have your own views on whether or not to award a mark for each composition – if you do, allow scope in your system for students to see an improvement over the months: it's pretty discouraging if you're still getting the same mark even at the end of the course! Instead, you may prefer to write a few appreciative and helpfully critical comments. (See **Mistakes: marking and correction** below.)

When you mark each composition, pay particular attention to the Writing skills covered earlier in the unit. Students can help each other a lot here, by evaluating and criticising each other's compositions. Surprisingly, if students know that other students are going to read their work, they tend to take a lot more care over it than if it's 'only' the teacher who's going to see it!

In an advanced class, each individual student may to a greater or lesser degree be 'good at writing'. It is essential to regard the Writing skills exercises in *Progress to Proficiency* as a starting point. Further remedial work may be necessary for students whose writing skills are particularly weak. In particular, the feedback you give to students when handing back their written work should take into account each individual student's strengths and weaknesses.

Mistakes: marking and correction

In marking students' written work, it is important to remember how discouraging it is to receive back a paper covered in red marks! It's better for students to locate and correct their own mistakes, rather than have corrections written out for them. This is particularly important when you believe that a student has made careless mistakes or slips of the pen.

In many cases, once mistakes are pointed out to students, they can often correct them themselves. A 'marking scheme' like the following is recommended, but whatever scheme you use make sure your students are conversant with the system you're using.

✗ = 'Somewhere in this line there is a mistake of some kind that you should find and correct'

✗ ✗ = 'Somewhere in this line there are two mistakes that you should find and correct'

<u>An incorrect word or phrase underlined</u> = 'This particular word or phrase is not correct and you should correct it'

G = GRAMMAR 'Somewhere in this line there is a grammatical mistake that you should find and correct'

V = VOCABULARY 'Somewhere in this line there is a vocabulary mistake that you should find and correct'

Sp = SPELLING 'Somewhere in this line there is a spelling mistake that you should find and correct'

P = PUNCTUATION 'Somewhere in this line there is a punctuation mistake that you should find and correct'

WO = WORD ORDER 'Some of the words in this sentence are in the wrong order, please rearrange them'

ST = STYLE 'The style you have used here is not really appropriate to the task – it may be too formal, or too informal'

? = ?? 'I don't quite understand what you mean'

And equally important, remembering that all learners need encouragement and praise as well as constructive criticism, some more positive or encouraging marks should be included:

✓ = 'Good, you have expressed this idea well!' or 'This is an interesting or amusing point'

✓✓ = 'Very good, you have expressed this idea very well!' or 'Very interesting or amusing point!'

As the symbols shown here would appear on the side of the page in the margin, make sure your students do leave a wide enough margin for your comments!

In speech, although work on improving students' accuracy is essential, it is far more important for learners to be able to communicate effectively. It is very difficult to develop confidence if one is afraid of making mistakes. In real life, after all, people have to communicate with each other *in spite of* the mistakes they may be making and their less-than-complete command of English.

Students should certainly be corrected when they make serious errors, but it is usually best to point out any mistakes that were made *after* the groups have completed an activity, rather than interrupting the flow of the activity. While students are working together in pairs or groups, and you are going from group to group listening in, you may be able to make the occasional discreet correction without interrupting the flow of the discussion, but normally it is better to make a note of some of the errors you overhear and point them out later.

You may hear your students making mistakes in pronunciation, grammar or style, but rather than mentioning every mistake you have heard, it is more helpful to be selective and to draw attention to specific points that you think your students should concentrate on improving. It may be less confusing to focus on just one type of error at a time by, for example, drawing attention to pronunciation errors after one activity and then to grammatical errors after another. Accuracy is something that takes a long time to develop and it cannot be achieved overnight!

There are no exercises in *Progress to Proficiency* specifically devoted to pronunciation. This does not imply that phonology is unimportant. Indeed, it requires constant attention, particularly when you are giving students feedback on their performance in spoken activities. At this level, correction is likely to be the most effective method of dealing with phonology. In the Interview paper in the Proficiency exam, pronunciation is one of the aspects that will be assessed.

Speaking: discussion & Communication Activities

Every unit contains a variety of questions for students to consider and then discuss in small groups. These should be regarded as 'discussion opportunities', and if they have a lot to say, these discussions may go on for quite a long time. Conversely, if your students have little to say about some of these questions, they may be omitted. In other words, the amount of time that should be devoted to these is unpredictable and you will need to 'play it by ear' when deciding when to move on to the next section.

If a particular topic is especially popular, you may decide to ask students to do some supplementary written work, outlining their own ideas or summarising the discussion they have been involved in. This option is not included in the Student's Book rubrics, and is left to the teacher's discretion.

Besides the discussion activities, there are photographs to talk about and Communication Activities, which provide students with plentiful preparation for the Proficiency exam **Interview (Paper 5)**. Many of the activities reflect the kind of tasks expected of candidates in the exam, but there are also some sections specifically devoted to preparing for the examination Interview: 11.9, 17.10 and 18.6.

The Communication Activities involve an information gap, where each participant is given different information which has to be shared with a partner. These are shown with the symbol 🏃‍♂️ in the Student's Book and the Teacher's Book. In some cases, each student reads a different part of a reading text or has some information to study, which they have to tell their partner(s) about in their own words.

The Communication Activities are 'scrambled' at the back of the Student's Book, so that the students (working in pairs or groups of three) cannot see each other's information. Exchanging information and ideas using this technique tends to be very realistic and motivating for students.

Guide to the Communication Activities

1.4B	1 + 32 + 34	Mark Wallington's walk
2.2F	3 + 22	Photos to describe
3.4F	41	Model answers & summary*
4.6D	25 + 30 + 39	Dictionary extracts
5.10C	5 + 23	How wine and beer are made
6.2C	4 + 19	Continuation of passage
7.1D	2 + 8 + 17 + 45	How to handle customers
7.8A	44	Green Consumer Guide
8.6B	6	Model summary*
8.7D	24 + 36 + 38	Animal stories
12.2C	9 + 26	Refrigerator & vacuum cleaner
12.10A	11 + 27 + 40	Modern design
13.8B	12 + 29	Edward Hopper paintings
14.2E	7 + 46	Money-making schemes
15.3A	16 + 33	Stills from silent movies
15.3B	14 + 31	Descriptions of films
15.3C	15 + 21	Questions to discuss
15.10B	18 + 35 + 42	Story in pictures
17.2C	10 + 37 + 43	Lives of war poets
17.10B	13 + 28	Passages
17.10C	20	Discussion activity

* These are not 'communicative' activities, but model answers for students to see.

Verbs and idioms

At the end of each even-numbered unit there are exercises on idioms or verbs and idioms. These sections concern phrasal verbs, idiomatic phrases and also the collocations in which certain common verbs are used. The exercises needn't be done at the end of the unit: they can be fitted in when there is a little spare time during the lesson, or set for homework and checked in class later.

These sections deal with the idioms, collocations and phrasal verbs connected with the following words:

2.9	*keep & hold*
4.10	*make & do*
6.11	*come & go*
8.12	*bring & get*
10.11	*put & set*
12.11	*give & take*
14.9	*good & bad*
16.12	*mind, brain & word*

In addition, there is work on prepositional verbs and phrasal verbs in 12.3 and 14.3 respectively.

The exercises are not intended to provide comprehensive coverage of phrasal verbs or idioms. Students should make a note of any phrasal verbs or idioms that they come across and look them up in a dictionary, paying particular attention to the examples given there. *The Collins COBUILD Dictionary of Phrasal Verbs* is recommended for students with a particular interest in this area of vocabulary.

Exam advice and tips

★★ Scattered throughout the book, students will come across paragraphs like this. These sections contain advice which students may find helpful in the exam as well as tips to help them with their studies. These are offered to students as ideas that 'might work for you' and are not intended to be followed unquestioningly. Students should be encouraged to build on their experience of previous exams they have prepared for, refining techniques that have worked well before and discarding ones that may have restricted their success in the past.

Symbols

▓ indicates Communication Activities, where individual students are given different information that they have to communicate to each other. These are printed at the end of the Student's Book in random order so that students can't see each other's information. There is a complete 'guide' to these opposite.

▭ indicates that there is recorded material on the cassettes. Every unit has accompanying recorded material.

◢ indicates that students should use a fluorescent highlighter for an activity. A pencil may be used instead, if preferred, to underline or put (rings) round the words, but a highlighter is much more effective.

⚠ indicates a piece of advice or a warning.

1 Free time

➡ See page 7 of the Introduction for more information on the **Topic vocabulary** sections, and page 17 for information on **Mistakes: marking and correction**.

A   These questions form the basis of a warm-up discussion. You may prefer students to do this in groups of three or four.

After some minutes' discussion, call on selected pairs to report back to the class on the most interesting things they found out from each other.

Encourage questions on vocabulary connected with the topic while students are taking part in their discussions, and afterwards.

B   A short discussion in pairs about the hobbies shown in the pictures will help students to approach the next section more confidently. Some of the pictures are deliberately ambiguous in order to provoke discussion.

C   ▭ This is an exercise in listening for gist and, with students who are good at listening, may only need to be played once. To help students with the task, pause the tape after each speaker so that everyone has time to make notes before the next speaker begins.

Suggested answers

Karen: Cooking (together with her husband)
        She treats it like painting, and now enjoys something she used to loathe
Tim: Music: composing songs
        (No reason given, but presumably he enjoys it because he has a talent for it)
Jacqui: Riding a horse
        Having a 'friend'   being in the country with your own thoughts
Mike: Tennis and squash
        Meeting people   easy and rewarding for beginners   involvement in tactics and strategy
Ishia: Making pots
        Physical sensation of working with clay   making complicated 'advanced' pots like teapots, in different styles   the bright colours

Transcript

Presenter: We asked five people to talk about their hobbies or leisure interests. First of all, Karen.

Karen: Ah, now my hobby began through something that I've loathed, I think since a past life. I've always loathed cooking and when I met my husband, oh... just about ten years ago – he's Russian, and... um... Russian men have this tendency to believe that women work and cook and do everything else as well. And so he said, 'Oh you... you like cooking?' I said, 'No. I don't actually go in the... in the kitchen usually.' 'Ah,' he thought, 'Mm,' he thought, 'I can cook a bit. Er... let's cook together.'

So he refused to go in the kitchen on his own and I never went in the kitchen on my own and I did start cooking. And the only way I could look at it was as a sort of... more like painting than actually the ph... physical act of cooking and then I actually really began to enjoy it.

What about you, Tim? What do you enjoy doing?

Tim: Um... well, I suppose... would you call it a hobby? Music really is the... the other side of things that I do. I've got a little studio at home with a four-track tape recorder and synthesisers and drum machines and guitars and all that sort of thing. And... er... I spend lots of time playing with the equipment and not enough time writing music, and actually doing anything about it. I spent a long time a few years ago with a record that I thought was going to be absolutely the smash hit of the year and I ended up having an interview with this very very big, very fat music producer who sat back with a big cigar in his mouth and told me that my education was standing in my way because the m... lyrics were too clever! So I was very flattered by that.

Presenter: Next we hear from Jacqui.

Jacqui: Recently... um... I sort of went back to my childhood and I've bought a horse. Yeah, and... er... I mean, I was quite... quite good when I was younger, I used to compete, but this time I've decided not to compete because that would... I felt would be quite stressful. And... I... the reason I just love riding is because (a) you've got a friend but (b) you... I'm not completely friendless, but a friend who doesn't answer back, that's the best thing! And (b) you... I mean I live in the country near Henley and you ride off into the woods and I mean sometimes you don't see a car or... or a person or anything for hours and there's just the countryside and your own thoughts and I think that's what a hobby should be. It should be something you enjoy and maybe something completely different from your own work.

What about you, Mike? Have you got any hobbies?

Mike: Well... er... I have... er... I suppose the main things I do with my leisure time are a couple of sports that I play. Er... mainly tennis, but I... I've recently started to play squash again, and you know squash has a... a terrible image recently, you know, of being a terribly yuppie sport and being very dangerous and stuff. But the thing you find out when you... when you join a public sports centre in the way I play is that, you know, just everybody plays. And what's great about squash is – there are a number of things which I like about it – one is that when you play in the squash leagues that they organise you're not forever looking for somebody to play, there's just four or five other people who you phone up and say, 'Well, we're in the same league, we'll play' and you meet literally all kinds of people. And our league is a mixed league and there are several very good women players in it as well, which is really interesting to watch these women play.

But squash is fun, I think, mainly because it's so easy at the beginning. Two people who've just started can have a good time playing squash right away because the ball always comes back, and... er... two better people can have a harder game. But... er... a... and you get involved in the strategy of it very quickly, whereas in tennis you really have to be really very good before you start thinking about, 'Well, gee, where am I going to play this ball?' It's an achievement in tennis just to hit the ball back at all. But in squash you're right away involved with where you should play the ball and... er... the tactics and strategy of it, which is what I find more interesting about it.

Ishia, what about you? Have you got a hobby?

Ishia: What about me? Well, I'm afraid it's not squash. I'm certainly not sports . . .

Mike: You surprise me!

Ishia: I know I'm... um... actually what I really... I used to have a hobby that I really enjoyed doing and it was making pots, which I love and I'm really sad because I just don't have the time to do it any more. And I do spend a lot of time looking at pots, I mean I just love them, I mean I head for them in the... in any museum, any gallery, wherever. I always go and have a look at the pots and literally my fingers itch because I want to make them, because it's such a *wonderful* sensation, it's such a marvellous thing to do. And I did it for quite a long time and I made teapots by the end, which was quite advanced and great fun because you... you, you know, you got a bit of everything then: you made the actual shape, you then had to fit a handle which was very difficult, and a lid and a spout. And they all had wonderful personalities, so you could make them sort of cheerful round ones or quite severe ones or quite elegant ones. Um... and I loved bright colours. And I did a lot of... a lot of work in terracotta clay not in... not so much in stoneware, which is very sort of English and very... very lovely. But the stuff that I really liked was... was sort of beautiful sort of bright blues and bright greens and lovely red clay. And I miss it!

(Time: 5 minutes 30 seconds)

D   A few minutes' preparation alone is desirable to give everyone time to gather their thoughts before launching into a discussion on the pros and cons of each sport or pastime.

Again, encourage questions on relevant vocabulary. During this kind of activity, students may also use their dictionaries. However, it may be best to ban the use of bilingual dictionaries in this kind of activity, in favour of English–English dictionaries.

1.2 Learning a musical instrument

➡ See page 10 of the Introduction for more information on the Reading sections.

➡ If time is limited, and you would like everyone to prepare the reading passage before the next lesson, discuss section E first, moving on to A later.

A   As with 1.1B, students need time to prepare themselves by considering the theme of the passage before starting to read it.

The instruments shown are: piano   violin   maraca   harmonica   drums   French horn   accordion   guitar   saxophone
– though there may be some discussion about this.

B   Generally, with a reading passage of this length, students should be asked to read it through at home before the lesson, and perhaps also answer the comprehension questions and vocabulary questions. If this is done there is more time in class for everyone to DISCUSS the answers and for any follow-up work.

Students should answer the questions in note form – full sentences are not required in this case.

Answers

1   piano   violin   maraca   harmonica   drums   brass (e.g. French horn)
    guitar   electric accordion   saxophone
2   a sense of accomplishment, a creative outlet and an absorbing pastime
3   low back pain   shoulder strain   bleeding   unsightly swelling
4   You get depressed because you can't play it well enough – or you get
    depressed because you spend so long practising that there's no time for
    anything else
5   a   piano: expensive, difficult to play, not sexy
    b   violin: notoriously difficult
    c   maraca: mildly entertaining, but only to babies
    d   harmonica: you quickly get bored with it
    e   drums: very difficult to learn, but people think it's easy and fun
    f   guitar: too popular, most people will play it better than you
    g   electric accordion: anti-social
    h   saxophone: playing it in public may destroy your credibility
6   Brass instruments (e.g. French horn) – if you like making rude noises.
    And the saxophone – if you really do learn to play well.
7   The drummer attacked someone who came up to him and there was a
    fight

C   [icon]   This exercise draws attention to some of the vocabulary in the passage. Make sure everyone has time to do the highlighting , as only this can focus on the use of the words in context. Just matching the words and phrases is not enough.

Answers

grudge – dislike   *syndrome* – condition   *maudlin* – self-pitying
endeavour – effort   *be misled* – get the wrong idea
physical coordination – control of one's movements
nuance – subtle variation   *unruffled equanimity* – perfect calmness
charisma – charm and magnetism

E   Allow enough time for discussion and comparing ideas. Everyone has their own methods of learning vocabulary items, and students may be able to learn from each other some useful techniques which might work for them. There is, of course, no 'best way' of memorising vocabulary, and you and your students may disagree with some of the ideas in this section.

An extra point: As time passes, if the highlighting ink fades, students can re-highlight the words they still want to be reminded of.

1.3   Comparing and contrasting   Grammar review

➡ See page 12 of the Introduction for more information on the **Grammar review** sections.

A   The contrasted sentences in this section illustrate some of the ways in which different structures are used to convey different meanings. There is, of course, no need for students to actually rewrite each sentence – but they could highlight any structures they want to remember.

   With this kind of exercise, encourage everyone to do the easier ones first, and come back to the trickier ones later. If a pair is having difficulty with a particular question, they should ask another pair for help.

   At the end spend a few minutes on a feedback session, discussing any questions that arise. Note that these are **Suggested answers**, which may be open to discussion. Other interpretations may be possible, particularly if a sentence is given an unusual intonation, or if particular words are stressed.

Suggested answers

1 Like you, I wish I could play the piano.
    – We both wish we could play the piano.
    I wish I could play the piano like you.
    – You are a better player than me.

2 Your essay was most interesting.
   – *Your essay was very interesting.*
   Your essay was the most interesting.
   – *Your essay was more interesting than any of the others.*

3 The cliff was too hard for us to climb.
   – *We couldn't climb the cliff because it was so difficult.*
   The cliff was very hard for us to climb.
   – *Although it was difficult to climb the cliff we managed it.*

4 She is a much better violinist than her brother.
   – *They both play well, but she plays better.* OR *She plays well, unlike her brother.* (This seems more positive than the second sentence, because of the use of *better*.)
   Her brother is a much worse violinist than she is.
   – *Neither of them are much good, but he plays rather badly.* (This seems more negative than the second sentence, because of the use of *worse*.)

5 Claire is Britain's second most popular name for girls.
   – *In the Top Ten of first names, Claire is number 2* (after Sarah).
   Claire is Britain's most popular second name for girls.
   – *There are many popular first names, but Claire is the most popular second name* (as in Sarah Claire Brown).

6 She swims as well as she runs.
   – *She is good at both running and swimming.*
   She swims as well as runs.
   – *She takes part in both sports.*

7 Bob isn't too bright, like his father.
   – *Both of them are rather dim.*
   Bob isn't as bright as his father.
   – *His father is more intelligent.*
   Bob's father is bright, but Bob isn't that bright.
   – *They are both quite intelligent, but Bob is rather less intelligent.* OR *His father is intelligent, but Bob is not particularly intelligent.*
   Bob isn't all that bright, like his father.
   – *Neither of them is particularly intelligent.*

B   Suggested answers (many alternatives are possible)

1 *Example: make sure everyone understands what they are supposed to do.*
2 plays *tennis* so well
   is such a brilliant *tennis* player
3 as *fast* as anyone else in her class
   so *fast* that she overtook me on the first lap

4 is a great deal less *energetic* than
   is not at all *energetic* – unlike
5 takes a lot longer than
   requires considerably more time and effort than
6 the least interesting hobby
   one of the most expensive hobbies
7 I'd rather go out for the evening
   I prefer to go to a club with my friends rather

C   Corrections

1 It isn't true to say that London is **as large as** Tokyo / **larger than** Tokyo.
2 He's no expert on cars: to him a Mercedes and a BMW are **alike** / **the same**.
3 Her talk was most enjoyable and much more informative **than** we expected.
4 Don't you think that **the more difficult something is, the less enjoyable it is**?
5 **Fewer** people watched the last Olympics on TV than watched the soccer World Cup.
6 Who is the **least** popular political leader **in** the world?
7 My country is quite **different from** / **to** Britain.

D   This section could be done entirely in class, or the written work could be set for homework.

At the end, allow time for feedback and questions. Maybe point out that this section has only covered certain aspects of comparing and contrasting, and that students who still feel unclear may need to refer to a grammar reference book, such as *Practical English Usage*.

Extra activity As a follow-up, this **Comparison game** may be appropriate:

Working in pairs (or teams), students note down some things that are similar in some ways and different in others, then the other pair (or team) has to explain the differences and similarities. Like this:

What's the difference between a chair and a table?
– *They both have four legs, but a chair is for sitting on and a table is for sitting at. A table is usually higher and heavier than a chair.*

Examples of other suitable pairs:
   police officer – judge   tree – bush   fountain pen – pencil
   knife – scissors   computer – typewriter   tea – coffee

1.4   A 300-kilometre walk

➡ See page 13 of the Introduction for more information on the **Questions & summary** sections.

Most students find writing summaries one of the hardest parts of the Proficiency exam, but with adequate preparation it becomes much less formidable. The work in this section, and similar sections in later units, helps students to prepare progressively for the summary writing they will have to do in the exam.

A   Preliminary discussion helps students to anticipate what the passage is likely to be about, building up certain expectations. Looking at the map will help too.

B   The class is divided into groups of three. Each student has a different part of the same text which they will have to tell the others about in their own words later.

Student A looks at Activity 1 on page 289 in the Student's Book. Student B looks at Activity 32 on page 304, and student C looks at Activity 34 on page 305. If necessary, in a group of four, two students can share the same information.

Everyone should make notes while they're looking at the passage, to help them to remember what they read, and to make it easier to tell the others about it in their own words in C.

C   Make it clear that the idea here is to use your own words, not quote from the passages. In the exam, one of the difficulties many students have is avoiding quoting verbatim from the passage. There will be ample practice in this as the course progresses.

D   This summary is intended as a model for the task in E.

E   No word limit is set for this task – it's best just to see how it comes out this time, and for students to discover what problems they encounter when trying to use their own words.

This Model summary, in common with the ones in later units, may be photocopied for your students to see, if you wish.

Model summary (about 100 words)

In spite of the bad weather, Mark Wallington has good
memories of his walk. During the worst of the weather he

was able to rest and shelter at St Davids, which is a
delightful little place. When the sun came out again he
resumed his walk, and was surprised again and again by the
marvellous views of the islands and beaches. For three
days the weather was pleasant by day and, as the nights
were calm, he enjoyed camping out. At the end, after
walking 300 kilometres, he was able to look back on it
with a satisfying feeling of accomplishment.

1.5 Adjective + noun collocations — Vocabulary development

➡ See page 9 of the Introduction for more information on the **Vocabulary
development** sections.

A   This short section is an introduction to the subject of collocations.

Answers

a *deep* lake   a *close* friend   a *valuable* piece of advice
a *noisy* room overlooking the street
a *quiet* room overlooking the garden   a *nearby* shop
an *expensive* meal   a *profound* book   a *loud* noise   a *silent* movie

B   The aim of this section, and of section C, is to encourage students to be
creative, to pool ideas, and to use a dictionary for inspiration whenever
necessary.

Suggested answers

enjoyable/pointless activity   ferocious/cuddly animal
readable/absorbing book   naughty/local boy   strenuous/physical exercise
enjoyable/terrible film   dear/old friend   exciting/thrilling game
pretty/little girl   serious/mysterious illness   great/slight interest
worthwhile/demanding job   handsome/tiresome man
disappointing/delicious meal   beautiful/impressive painting
talented/professional photographer   delightful/depressing place
catchy/memorable song   funny/frightening story
hard-working/charming student   entertaining/informative talk
well-informed/intelligent teacher   attractive/sensible woman

C   There are many possible collocations in this exercise. It may be
necessary to remind students to skip the ones they can't do easily, and come
back to them later on – or ask another pair for their ideas.

Suggested answers

1 *Ask the class to suggest other collocations before they do the exercise:*
   e.g. a light wind   a pale complexion   a bright light
   a colourless town
2 a famous film star   a well-known actor   a notorious murderer
   an infamous tyrant   a distinguished professor
3 an extensive vocabulary   a long list   a wide selection
   a broad education
4 an old car   an elderly gentleman   an ancient castle
   an old-fashioned radio
5 a new fashion   a modern building   an up-to-date dictionary
   a recent development   a fresh egg
6 a considerable advantage   a major disaster   a strong influence
   an important point   a significant number   a vital ingredient
   an essential precaution
7 an insignificant amount   a minor operation   a small difference
   a little girl   a trivial mistake
8 a strange dream   an unusual name   a rare species
   a peculiar smell   an uncommon occurrence

1.6 It's only a sport!   Reading

A   This section not only leads students into the reading passage, but
introduces some useful vocabulary.

B   **Suggested adjectives**

*competitive   confident   dedicated   determined   disciplined   easygoing
emotional   exuberant   humorous   intelligent   methodical   modest
obstinate   painstaking   persistent   resourceful   self-deprecating   sociable*

C   Point out that true/false questions often look deceptively easy. In some
ways the techniques required in answering them are similar to those required
when answering multiple-choice questions: looking carefully at each part of
the sentence and comparing the information given with relevant parts of the
text. Highlighting or underlining quotations from the text helps when
answering true/false or multiple-choice questions – and makes it easier to
justify your answers to a partner.

Answers

TRUE: 2   6   7   10   FALSE: 1   3   4   5   8   9

D   Giving paragraph numbers rather than the exact line numbers encourages students to read through the sentences more carefully, and draws their attention more effectively to the contexts in which the words are used.

Answers

dull routine – chore   *to an extreme degree* – with a vengeance
disappointing – not all it's cracked up to be   *disappointed* – disillusioned
former – erstwhile   *attractively* – endearingly   *lively* – exuberant
attract publicity – hit the headlines   *well-known* – high-profile

➡ Any discussion of students' reactions to the passage might be saved until after 1.7 has been done, when students will have heard another point of view.

1.7   It's a nice way to live!   Listening

A   Allow time for everyone to discuss any previous knowledge they have of the subject and to make some suppositions about the answers to the questions. Reading the questions through in advance will make it easier for them to follow the interview when they listen to it.

B   ▭ This is an exercise in listening for specific information. The questions don't cover every point made. It may be necessary to reassure students that even if they can't catch every word the speaker says (and she does speak rather fast some of the time) it won't stop them getting the answers to the questions.

Point out that brief notes are sufficient for this exercise – complete sentences are not necessary.

Answers
 1 Swimming, cycling and running
 2 Anything from half an hour to 15 hours (depending on the distances involved)
 3 Developing a well-toned body   A drop in your heart rate   Loss of weight   More energy
 4 You develop a positive self-image
 5 Everybody who takes part is a winner (especially if they finish the race)
 6 Tobacco companies
 7 They're living in a dream world
 8 1,500 metres swimming   40 km cycling   10 km running
 9 15-20 hours a week
10 3½ to 4 thousand kilometres   (She means 3½ to 4 thousand *metres*)

11   50-60 km
12   She drinks a lot of water and eats fresh, unprocessed foods

C This discussion activity follows on from what students have read about Zara Long in 1.6 and heard from Sarah Springman in 1.7. As not every question may be equally relevant to each group, it may be a good idea to recommend that they start with the questions which seem most interesting. At the end of the discussion, ask each group to report back to the class on the most interesting or controversial points which were made.

Extra activity This activity is particularly suitable for students who are keenly interested in the topic of this unit.

1   Choose one of your favourite sports or games (this could be a non-athletic game like chess, backgammon or Scrabble – preferably one that the rest of the class don't know too much about.
2   Make notes on how it is played, using a dictionary and consulting a book of rules if necessary. Do this as homework.
3   Give a short talk to the class about your chosen sport or game, and answer their questions about it.

Transcript

Sarah: My name's Sarah Springman, I'm an international triathlete and I've been taking part in my sport now since... er... middle of 1983.
Presenter: What exactly is a triathlon?
Sarah: Well, a triathlon is a... an event that includes swimming, first of all, then bicycling and then running. All one after the other, without stopping, and they can take from perhaps half an hour for a short distance novice event, which is enormous fun and not terribly difficult to do at all, right up to the really rather longer and more gruelling events that take maybe twelve to fifteen hours to finish, but those are a bit crazy.
Presenter: What are the satisfactions of the sport?
Sarah: Well, I think the satisfactions really begin with the training and with the change in your outlook on life. Simply... simply put, if you're somebody who doesn't exercise at all and suddenly you indulge in a very sensible programme of swimming, bicycling and running, you actually are training all parts of the body really – and the swimming trains the upper part of the body and of course the cycling and the running covers the lower part. So you're actually developing a well-toned... um... all-round body, you're developing your heart and your lungs, your blood pressure drops, your resting heart rate drops – I think my resting heart rate has, at the very lowest level, gone down to 28 beats a minute, which again is... is... is unusual. But for people who have an average resting heart rate of 72 beats a minute, for example, if you can drop that to in the fifties, then clearly when you're resting, your heart isn't working quite so hard. So there are all these wonderful benefits which... which come. Er... you lose a little weight, and more...

more than anything you seem to have the energy to do an awful lot more things than people who are more sedentary, so you have a positive self-image and you feel that much more confident about life.

So I think that is the core satisfaction that comes from knowing that you are doing something that you enjoy and that comes from actually feeling good about it. And I think the races are on top, I think they're fun, I think they're a way of pitting yourself against other people, and it's very nice to be the winner but you're a... you're only the winner, as it were, if you're the first across the line, and there's always somebody around who's better than you, so that's not really a very valid marker in my mind. It's to know that you're doing the best you can and achieving your best potential. And I think that is what most people who take part in triathlon have to be satisfied with: the fact that they're there, they're on the start line, and more than anything they finish the race. Everybody who takes part in it is a winner, and it's not necessarily just the fastest woman or... or man. And I think that's an important ethic to have and it's one we try and put across in... in our sport.

Presenter: What is her attitude to sponsorship?

Sarah: I think, I'm afraid, that money makes the world go round and if you have sponsorship then you can put on a wonderful event and many many more people benefit. So I think that as long the sponsorship is... is a valid sponsorship, i.e. it is *not* tobacco sponsorship for sport – I feel very strongly about this, I would never *ever* allow myself or I would strongly discourage... um... any of the national governing bodies or the International Triathlon Union if they every *dreamt* of allowing tobacco to sponsor... um... a triathlon – and fortunately I think everybody is pretty much of the same opinion a... as I am.

Presenter: How does she find enough time to do her job and take part in her sport?

Sarah: You know, life is always a balancing act, nothing is ever perfect and the athlete or the individual who assumes that life is perfect is living in a dream world, I'm afraid. And so we've just got to get up and get on with it and do the best that we can. And as long, my feeling now is, as long as I'm making a contribution somewhere along the line then I feel that I'm not wasting my time. And if I'm teaching undergraduates to enjoy and understand... um... engineering principles then that... that's exciting. If I'm encouraging other women to come into the sport that's wonderful.

But, um... you know, life is... life is there for variety and you have to remember what your main goals are and bear those in mind at all times, but allow a little freedom to have some fun and do some other things on the way. You're a long time dead, as they say!

Presenter: How much time does she spend training each week?

Sarah: It depends on the distances you're training for. At the moment I'm training for the Olympic distance, which is a 1,500-metre swim, a 40-kilometre bicycle ride and a 10-kilometre run, and so that event will take me around two hours. So in contrast to an event that takes me ten hours I clearly don't need to train quite so long.

So perhaps, maybe fifteen to twenty hours at the moment, and I would swim maybe three or four times a week, and get up at six o'clock in the morning and go swimming at 6.30, swim maybe 3½ –4,000 kilometres. (*She really means metres*) Um... then I might bicycle perhaps five times a week... er... I might do one long ride which is about anything, say anything between... um... 50 to 60 kilometres, something like that, and I might do a 16-kilometre time trial one evening, I might do a set of interval sessions, and a couple of steady rides. And then on the running I might do a very hard interval session, I might do a tempo run when I'm running quite hard so I'm a bit breathless but not absolutely flat out, maybe a long run, a couple of steady runs as well, maybe some circuit training, a few sit-ups and press-ups, you know keep the middle part of the body well looked after. And try and do some stretching as well, that's very important, a little yoga, a little relaxation. Of course, inevitably time is always short and that's the one thing that goes and then you get a little nagging injury and you have to pay attention to it again.

So it's really an all-round thing, but there's nutrition as well which is very important, what you eat... 'You are what you eat,' they say. Your body's 70% water so you have to make sure you drink lots and lots of water and... er... eat all the right foods, fresh foods, nothing too processed. And you know, i... it's all right, it's fun, it's a nice way to live.

(Time: 6 minutes 30 seconds)

1.8 Using participles
Advanced grammar

➡ See page 12 of the Introduction for more information on the **Advanced grammar** sections.

A Suggested answers

1 Standing at the top of the hill, I could see my friends in the distance.
 – *I was at the top of the hill and my friends were in the distance.*
 I could see my friends in the distance standing at the top of the hill.
 – *My friends were at the top of a distant hill, and I could see them there.*

2 Before preparing the meal he consulted a recipe book.
 – *He couldn't start cooking until he had found the recipe.*
 After consulting a recipe book he prepared the meal.
 – *He looked for the recipe and then started cooking.*
 (There is only a slight difference in emphasis between these sentences.)

3 Finding the window broken, we realised someone had broken into the flat.
 – *We saw the broken window and this made us realise that there had been a break-in.*
 We realised someone had broken into the flat, finding the window broken.
 – *When the burglar found the broken window, he used it to make his entry.* (This suggests that the window was already broken before he arrived and that it made it easier for him to get into the flat.)

4 While preparing the meal, he listened to the radio.
  – The radio was an accompaniment to the main task of cooking.
  While listening to the radio, he prepared the meal.
  – Cooking was an accompaniment to his main interest: listening to the radio.

5 Crawling across the road, I saw a large green snake.
  – This sounds strange, and without a context could be understood to mean that the speaker was crawling across the road and came across a snake.
  I saw a large green snake crawling across the road.
  – The snake was crawling across the road when I saw it.

B Studying the examples should be done in silence in class – or if possible, set for homework.

➡ Any of exercises C to F can be done in pairs in class – or as homework and then discussed in class later.

C Answers

1 arranged
2 arriving
3 reaching
4 Shaken
5 finished
6 required
7 completing
8 lifting something heavy

D Answers

1 Not having a car, I usually travel by bus.
2 Chanting loudly, the demonstrators marched into the square.
3 Finding their way blocked by the police, they turned back.
4 Ever since watching the match on TV, she's wanted to take up golf too.
5 Having heard that he collects butterflies, I asked him to tell me about it.
6 Finding none of her friends (waiting) outside the cinema, she went home.
7 Not knowing much about art, I can't comment on your painting.
8 Sitting smoking at the back of the room (there) were three old men.
9 Drunk too quickly, coffee can give you hiccups.
10 Feeling a bit under the weather, I went to bed early.

E   Corrections

1 Looking out of my window, I saw a crowd of people in the street.
2 We thought he looked ridiculous wearing bright yellow trousers.
3 His father treats him like an adult because he is rather tall for his age.
4 Having been given such a warm welcome he felt very pleased.
5 If washed in hot water this garment will shrink.

F   If you think this exercise might be too hard for your students as it stands, write up the 'missing verbs' on the board to help them:

face   hear   look   open   open   realise   shout   sit   think   wonder

Answers

On **opening** my eyes, I knew that I was in a strange, dark room. **Thinking** that I might still be dreaming, I pinched myself to see if I was still asleep, but, **realising** that I really was awake I began to feel afraid. I found the door in the darkness, but it was locked. I decided to call for help but, after **shouting** for several minutes, I knew no one could hear me. I went to the window, and cautiously **opening** the shutters, I discovered that the window was barred and, **looking** outside, all I could see was darkness. My heart sank. **Faced** with an apparently hopeless situation, I sat down **wondering** what to do. I remained there **sitting** on the bed in silent desperation for several minutes.
    Suddenly, **hearing** a key being turned in the lock, I . . .

1.9 'Golden rules'   Writing skills & Composition

➡ See page 16 of the Introduction for more information on the **Writing skills & Composition** sections.

In future units, the sections on Writing skills and Composition are separate.

A   This is a discussion activity – these steps are not definitive, which is why the title is in inverted commas. Students should be encouraged to develop their own 'rules' and then be reminded to stick to them in future written work.

Suggested sequence (open to discussion)
GOLDEN RULES FOR WRITING A COMPOSITION
1 Look carefully at the instructions
2 Discuss what you're going to write with someone else
3 Do any necessary research   ⟫➡

4   Think about what you're going to write
5   Jot down all the points you might make
6   Analyse your notes, deciding which points to emphasise and which to omit
7   Use a dictionary to look up suitable words and expressions and write them down
8   Write a plan, rearranging the points in the order you intend to make them
9   Write a first draft, perhaps in pencil
10 Proof-read the first draft: eliminate errors in grammar, spelling and punctuation
11 Show your first draft to someone else and get feedback from them
12 Take a break
13 Look again at the instructions
14 Edit your first draft, noting any changes you want to make
15 Write your final version
16 Proof-read your final version, eliminating any mistakes you spot
17 Have a rest
18 Get feedback from other students on your final version (they are 'your readers')

B   Only the following steps from the list in the Student's Book might be feasible under exam conditions:

1   Look carefully at the instructions
2   Think about what you're going to write
3   Jot down all the points you might make
4   Analyse your notes, deciding which points to emphasise and which to omit
5   Write a plan, rearranging the points in the order you intend to make them
6   Look again at the instructions
7   Write your final version
8   Proof-read your final version, eliminating any mistakes you spot

C   The answers to these questions are a matter of opinion, but here are a few suggested answers to help students who lack inspiration:

Further information:
    type of ball, shape of racket, scoring system, type of court
Assumed knowledge:
    as above + the reader is assumed to know enough about tennis to be able to compare it with squash
Effective vocabulary:
    all walks of life   a major achievement   hunting for lost balls

Effective style and sentence structure:
    You don't have to be . . .   With tennis . . .   With squash . . .
    It does help to be . . .   Perhaps it's because . . . that . . .

D   Treat this and the next few compositions as a 'diagnosis' of each student's composition writing. What are the major points each should concentrate on improving?

Make sure everyone understands your system of marking written work and the meaning of the symbols you use. At this level there's no point in your correcting every little mistake that students have made – it's better for them to locate and correct their own mistakes, with some guidance in the form of symbols in the margin – see **Mistakes: marking and correction** on page 17.

Encourage students to read each other's work. The kind of feedback they give each other might include comments on and questions about:

- the content in general
- the style and how easy the piece was for them to read
- information or ideas that seemed particularly interesting or amusing
- information which was missing from the piece
- sentences which were less easy to follow

➡ As this is probably the first composition that the class will have done for you, it's a good idea to PHOTOCOPY their work and keep it on file. Then, later in the course, you can compare their compositions with this earlier one and see how your students' written work has improved. The students themselves may find it reassuring to look at these early compositions again later, to see that they have made progress. At this level it's often difficult to realise that your English actually is improving.

Finally . . .

Recommend to everyone that they should spend half an hour reading through the whole of this unit at home before moving on to Unit 2. This will help them to memorise the vocabulary and other points covered in the unit.

Flipping through earlier units in the book regularly, recalling previous lessons, is a simple yet surprisingly effective revision technique too.

2 Adventure

A   This is not just a warm-up discussion: it gives students the opportunity to consider some of the vocabulary related to the theme of this unit.

Among the qualities listed, the ones which are probably *least* important are:

arrogance   charisma   compassion   dignity   humility   intelligence knowledge   modesty   – but clearly this is a matter of opinion.

Background

The article is a review of one of Dervla Murphy's books. Most of her books concern travels she has made to exotic places, mostly in the company of her daughter Rachel. Among these are:

Full Tilt: Ireland to India with a Bicycle (1965)
On a Shoestring to Coorg: Experience of South India (1976)
Where the Indus is Young: A Winter in Baltistan (1977)
A Place Apart (1978) – a study of life in Northern Ireland
Eight Feet in the Andes: Travels on a Donkey from Ecuador to Cuzco (1985)
Muddling through in Madagascar (1985)
In Cameroon with Egbert (1989)

B   Answers

1 Juana (4), Dervla (2), Rachel (2)
2 In the Murphys' eyes: Juana, the mule;
   in the reviewer's eyes: 9-year-old Rachel
3 Three months ¶ 5 – one week less than the *conquistadores* ¶ 12
4 In a tent ¶ 11

C   In some of the passages in this book the paragraphs are numbered, but not the lines. If you wish to refer to particular lines in the text, you can do this by saying 'Line 4 of the 10th paragraph', for example.

Answers

saunter – stroll   *madcap schemes* – crazy plans   *frolic* – amusing game
heartening – encouraging   *overenthusiastically* – without restraint

day one – the beginning   *fretting* – fussing and worrying   *coveted* – envied and wanted   *homespun* – unsophisticated   *sticky moments* – dangerous incidents   *trusting soul* – someone who believes other people are honest

D   Answers

1 She is sceptical and is sarcastic about their unadventurousness and greed
2 two: South India and Baltistan (part of Kashmir)
3 Rachel was going to go to school
4 She lost patience   she joined in with religious festivals too enthusiastically   she wore unsuitable shoes which gave her blisters
5 pejorative – her views are considered to be unoriginal or naive by the reviewer
6 potatoes, tinned sardines, noodles   Juana ate alfalfa (grass)
7 She was stolen (and then presumably recovered because 'all ends happily')
8 Worst: Juana was nearly killed falling over a cliff
   Best: the views and the kindnesses

E   The ironic/sarcastic turns of phrase are underlined here. This may be open to discussion, and students need not be expected to spot all of these:

ONCE upon a time, with travel writing, the rewards won related to the risks taken. No longer. Travel writers travel by public transport; often they just hop in the car. They travel round British seaside resorts; they saunter up low mountains in the Lake District. Greatly daring, they visit islands off the coast. There is no point in travelling hopefully; far better to arrive as quickly as possible and collect your multi-national publisher's advance.

2.2 Articles and determiners   Grammar review

➡ Not all students have difficulties with articles in English. If these exercises present no problems for your students this section can be omitted, or set for homework and discussed later in class.

A   Answers

1 What was the mule like? = Could you describe their mule?
   What are mules like? = What is a mule like?

2 Do you like tea now? = Have you overcome your dislike of tea?
   Do you like the tea now? = Is the tea all right for you now?

3 Would you like some coffee now? = Would you like a coffee now?
  Would you like your coffee now? = Would you like the coffee now?

4 Every difficulty was foreseen. = Each difficulty was foreseen. = All the
  difficulties were foreseen.
  Some difficulty was foreseen. = We expected a certain amount of
  difficulty.
  No difficulty was foreseen. = We didn't expect any difficulty.
  Some of the difficulties were foreseen. = Not all of the difficulties were
  foreseen.
  The difficulty was foreseen. = We expected a particular difficulty.

5 He's not *the* Michael Jackson. = He's not the famous Michael Jackson.
  He's not Michael Jackson. = Michael Jackson is not his name.

6 Who's coming to dinner? = Who has been invited to eat with us?
  Who has been invited to the banquet? = Who's coming to the dinner?

B   Allow a little time for everyone to study the examples before they do
the exercise.

Suggested answers

advice – hint   tip   piece of
applause – round of
behaviour – action
clothing – coat   shirt   article of
fun – game   joke
information – fact   piece of
laughter – chuckle   laugh   (also a shriek of laughter)
luggage – suitcase   item of
music – song   tune   piece of
news – article   report   item of   piece of
progress – improvement
rain – drop of   fall of
research – analysis   piece of
snow – fall of   flake of
spaghetti – piece of   plate of
teaching – class   lesson
transport – car   train   means of
travel – journey   trip
wealth – asset   fortune   possession

C   Again allow time for students to study the examples before doing the
exercise.

Answers

1 knowledge   2 experience/adventure   3 success/experience   4 wood
5 adventure/experience/thought   6 pleasure   7 imagination   8 failure
9 butter/cheese/soup   10 cheese   11 knowledge/love   12 coffee

D   Suggested answers

The Murphys clearly see not Rachel but Juana, **their/the** beautiful glossy mule, as **the** heroine of **the** /**their** story. She cost £130 and they fuss over her like **a** film star, fretting about **her** diet, **her** looks, **her** mood. Juana is coveted by all; as **the/their** journey proceeds it is shadowed by **the/their/a** parting from her. There is **a/the** terrible moment when she falls over **a** precipice to Ø certain death but for **a** divinely placed single eucalyptus tree in **her** path.

She worries that Ø religion is so little comfort to **the/a** Peruvian Indian, that **the/their** babies chew Ø wads of Ø coca, that **the** boys Rachel plays Ø football with on **their/Ø/the** sloping pitches have no future, that she cannot repay Ø/**their/the** kindnesses: **the/an** ancient shepherdess who shared **her** picnic lunch of Ø cold potato stew on **a** cabbage leaf, **the/an** old man who set **his** dog to guard **their** tent at night.

E   Corrections

1 Politics **doesn't** interest him, except when **an** election takes place.
2 **Grapefruit** is my favourite **fruit**, but I don't like **bananas**.
3 The news **is** depressing today: two **aircraft** have crashed.
4 There **is a** crossroads at **the** top of **the** hill.
5 Mathematics **was the** most difficult subject at Ø school for me.
6 **The** Hague is **the** capital of **the** Netherlands, but Amsterdam is **the** largest city.

➡ Here are some nouns that tend to cause confusion, and which may lead students into making errors.

Nouns that are singular but look plural:
  athletics   economics   maths   measles   mumps   news   physics   rabies
  the Netherlands   the Philippines   the United States   the West Indies

Nouns that have irregular or unusual plurals:
  analysis – analyses   crisis – crises   criterion – criteria   fungus – fungi
  goose – geese   hypothesis – hypotheses   ox – oxen   phenomenon – phenomena

Nouns with identical singular and plural forms:
  aircraft   crossroads   deer   fish   grapefruit   rendezvous   salmon
  series   sheep   species   trout

Nouns that are always plural:
>*binoculars clothes glasses/spectacles handcuffs*
>*headphones/earphones headquarters jeans knickers pliers police*
>*premises pyjamas scales scissors shorts sunglasses tights trousers*
>*tweezers*

F   Student A should look at Activity 3, while B looks at 22. This activity gives students some freer practice in using articles and determiners, first orally and then in writing.

2.3 Climbing mountains   Listening

A   These pre-questions, for discussion in pairs, will help everyone to approach the listening tasks more confidently.

➡ There are no pauses between the sections on the tape. You will need to stop the tape at the places shown by ★ ★ ★ in the Transcript below.

B Answers
1 physical exertion – he likes to be fit – mountaineering is a very good cardio-vascular exercise
    views   (no reason given, but presumably because they are spectacular)
    danger – the thrill of being at the end of a rope and having to 'do it right'
    company – he has made good friends with fellow climbers
2 rock-climbing: acute terror   mountaineering: worry, chronic anxiety
3 Alastair himself was unconscious – his partner had to save him
4 Because there was no evasive action they could take
5 Because there was a cable-car station at the top, where they knew they could shelter

C Answers
1 pyramid   36   2 or 4   stores/supplies and equipment
2 north   (local) porters   the members of the expedition
3 Camp Two   fixed   safe   climbing   walking
4 wash   change their clothes   teeth
5 cramped   comfortable   safe

D Answers
YES answers: 1   4
NO answers: 2   3

E   This is a follow-up discussion.

Transcript

Presenter: Alastair Miller was a member of a recent British Combined Services expedition to Everest. We talked to him about climbing mountains and asked him what he enjoys about mountaineering.

Alastair: I enjoy the sheer physical exertion because I enjoy being fit anyway and I do a lot of sport and running and that sort of thing and I like just to be physically fit, and I find mountaineering is a nice way of doing that and probably that's one of the best ways because you're not actually running and pounding your knees and Achilles tendons and things. But if you're walking hard at altitude and uphill then that's probably as good a cardio-vascular exercise as anything. So I enjoy that aspect of it.

I enjoy the... the views, er... I enjoy the danger to a certain extent. I mean, I wouldn't go somewhere if I thought that I was going to kill myself, although I recognise that there is a risk of it. But I enjoy the... the thrill of being out on a... on the end of a rope knowing that if I don't do it right, then I am going to fall. Um... but hopefully that I'm going to get held and I'm not going to do a lot of damage, I wouldn't like to go climbing solo in a situation where if I fell I was going to kill myself. I enjoy the... the company, because I think you... you make tremendous friends on these expeditions and I've got friends that I've climbed with who are amongst my... my best friends ever really and I've climbed with them on... numerous other times now.

Presenter: As he admits, climbing mountains can be dangerous. Has he ever been frightened?

Alastair: Oh yes, I'm sure I have. Er... it's difficult to define specific instances but again I think there's a distinction between rock-climbing and... and mountaineering where... and the... the mode of being frightened is... is slightly different. In... in rock-climbing it's much more acute, if something goes wrong you know you're going to fall off. And in fact the worst... my worst accident... I didn't really have time to be frightened in, because it happened all so quickly, and that was... we were climbing... we were rock-climbing in... in Yosemite Valley in California, and the thing that I was tied on to on the cliff just pulled out and I fell the whole rope-length between myself and my partner. And as I fell past him I remember shouting, 'Stop me!' and I do have a vague recollection of falling but then I obviously hit something on the way down and was unconscious at the end of the rope, and so it was probably a lot more frightening for him than it... it was for me. So that's the sort of acute terror that you get from rock-climbing.

In mountaineering I think it's more the worry that you're going to get lost, the weather's going to come in, er...you're going to get hit by an avalanche, so there's the sort of more a chronic anxiety level there and I'm aware of that all the time. The weather...it never seems to be absolutely perfect conditions wherever you are, whether it's Himalayas or Alps, you're always aware there's that little wisp of cloud on the horizon which in a couple of hours could build up into a major storm.

And the other frightening experience was climbing a route called the Frendeau spur on the Aiguille du Midi in the French Alps in about 1980 I think it was, and we… we came to the top of that in a… in an enormous thunderstorm and as we were climbing the final snow slopes there was lightning literally striking the snow behind us, and setting off mini-avalanches and that was very frightening. But you just had to be philosophical because there was nothing you could do to avoid this lightning and if it hit you then that was it. The only comfort about that was that it's a mountain that has a cable-car station at the top, so although we were climbing up towards the top of the mountain, we were actually climbing towards safety and were able to scurry into the… into the cable car station and… and shelter from the storm overnight and… er… get the first cable car down the next day and have a beer to celebrate still being alive!

★★★

Presenter: What is it like taking part in an expedition to climb Everest?

Alastair: A lot of it is boring, a lot of it's hard work, a little bit of it is frightening as we've discussed, and some of it is fantastically exciting and exhilarating and that's the bit that you remember and that makes up for everything else.

Then the major problem on any expedition, and certainly a large expedition climbed in the sort of style that we did, is… is the logistics of it. And to get all… as I'm sure people will know, it's… it's what's called a 'pyramid effect': you've got 36 people at the bottom and you want to get two or four maybe at the top, so you slowly have to build up stores higher and higher up the mountain… er… to… in order to place your last four people on the summit. So you… there's an awful lot of carrying of stores and things. Now, on… on this particular side of Everest there are not a lot of local porters around, as there are on the south side, so on the south side you probably engage two hundred local porters who will carry your equipment up through the Khumbu Ice Fall into the area where you're going to be climbing from. On the north side you don't have that facility and you have to engage yaks. And so we had about 80 yaks loaded with kit, and they had to be looked after. The yaks would only go just a little bit above Camp One and from there on it was just expedition members doing all the carrying.

So that was how it worked. So you'd maybe do a week of carrying between One and Two, go down for a rest, and then come back up and find you'd be carrying between Camps Three and Four, or maybe eventually with luck, you'd actually get to be one of the lead teams and you'd be pushing the route out and of course that was when it became exciting and exhilarating to be places where nobody else had been. It was always exciting to… to be somewhere where you'd never been before, and I remember the first time I went up above Camp Two, I… it was absolutely brilliant: we were on fixed ropes which other people had put in so we were entirely safe, but for the first time we had crampons on and we were actually properly climbing rather than just walking.

A lot of it's uncomfortable, certainly above base camp, the facilities there . . . Camp One you might have, if you were feeling very brave, had a wash, but certainly above there you wouldn't do anything for a week or ten days, you would just not change your clothes, only clean your teeth, but everything else was just in the same clothes crawling in and out of your tent and sleeping bag. Above Camp Two, which was at 20,000 feet [6,000 m] on the… on the very steep bit of the climb at Camps Three and Four we lived in snow holes, which we'd had to dig out ourselves and they were quite cramped and of course they… although they're comfortable and they're safe because if an avalanche falls across the top of a snow hole it might bury you in, you might have to dig yourself out, but it's less serious than being swept away if you're in a tent.

★★★

Presenter: So, after going to Everest, what is there left to do now?

Alastair: I think I would go back to my old plan of making it a small group of friends going to climb a lower mountain where you didn't have to use oxygen and of higher technical interest. There's a... there's a beautiful mountain called Ama Dablam in the Everest region, which I think is only about 23–24,000 feet [7,000 m], but it's technically quite demanding and that... it's a beautiful mountain, it looks like the Matterhorn, and I'd love to go and climb that. But there are a number of other mountains of about that height that I would like to go to.

I've never been to South America and I'd love to go and climb in the Andes, I've done very little in North America. There are a lot of other mountains around the world I'd like to go and see.

(Time: 7 minutes 30 seconds)

2.4 Brazilian Adventure   Reading & summary writing

Background

Peter Fleming (1907–1971) was the brother of Ian Fleming, creator of James Bond. He is best remembered for his travel writing which describes relatively 'safe' adventures in an amusing way.

Brazilian Adventure (1933) describes his experiences of an expedition to Brazil, which he joined after seeing this advertisement in *The Times*:

> **EXPLORING** and sporting expedition, under ex-perienced guidance, leaving England June, to explore rivers Central Brazil, if possible ascertain fate Colonel Fawcett; abundance game, big and small; exceptional fishing; ROOM TWO MORE GUNS; highest references expected and given.– Write Box X, *The Times* E.C.4.

– Colonel Fawcett had disappeared on an expedition to find Eldorado and was never heard of again.

Peter Fleming's other books include *One's Company: A Journey in China* (1934) and *News from Tartary* (1936).

A Answers

1 Four people were directly involved in the expedition: the leader (Bob), the Organizer, Major Pingle, Captain John Holman. And peripherally: Major Pingle's German partner.

2 Bob, the leader   the Organizer

3 Not very

4 Yes, but that wasn't his real name

B Answers

1 Not a lot: at any rate, he had only shot one jaguar
2 To go by lorry instead of train OR to go by train instead of road
3 He was worried
4 A man who has had many adventurous experiences – or so he claimed
5 Captain John Holman
6 At his headquarters in São Paulo, Brazil
7 By telegram
8 None
9 Buying provisions, employing guides and making all the necessary arrangements
10 An entertaining fiasco, but probably not a disaster

C Answers

1 kinds of expedition   2 actors   3 understatement   4 unwilling
5 up-to-date   6 you can't do without   7 very little information
8 untrue or exaggerated

D   These are questions for discussion, but to settle any arguments students might like to know that the book was published in 1933. The tone of the passage might be described as 'ironical, deadpan, humorous or amusing'.

E Model summary   (This may be photocopied for students to see, if required.)

In spite of his charm and appearance, the vagueness of the Organizer did not inspire confidence: he was unwilling even to commit himself on their means of transport from Rio to São Paulo. He had given the responsibility for making the arrangements to a Major Pingle in Brazil, but it was unclear what arrangements he was making — if any — as only one message from him had been received, and that had been lost by the Organizer.

2.5 Words easily confused   Vocabulary development

➡ A useful source of words that particular nationalities tend to find confusing in English can be found in *Learner English* edited by Michael Swan and Bernard Smith (CUP, 1987). This book also covers grammatical and phonological difficulties that particular nationalities have in English.

Here, by way of example, are a few words that are 'false friends' for Greek speakers or which they sometimes mix up – some of these are covered in the exercises in this section:

> *agenda – notebook   agnostic – strange, foreign   air – wind*
> *annoy – bother   cabaret – bar   ephemera – newspaper   fortune – storm*
> *house – home   idiotic – private   pneumatic – witty*
> *remember – remind   room – space   sympathise – like*
> *trapeze – table, bank   woman – wife*

A   Consult a dictionary if you are in doubt about any of the meanings.

B   **Answers**   (The words that fit are given, though some of the others might also fit if used humorously or imaginatively.)

3 difficult   emotional   moody   sensitive   touchy
4 attended
5 annoying   bothering   provoking
6 diary   exercise book   notebook
7 absent-minded   forgetful   inattentive (?)
8 advantages   benefits   rewards
9 farther   further
10 eventual   imminent   possible
11 apparent   evident   obvious
12 course   training
13 conference   congress   meeting (?)
14 hit   punched   slapped   smacked (?)   struck (?)   whacked
15 exclusive   private
16 at once   immediately   in a moment?   presently   shortly

C   Make sure everyone understands what they have to do in this activity before they begin writing sentences.

2.6 Keeping the reader's interest

A 　　Highlighting the phrases will help everyone to see how they are used in context. The other examples should be done by students using their own ideas, and no suggested answers are given here.

B The more effective features are in bold print, the less effective ones are underlined. This sort of thing is debatable.

The composition in the Student's Book is about 250 words long and seems to run out of steam after the first paragraph.

It had been a long, tiring journey to S_____. The ferry, which should have taken at most five hours, had had engine trouble and didn't arrive till 2 a.m. As the harbour itself was several miles from the main town – the only place where accommodation was available, and much too far to walk to even by daylight – we **hoped against hope** that the local bus service would still be running. **Sure enough** one tiny, ancient blue bus was waiting on the quayside, but **imagine our dismay** when we saw that **about 98** other passengers were also disembarking with the same destination. We **fought** our way onto the bus and waited for the driver to appear. A man **staggered** out of the bar nearby and **groped** his way into the driving seat – presumably he'd been drinking since early evening when the ship was supposed to arrive.

We were <u>very frightened</u>. Most of the passengers hadn't seen the driver come out of the bar. The bus went <u>very slowly</u> up the steep road. On one side the cliffs **dropped vertically down to the sea hundreds of metres below**. We arrived in the town at <u>3 a.m.</u>, but there was no accommodation. We found a taxi to take us to the other side of the island. We slept on the beach.

As it began to get light and the sun rose over the sea, **waking us from our dreams**, we realised that it had all really happened and that we were **lucky to be alive**.

C Here is an improved version of the second half of the composition, making a total of about 350 words. These paragraphs may be photocopied for your students to see.

We were absolutely petrified and we knew that most of the other passengers hadn't spotted the driver coming out of the bar and were blissfully unaware of what might be in store. It was a nightmare journey: the bus was so full that it could hardly get up the steep, narrow hill that led from the port to the main town. On one side of the road we could see the cliffs dropping vertically down to the sea hundreds of metres below us, and were afraid that at any moment we would all go crashing down to our deaths.

But we survived. We arrived in one piece,and although the whole journey seemed to have taken days, by the time we arrived in the town it was still only 3'clock. To our dismay,though, there was no accommodation to be had for love or money. Fortunately, we found a taxi which took us to the other side of the island where there was a beach, and we slept under the stars.

The next morning, as it began to get light and the sun rose over the sea, waking us from our dreams, we realised that it had all really happened and that we were very lucky to be alive.

© Cambridge University Press 1993

E   Doing this will help students to get ideas from each other – and gives a reason for writing an exciting story for D above. The pairs might be expanded to groups so that more people can read each other's work.

2.7 Position of adverbs   Advanced grammar

➡ As will become clear from this section, it's impossible to lay down hard-and-fast rules about adverb position.

Make sure, however, that everyone is aware of the difference of emphasis achieved by placing adverbs in less usual positions, particularly at the very beginning or very end of a clause. Often, this is done using a comma (rather like a pause in speech) – or after a dash at the end of a sentence – as in these examples:

Adverb position usually causes students problems.
Usually, adverb position causes students problems.
Adverb position causes students problems – usually!

A   Suggested interpretations

1 Tricia only wants to help. – *She's trying to be helpful, not interfere.*
   Only Peter wants to help. – *Nobody else wants to help, only Peter.*

2 Paul just doesn't like flying. – *He simply hates it.*
   Olivia doesn't just like flying . . . – *She also likes lots of other things.*

3 Pam doesn't really feel well. – *She's slightly unwell.*
 Jack really doesn't feel well. – *I assure you that he's not well.*
 Anne doesn't feel really well. – *She's not totally well.*

4 Tony and Jane still aren't married.
 – *Contrary to our expectations they haven't got married yet.*
 Still, Sue and Bob aren't married. – *Nevertheless, they aren't married.*
 Olivia and Paul aren't still married, are they?
 – *I know they used to be married, but I don't think / didn't think they were any more.*

5 I don't particularly want to see Lisa. – *I've no special desire to see her.*
 I particularly don't want to see Tim. – *He's the person I really don't want to see.*

6 I enjoy eating normally. – *I like normal kinds of food, not unusual ones.*
 I normally enjoy eating. – *I usually like eating.*
 Normally, I enjoy eating. – *I usually like eating, but in this case maybe not.*

7 Carefully, I lifted the lid. – dramatic and emphatic
 I carefully lifted the lid./ I lifted the lid carefully. – not particularly dramatic

B Notice that, in formal style, *hardly ever, never, rarely* and *seldom* can be placed, for emphasis, at the beginning of a sentence, but that the word order changes:
 Never have I been so insulted in my life.
 Seldom have there been so many people at a concert before.
This point is covered in 3.7 Using inversion for emphasis.

Suggested answers

1 We have **nearly/practically/virtually** finished our work.
 I **utterly** disagree with what you said.
 It is **hardly ever/rarely/seldom** as cold as this usually.

2 I don't **altogether/entirely** agree with her.
 Your work has **greatly** improved.
 He isn't **altogether/exactly** brilliant
 I enjoyed the show **enormously/greatly**.

3 The Olympics take place **once every four years.**
 I've warned you **again and again/many times/over and over again** to take care.

I don't have the information **at the moment**, so I'll call you back **before long/in the evening/within the hour**.
Most of the time I agree with what she says, but **from time to time/once in a while** we don't see eye to eye.
Although she had washed her hair **before breakfast/the previous day**, she washed it again **in the evening**.

4   I can't give you my answer **at once/immediately**, but I'll let you know **presently/eventually/later/shortly/soon**.
Let me know **afterwards/later** what you thought of the film.
It will **presently/soon** be time to go home, so you'll have to finish the work **afterwards/later**.

5   She was behaving very **foolishly/oddly/strangely**.
They congratulated him **discreetly/warmly**.
He held up the prize **carefully/proudly** and thanked everyone **sincerely/warmly/thoughtfully**.
I raised my hand **automatically/instinctively** to protect my face.
She took his hand **gently/lovingly/reassuringly** and looked **apprehensively/gloomily/lovingly** into his eyes.

6   **Luckily**, I found my wallet in the car.
Hopefully, I'll have finished the work soon.
Strangely enough/Unfortunately, she didn't get the job.
Amazingly/Funnily enough, they're getting married.

C   Suggested answers

1   After a while they replied to my letter.
2   I'm afraid that's a mistake I make again and again.
3   I often eat out in the evenings.
4   I've practically finished writing this report.
5   They reluctantly helped me. / They helped me reluctantly.
6   I particularly don't want to go for a walk.
7   Each branch of the company operates independently.
8   Presumably he will be feeling apprehensive.
9   You should always pay attention to your spelling.
10 She looked at me anxiously.
11 All enquiries will be handled discreetly.
12 He does lose his temper from time to time. / From time to time he does lose his temper.

2.8   Going for a walk?   Listening & composition

In this section the information and ideas given in the recording act as a basis for the composition.

A   Looking at the task before listening to the recording helps students to apply their previous knowledge and common sense to the task.

B   🔲 **Answers**

PRECAUTIONS

1 four
2 careful   trained
3 deteriorate/get worse   weather forecasts (especially in the newspaper)
4 time   darkness
5 speed/pace   slowest   behind
6 stop walking   somewhere to shelter   visibility to get better/improved visibility   walk on/go on walking   precipice

EQUIPMENT

1 plan   route
2 compass   landmarks   how to use it   your nose   sense of direction
3 warm   waterproof
4 proper walking boots   sandals   trainers
5 rations   chocolate   raisins   sandwiches   (and something to drink)
6 torch/flashlight
7 survival blanket   survival bag

And . . .
let someone know where you're going   what time you expect to be back report your safe arrival

C & D   Follow-up discussion   The groups should explain their ideas to the rest of the class.

E & F   The information given in the listening exercise, together with the discussions in C and D, now provides a basis for the composition which students are going to have to do. Insist that everyone makes notes (preferably in pencil) before they put pen to paper.

Transcript

Presenter: OK, so it's a... it's a lovely sunny day and you feel like going for a walk maybe up into the mountains. And off you go, hoping for a good trip. So far so good but according to Denis Rosser, you could be asking for trouble. Now what's all this about, Denis?

Denis: Well, yes of course, most of the time, the majority of the time you'll have a marvellous day, you'll get back safely, maybe you're feeling a bit stiff the next day, but there'd be no problem. But... er... you should bear in mind that there are risks in going walking in the mountains because they can be very dangerous places. First of all, you should never ever head off into the mountains by yourself. That's very important. It's best to have at least four people actually in your party, then if anything goes wrong, like someone breaks a leg, or sprains an ankle or something, one can stay with the injured person and two others can go off to get help. Er... so you should always be careful and not do anything you're not trained to do and take all the necessary precautions as well.

Presenter: What sort of precautions?

Denis: Well, it's a good idea to expect weather conditions to deteriorate. You... you really mustn't rely on the accuracy of weather forecasts. I mean, we all know about that generally – look at the gale the other year that we had! But... er... but you should especially not... er... rely on ones in the paper, which are often at least twelve hours old before you... you read them. And mountains also have what we call their own micro-climate, which means that they have their own weather systems the... which can often differ considerably from... er... weather in the surrounding valleys or low-lying areas. I... in the mountains, the weather can change very very quickly as well, you can suddenly get thunderstorms developing and clouds come down quite suddenly.

Presenter: Right, right, I understand.

Denis: So... er... (*cough*)... excuse me. When you set out, you should also allow yourself plenty of time, er... because you don't want to let darkness catch up with you while you're still out. It's... er... it's better to arrive in the valley low down when it's, you know, three thirty, four o'clock in the afternoon rather than having to scramble down... down some path at the last minute when darkness is coming down.

Another important thing is... er... not to leave anyone in your group behind. I mean, this might sound a bit silly but... um... the pace of the party really should... should... should be the same as the slowest member of the group and not the quickest.

And if the... the visibility does worsen, if fog comes down or if you run into low-lying clouds or something, and you don't know where you are exactly, it's advisable to stop walking and find somewhere to shelter, and sit and wait for it to get better. Otherwise you might walk straight over a precipice or something, which wouldn't be too clever!

Presenter: Oh dear! But I suppose if you've got a map and a compass and things then, I mean, it's less likely to happen, isn't it?

Denis: Er... well, yes I suppose so, but y... you must pr... you must plan your route first before you go really. I always mark my proposed route on the map with a... a yellow highlighter, which is a... a good tip, and you... then you know exactly where you are on the map all the time. And... er... and you must keep looking at your map, so... er... so you know while you're walking.

And you're quite right: you should... should be carrying a compass with you... um... it really is the only way of knowing which way you're going if you can't see the sun and... er... there aren't any landmarks or anything. And make sure you know how to use it properly. It's a... it's amazing how many people wouldn't like to admit to the fact that they can't use a compass. And the important thing is: don't just follow your nose and rely on your sense of direction because often that will mislead you.

Presenter: And what should you wear, I mean, what sort of clothes should you wear and do you need... do you need other equipment at all?

Denis: Well, you... you ought to take a rucksack with you really. Er... and even if it's hot and sunny when you set out, you've got to be prepared for... for wet and colder conditions to develop. So... um... er... you need waterproof clothing with you and... er... you'll also need warm clothing. Um... and of course proper footwear: it's not... um... there's no point in wearing sandals or trainers or something like that, you've got to have proper walking boots. If it's very hot then it's OK to wear shorts, but do take some trousers with you in your rucksack... um... and not jeans, because... er... they don't keep out the cold and... er... they'll make you feel even colder if they get wet, and in fact you'd be better off not hav... you know, having bare legs than jeans, jeans are really not... not good at all.

Also in your rucksack you'll need some... er... rations, emergency rations for... er... if you get stuck: chocolates, raisins, sandwiches, something to drink, things like that. And... er... a small torch is good if... um... if you do get caught in the dark. Er... and you should also pack a survival blanket or a survival bag... er... they're very lightwake... um... weight and... er... they take up... er... very little room. They're indispensable.

Presenter: Oh really? I mean, what... what exactly are they?

Denis: Well... um... a survival bag is a large plastic bag which you can climb into to protect you from the cold and wet, and... um... the survival blanket is a... a large plastic sheet that reflects the heat back to you. Um... either... either... either of them will save your life if you... if you have to spend the night in the open. Er... and... er... they're very... er... good... good... er... things to take with you.

Presenter: It doesn't exactly sound like a barrel of laughs, this trip, does it?

Denis: No... er... actually I shouldn't... er... I shouldn't panic people. The thing is if you take the precautions and you've got all this equipment and you know what you're doing, you're better prepared and therefore you can walk all day long feeling confident and... and you'll enjoy yourself more. And one... one more thing that's vital: before you set out, let someone know where you're going and what time you expect to be back... er... and in that way... um. When you do get back as well, you know, you... you must report your safe arrival to them, otherwise they'll be worried and they might send out a search party... er... when it's not necessary. But... er... er... if you do get into difficulties and people know, then there will be a rescue party there if you need it.

Presenter: Yes, you're right. Well, Denis, thank you very very much. I mean, I'm sure you're absolutely right, it's better to be safe than sorry – or maybe possibly to stay at home? Thank you very much, Denis.

Denis: Thanks a lot.

(Time: 5 minutes 50 seconds)

2.9 Keep + hold

➡ Every even-numbered unit has a page of exercises on collocations, idioms and phrasal verbs. There's no need to do this at the very end of the unit – it could be fitted in if there is spare time earlier in the unit, or started off in class and finished for homework, or done for homework and discussed in class.

This section contains a selection of expressions that advanced students might find useful, but it is by no means comprehensive. For more information on phrasal verbs and prepositional verbs, consult *Collins* COBUILD *Dictionary of Phrasal Verbs*, or an English–English dictionary.

A   This exercise covers collocations and some idiomatic phrases.

Answers

KEEP   a diary   a promise   a straight face   in touch with someone   someone company   yourself to yourself   someone in the dark   your fingers crossed

HOLD   a job down   a meeting   your breath   your head high   someone responsible

B   This exercise covers idiomatic phrases and some phrasal verbs.

Answers

1   walk at the same speed as
2   compete with the neighbours in acquiring material possessions
3   maintain the same level of excellence/progress
4   Don't tell anyone – it's a secret
5   be thinking of you and hoping that you have good luck
6   bear a grudge against me for it
7   stand up to logical examination
8   Wait   don't ring off/stay at the other end of the line (on the phone)
9   delayed
10   not revealing the whole truth/all the facts

C   This exercise covers phrasal verbs and some prepositional verbs.

Answers

1   hold out
2   held out

  3 keep off
  4 keep   down
  5 keep out of
  6 holding   back
  7 keep in with
  8 hold   back
  9 held out for
 10 hold on

D   This activity, which could be done in pairs or as homework, gives students a chance to use some of the expressions in their own writing. A prize might be awarded to the student who uses the most expressions!

3 People

A & B   As the article is quite long it should, ideally, be prepared before
the lesson. The preliminary discussion could take place before or after the
reading – or postponed until later with E below.

C   Answers

1 *Names*	*Who they were*	*Means of transportation*
b) (not stated)	depressed friend	float plane
c) Dave, Diane & kids	her nearest neighbours	boat
d) Lise	lighthouse keeper's wife	Coast Guard helicopter
e) Bob	lumberjack	on foot
f) three men	Dept of Fisheries scientists	boat

2 a) a mother and her two young sons – the mother couldn't have coped
with the simple life and the sons were TV addicts who would have been
bored, and annoying
  b) Frank and his spouse – Frank was recovering from an operation and
might have needed looking after
  c) a guitar-playing friend – the writer wanted peace and quiet, not guitar
music
3 Local people she never met but who somehow knew she was alone and
might need company, and who told Dave and Diane, Bob and the three
men from the Department of Fisheries to visit her
4 She is being ironic: to show that she had been dreading the friend's visit
and didn't want her to stay any longer
5 There was so much that it's difficult to single out one aspect; but she
certainly appreciated: watching the sea lions and whales, getting to know
the people she met there, learning about solitude and loneliness

D   Answers

foolproof – precarious   *unassailable* – vulnerable   *outraged* – unruffled
the bush – civilisation   *unsolicited* – invited   *positively* – not in the least
blissfully – unhappily   *egged on* – discouraged   *abhors a vacuum* – loves
an empty space   *came to nothing* – did happen   *flagged* – continued
tentatively – confidently   *bustle* – calm

E Follow-up discussion   If this discussion is absorbing it could become the basis for some written work, such as a short composition or paragraph. Or a fictional 'letter to a friend describing a stay in a small community', perhaps.

3.2 Reporting – 1 Grammar review

This section is far from comprehensive and some students may need more guidance and practice in this area of grammar. The transformation exercise in C can be treated as a 'test' of how confident and accurate your students are. It may be necessary to have recourse to less advanced materials, such as *Use of English* or *Communicative Grammar Practice* by Leo Jones or *English Grammar in Use* by Raymond Murphy.

A   Answers

complain – grumble   *confess* – admit   *disclose* – reveal   *emphasise* – stress
forecast – predict   *infer* – gather   *insinuate* – imply   *order* – tell
promise – guarantee   *reiterate* – repeat   *remember* – recall   *suppose* – guess
yell – shout

➡ Get everyone to write sentences using any words they were unsure of.

B   **Suggested answers** (by stretching the imagination, alternatives are possible with each structure)

They…   admitted   agreed   discovered   didn't expect   explained   hoped   imagined   implied   didn't know   learned   mentioned   pretended   never realised   reckoned   didn't remember   didn't reveal   didn't say   shouted   suggested   threatened   wished   **…that we had done it**

They…   agreed   asked   couldn't decide   didn't expect   hoped   learned   pretended   promised   refused   didn't remember   threatened   wanted   wished   **…to do it.**

They…   advised   allowed   asked   didn't expect   forbade   persuaded   reminded   didn't tell   wanted   wished   **…us to do it.**

They…   advised   asked   couldn't decide   explained   implied   didn't know   mentioned   didn't remember   didn't reveal   didn't say   shouted   suggested   **…when we should do it.**

They…   advised   asked   explained   implied   mentioned   reckoned   didn't say   shouted   suggested   **…that we should do it.**

They... advised asked couldn't decide discovered explained didn't know learned mentioned didn't remember didn't reveal didn't say suggested **...when to do it.**

They... asked couldn't decide discovered didn't know didn't remember didn't reveal didn't say **...if we had done it.**

The five verbs that don't fit are:
accused apologised dissuaded forgave warned

You accuse someone of doing something wrong
You apologise for doing something
You dissuade someone from doing something
You forgive someone for doing something
You warn someone about something OR *warn someone not to do something*

C Suggested answers

2 He refused to help me and told me that I would have to do it by myself.
3 She advised me not to write it all out in longhand.
4 He warned me not to feel too confident about my driving test.
5 She suggested that I should telephone him to see if he was free that night.
   She persuaded me to telephone him . . .
6 She warned me not to start giggling during the interview.
7 He persuaded me to type the letter out for him, promising to buy me a drink to thank me.
8 She accused me of borrowing her dictionary.
9 He threatened to call the police if I didn't move my car.
10 She agreed to accompany me.
   I persuaded her to accompany me.
11 She apologised for breaking my fountain pen.
12 He forgave me for my rudeness, knowing that I was upset.

3.3 Who's talking?   Listening

A [cassette icon] The recording consists of five separate monologues. Pause the tape after each monologue for pairs to discuss their answers before they hear the next one. The answers given below are suggestions only. Plausible variations should be accepted if they can be justified.

Answers

FIRST SPEAKER

1 angry; at home
2 her husband (or older child?)
3 books or papers? (toys??)
4 the children (from school) or some people (from the station?)
5 indifferent – or defiant?
6 he wants to avoid conflict?

SECOND SPEAKER

7 a female stranger
8 he mistakes her for a well-known TV actress
9 TV stars or characters in TV programmes
10 doesn't want to get involved? aloof?

THIRD SPEAKER

11 a friend
12 the team captain, the organiser
13 sports kit and equipment
14 the sports field
15 the match

FOURTH SPEAKER

16 the manager of a factory or power station
17 reporters
18 an accident, causing pollution or a radioactive leak
19 . . . any accident of this kind ever happening again?

FIFTH SPEAKER

20 a busybody?
21 a child
22 flowers
23 intimidated?
24 . . . to make you cry

Transcript

(The Presenter gives the number before each speaker.)

First speaker: . . . Oh, look at this! They're all over the place! I'm fed up with it, really I am. If I've told you once, I've told you a thousand times. Why should I have to do it for you? You're the one who put them there and they're yours not mine. Oh yes, I know, you're 'going to do it later'. I wish I had a pound for every time I'd heard that. Look, I've got better things to do, all right? Oh, don't look like that, of course it matters, it's symptomatic of your whole attitude, this. Oh God, it's almost time to pick them up now and I've got nothing done at all this afternoon, thanks to you. Yes, it is your fault and don't pretend it's not and they're just as bad. They think if you can get away with it, so can they. It's just not fair. Look, I'm warning you, if you don't make an effort to change . . .

Second speaker: Excuse me, um...aren't you... er... ? Oh... haha... no, course you're not, sorry. Silly of me. It's just that... er... in this light, but... er... now I can see I was wrong. Yeah. And you're quite a bit taller too. Sorry again. Has anyone mentioned the resemblance before, I wonder? No, no, I suppose not. Oh, don't you? Oh, you know, Jane... um... Jane... whatsername, can't remember her other name. She was in that sitcom: you know, she played the daughter and Geoffrey Palmer played the father. No, not, Geoffrey Palmer the other one, um... the one who's in the coffee commercial, what's he called? Er... oh, you know, the mother was played by that blonde actress, the one who was in that accident recently. Miracle she wasn't killed, apparently. Anyway, she was the mother and this Jane was the daughter, and you look just like her, you know. So can I . . .? Oh.

Third speaker: Well, I said I was no good at it and I told her not to include me but she insisted and said I was 'just being modest'. So I had no choice – well, I could have refused in *theory*, but I didn't want to let everyone down and she said it was too late to find anyone else. So I called off my other arrangements and got all the stuff you're supposed to have and got the bus all the way out there, and there I was all ready to go with all my things and just as it was about to start the heavens opened! Yes! So everyone took shelter and waited for it to stop, but it just got worse and worse. Anyway, after an hour or so of this, the ground was just – well, you can imagine, so they called it off and we all went to have a drink, which was fun, seeing everyone again after all that time. Still, I was a bit upset because she told me they wouldn't be needing me next time, and I'd taken the trouble to get all the stuff, not to mention the cost of it all, and now it looks as if I'm never going to have a chance to use it.

Fourth speaker: No, no... there's absolutely no truth in the rumour, none whatsoever. I've been assured by my staff, that every possible precaution is routinely taken and nothing like this could possibly have happened. The odds against it happening are literally thousands to one. So, well you see it couldn't have happened. However, to set the public's mind to rest, the whole area is to be closed to visitors for a period of ten days while tests are made, I m...thorough scientific tests made by our own team of experts. But, as I said, there is absolutely no danger to the public at this moment in time. Nor is there any likelihood in the future of . . .

Fifth speaker: No, no, no, I don't think s... no, you shouldn't. Look, I know there are lots of them but... but it's wrong. Now, what if everybody did it, there'd be none left, would there? And... y... you've got so many of them. It must have taken you ages... look, no, stop... stop please, you can't put them back, not... no you can't put them back now. Look... it... it's just not possible. Please don't give them to me, I don't want them. Look, the important thing is that you don't do it again. They... they're here for everybody to enjoy, you see? I mean, how would you like it if somebody came into your garden and started taking yours? Quite honestly, you're a very, very . . . Oh, no, please, sorry, look, don't get upset. I didn't mean... Look... please don't. Look, I'm sorry, I didn't mean . . .

(Time: 4 minutes)

B Suggested adjectives (these are open to discussion)

First speaker: irritable, short-tempered, excitable
Second speaker: diffident, nervous, introverted
Third speaker: reasonable, pleasant
Fourth speaker: self-important, assertive – or possibly: shifty, deceitful, corrupt, untrustworthy?
Fifth speaker: meddlesome, interfering, bossy

C This part is quite time-consuming and is best set for homework. If so, play the tape again and ask everyone to make notes to help to remember what each speaker says.

Suggested reports

FIRST SPEAKER
She accused her husband of not tidying up the flat and reminded him that she didn't have time to do it herself. She suddenly realised that she had to leave to collect the children from school, but that didn't prevent her from warning him that he should mend his ways.

SECOND SPEAKER
He had started talking to someone he thought was a well-known actress. When he realised he was mistaken he apologised but he continued trying to make conversation with her. She ignored him and left him still talking.

THIRD SPEAKER
She said she was upset because she had cancelled other arrangements and bought a lot of equipment in order to take part in a match of some kind. When the match was called off she was left with all the equipment unused, and no prospect of being able to use it in the future. She had enjoyed meeting her friends again, though.

FOURTH SPEAKER
He denied that there was any risk to the public, claiming that such an accident couldn't have arisen. However, he announced that the area would be closed to the public for ten days.

FIFTH SPEAKER
She saw a little girl picking flowers and told her to stop. When she told her not to do it again the little girl started crying, which disconcerted her.

3.4 Women's rights

Background

Women's Rights: A Practical Guide was first published in 1974. The authors are a journalist and a solicitor. As far as the figures quoted in the first paragraph are concerned, not much seems to have changed since then.

A & B Preliminary discussion This will help students to approach the tasks more confidently.

C Answers

oppression – tyranny *deprived* – robbed *doubly* – in two different ways *chattels* – possessions *legal reprisals* – punishment *confined* – restricted *upheld* – supported *provide* – sustain/support *resolutions* – decisions *indispensable* – essential *conceded* – given unwillingly *gains* – the rights they had won *maternal deprivation* – children suffering through their mother's absence *emerged* – were revealed

D, E & F There are Model answers in Activity 41. Strictly speaking, only people who owned property were enfranchised before 1832. Only very few of these property owners were actually women.

3.5 Discrimination

A & B Answers

Illegal in England and Wales (**✗**): 1 3 6a 6c 8 9
The others are permissible, even though many of them would be frowned on by most people these days.

Transcript

Presenter: The Sex Discrimination Act (and also the Equal Pay Act) was probably the greatest step forward for women in Britain since they won the vote in 1918 – and even then it was only married women over thirty that could vote. According to these Acts it is against the law to discriminate against anyone in employment, training, education and in the supply of goods, facilities and services on the basis of their sex – they also apply to sex discrimination against men. We take all this for granted now, I think, but the provisions of the Acts are not entirely straightforward, as Victoria Lawrence explains.

Victoria: I'd like to look at what is and what isn't legal – there are still many cases where it's perfectly legal to discriminate against women. I'm looking particularly at the Sex Discrimination Act here. For example, there's a difference between public and private places – so it's against the law for a woman to be refused service in a restaurant or pub, unless she's under age or drunk of course, but a private club can impose any rules it likes and it can choose to admit only men – or another club can choose to exclude men, for that matter.

Presenter: Mm. Education is another important area covered by the act, isn't it?

Victoria: Yes, it is, but there are differences between single-sex schools and coeducational schools. Now, the former may offer special subjects that the other one doesn't – perhaps those are ones that are more popular with girl pupils. However, in a mixed school every subject must be available to all the pupils. And it must be said that most teachers these days do encourage girls to continue with maths and science courses and they don't encourage them to switch to arts subjects like when I was a girl. And girls-only schools offer a full range of technology and science subjects these days.

Um... one thing: the Act doesn't cover textbooks, so if, for example, a school is, by any chance, still using a... one of those old-fashioned books that has a chapter, say, about explorers which are always male explorers and never female explorers, this would still be perfectly OK in the eyes of the law. Of course, these days there aren't that many... er... books like that that slip through the net – after all most... er... editors and most teachers are in fact women, and so you don't see many books like that in schools these days... you don't... don't see any new books at all which reinforce those old stereotypes.

Presenter: Oh, you mean: 'men are brave and strong and clever', and 'women are submissive, weak and homeloving'?

Victoria: Exactly the type of thing I mean, yes. Um... another area that's covered by the Act is advertising: a company can now be taken to court if it places an advertisement like, for example: 'Men only need apply' or 'Pretty girl required'. And... er... not only that, but any words that suggest the sex of applicants are prohibited, and this would include words like 'milkman', 'cleaning lady', 'waitress'.

Um... there are of course exceptions to this, and this is where offence might be caused to members of the opposite sex or in fact jobs that require physical contact with the opposite sex. And I can give you some examples of those: um... yes, an attendant in a woman's... women's lavatory, or a... an airport security guard, someone who has to frisk the women passengers. Er... also excluded are jobs that require a resident couple. And ads for jobs in countries whose laws and customs are such that, quote: 'duties could not be performed effectively by a woman'.

Oh... um... by the way, some particular areas of employment are not covered by the Act, and those include the mining industry, prisons and religious organisations. Oh, and the armed forces too.

So if an employer refuses to give a job to a woman because 'women aren't strong enough to do heavy lifting' they are breaking the law – but they are within their rights to say to an individual person, a woman or a man, 'I'm afraid you're not strong enough to perform this job'.

Presenter: And it also depends on the size of the organisation, doesn't it?

Victoria: Yes, it does indeed, er... companies employing no more than five staff are exempt, and jobs in private households are exempt too.

Presenter: Now presumably discrimination isn't just visible in advertisements?

Victoria: Ah no, no, they're just the tip of the iceberg. If we take just the interviews and job applications: let's suppose four people, all with exactly the same qualifications, apply for the same job and only three are called for the interview. Now, if the person not interviewed is a woman and the other three are all men, she can report the firm to the Equal Opportunities Commission, who would in fact take them to court.

And it's also worth mentioning here that in *factories* there are other so-called 'protective' laws controlling the hours that women are pre… permitted to work. So, they can't work at night, they can't work more than 48 hours a week… er… including overtime, and they can't work more than twelve hours in any one day, which includes meal breaks. Also they can't start before 7 a.m., they can't work on Sundays, and they have to finish work by 8 p.m., and 1 p.m. on Saturdays.

I… it's weird, isn't it? But these provisions date back to the first half of the century – and they don't all apply to *non*-industrial or commercial undertakings, like shops or offices, and neither do they apply to managerial or clerical work.

Mind you, I do have the feeling that they were designed less to protect women than to protect husbands and children from neglect! No, well, no law can protect women from having two full-time jobs . . .

Presenter: One in the factory and another in the home looking after a family, you mean!

Victoria: Yes, exactly. Yes.

Presenter: Victoria, thank you very much.

Victoria: Thank you.

(Time: 6 minutes)

C   Answers

businessperson   camera operator   chair/chairperson   head teacher
police officer   sales assistant   spokesperson   politician
cabin attendant/flight attendant   cleaner

D   Answers

2 We must find the best **person** for the job.
3 Prehistoric **people** lived in caves.
4 Nylon is an **artificial** substance.
5 There is a shortage of **staff**.
6 Pollution is a problem for **humanity**.
7 Her son has now reached **adulthood**.

E   Follow-up discussion   Perhaps arrange the groups so that each one contains both male and female students. On the other hand, it might be fun to have single-sex groups to start with, and then get them to report to the whole class later.

⚠ The first question about racism might arouse strong feelings in some classes: if any students may have been victims of racism, this question should be skipped.

3.6 Punctuation

A Answers

; semi–colon   : colon   ! exclamation mark   ... ellipsis/dot dot dot
- hyphen   — dash   " " inverted commas/quotation marks   * asterisk
( ) brackets/parenthesis   [ ] square brackets   / stroke/oblique
' apostrophe

Some further points:

- A *full stop* is also called a *period* – especially in American English.
- *Quote ... Unquote* is sometimes said instead of the cumbersome *Open inverted commas ... Close inverted commas.*
- In handwriting it's more usual to use double quotes (" ") than single quotes (' ').
- Dashes are more common in informal style than in formal writing – especially to add afterthoughts.
- Semi-colons are uncommon in informal style. Instead we tend to use a comma, or a full stop and a new sentence.
- Colons are used before explanations, and before a list, and also to introduce a quotation – but not to introduce direct speech, where a comma is more commonly used:

    He said, "Quotation marks are used to quote direct speech. Notice where the quotation marks and other punctuation marks are in relation to each other."

B   For the answers, students should compare their work with the text in 3.4B – some variations are possible. Discuss these with the class if necessary.

C Corrected sentences (with comments)

1 Sitting on the beach, we watched the windsurfers falling into the water. – Participle phrases usually require a comma unless they are the complement of verbs like *watch, see, hear, find, notice*, etc.
2 The aspect of punctuation which is most tricky is the use of commas. – Commas are not used to separate identifying/defining relative clauses from the noun phrase. But commas *are* required before (and after) non-identifying relative clauses: *My best friend, who lives over the road, is rather shy*.
3 Could you tell me when to use a semi-colon? – Commas are not used in indirect speech after the reporting verb.

4 Feeling completely baffled, we tried to solve the problem with which we were faced. – Participle phrases (as in 1 above) AND commas not used in identifying/defining relative clauses.

5 Although I was feeling under the weather, I went to work this morning. – A comma usually follows a subordinate clause when it precedes the main clause, though not always in shorter sentences.

6 There were, surprisingly, no punctuation mistakes in his work. – Adverbs which 'comment' on the whole sentence require commas. In this example, *Surprisingly, there were no . . .* might be more usual. And *There were surprisingly few punctuation mistakes . . .* would also be possible.

D   Corrected version (several variations are possible)

```
I have known Jan Smith, both professionally and
personally, for several years.
        Since 1992, when she first joined my department, she
has been a reliable, resourceful and conscientious member
of my staff with a thoroughly professional attitude to her
work. She has cheerfully taken on extra responsibilities
and can be relied on to take over when other staff are
absent or unavailable.
        She particularly enjoys dealing with members of the
public, and has a knack of putting people at their ease.
She is adept at defusing delicate situations with an
appropriate word and a smile.
        As her portfolio shows, she is also a very creative
and talented person, and her work shows great promise.
        During her time with us her attendance has been
excellent.
        She is an intelligent, thoughtful and imaginative
person. I have no hesitation in recommending her for the
post.
```

E   Written follow-up   It may be necessary to collect in all this work and check the punctuation. You may also need to settle any disagreements, remembering that the rules of punctuation in English are relatively *flexible*.

3.7 Using inversion for emphasis   Advanced grammar

A   **Suggested answers**

1 At no level of society do women have equal rights with men.
    – *Emphasis on* no *makes the sentence stand out and seem more
      dramatic.*
    Women do not have equal rights with men at any level of society.
    – *Straightforward and unemphatic – unless read aloud like this:* They
      do not have equal rights with men at *any level* of society.

2 It occurred to me later that I had made a big mistake.
    – *Normal straightforward word order with the emphasis, as written, on
      the last phrase.*
    Not until then did it occur to me that I had made a big mistake.
    – *Emphasis on the time and the delayed reaction to what had
      happened.*

3 Rarely have I felt so upset about being criticised.
    – *Emphasis on* rarely. *This sentence sounds very formal or literary, and
      might sound pompous if spoken rather than written.*
    I have rarely felt so upset about being criticised.
    – *Straightforward and informal style.*

4 So lonely did he feel that he went round to see his ex–wife for a chat.
    – *Emphasis on the depth of his loneliness.*
    He felt so lonely that he went round to see his ex–wife for a chat.
    – *As written, no particular emphasis, but when speaking the same
      sentence we could give the same emphasis as the first sentence by
      means of stress:* He felt *so lonely* that he went . . .

5 Little did they know that the sheriff was about to draw his revolver.
    – *Emphasis on their unawareness, more dramatic than the second
      sentence.*
    They didn't know that the sheriff was about to draw his revolver.
    – *Unemphatic, matter-of-fact narrative.*

6 At the top of the hill stood a solitary pine tree.
    – *By saving up the pine tree to the end, suspense is created. By
      changing the word order from what is 'normal', both parts of the
      sentence are emphasised.*
    A solitary pine tree stood at the top of the hill.
    – *This is the 'normal' straightforward word order.*

7 Bang went the door. In came Fred. On went all the lights. Out ran the cat.
    – *The repeatedly 'unusual' word order makes this line more dramatic.
      However, this is rather overdone here and something like this might*

be preferable: The door went bang as Fred came in. On went all the lights and out went the cat like a rocket.

The door went bang. Fred came in. All the lights went on. The cat ran out.
– The sentences seem too short in this line, and it sounds rather lifeless.

➡ Point out that sentences 6 and 7 don't require an inverted verb, only a change in word order, with the subject coming after the verb.

⚠ Point out that there are restrictions on the use of inversion, as these 'counter-examples' show:
  *Bang went it. *In came he. *On went they. *Out ran it.
  *Out went we. *Down came it. *Up they put their umbrellas.
  *Back went we. *Out I threw them.

B   Suggested answers

1 Little **did she/anyone realise** that she would win the competition.
2 Not only **does she play** the piano brilliantly but she **sings well/is an accomplished violinist** too.
3 Never in my life **have/had I been** so humiliated!
4 Nowhere in the entire town **were we** able to find a room for the night.
5 No sooner **had I got into** the bath than the phone **started ringing**.
6 So difficult **was the work that I was unable to finish it.** *many variations possible*
7 Under no circumstances **should/must** the fire doors **be locked/blocked**.
8 Not until **everyone** had finished **were the rest of us** allowed to leave the room. *many variations possible*
9 Only after **a long search/chase were** the police able to catch the thieves.
10 Not once during her entire **life has she been** in trouble with the law.
11 Not only **is** he rather naive but he also **seems to be** very sensitive.
12 No sooner **had we started** our picnic than **it started to rain.** *many variations possible*

C   Suggested answers

1 Out we went in our best clothes. Down came the rain.
2 Up went the umbrellas. Home we went, wet through.
3 Sitting beside her in the train was a tall dark stranger.
4 Lying under the table was a fat tabby cat, washing itself obliviously.
5 The edge of the cliff gave way and down she fell.
6 Behind the wall was a ferocious dog barking furiously.
7 Off drove the thieves with the police in hot pursuit.
8 Only/Not until then did I realise that I had made the biggest mistake of my life.

3.8 Opposites

A Suggested answers

1 sophisticated/worldly/crafty   2 cowardly/timid
3 unrepentant/unapologetic   4 accelerated/speeded up   5 innocent
6 hindered me/got in the way/obstructed me   7 saved it/put it by
8 closed it/pushed it to   9 made me more worried/upset me
10 stayed calm/kept his cool   11 synonym   12 closed it quietly

B Answers

inadvisable inappropriate unaware unbearable unclearly
incompetent inconsiderate inconsistent inconspicuous
unconventional unconvincing undecided indecisive undesirable
undignified indiscreet indistinct inefficient uneventful unexpected
inexplicable unfaithful unforeseen unforgettable infrequent
ungrateful ingratitude unimaginative unmanageable unpredictable
unrewarding insincere insincerity unsociable unsophisticated
instability unstable insufficient intolerant untrustworthy
invisible unwanted unwelcome

C Answers

disagreeable disapprove disarm disconnect discontented disentangle
illegible illegitimate illogical disloyal immature disorganised
impatient impersonal impossible irrational irregular irrelevant
disrespectful irresponsible dissatisfied dissimilar

E Answers

clumsy – careful   *complimentary* – critical   *fearless* – fearful/cowardly
neat – untidy/messy   *rare* – common   *restless* – calm   *tactful* – tactless
talkative – quiet/taciturn   *thoughtless* – considerate/thoughtful
trivial – significant/serious

beauty – ugliness   *knowledge* – ignorance   *noise* – silence/quiet/tranquillity
praise – criticism   *pride* – modesty   *promotion* – demotion
solitude – company   *success* – failure

F Answers

conceited – modest   *deceitful* – truthful/trustworthy/open/frank
fussy – easygoing/laid back   *lazy* – hard-working   *malicious* – kindhearted
mean – generous/kindhearted   *narrow-minded* – liberal
neurotic – easygoing/laidback/nonchalant   *pretentious* – unassuming
secretive – open/frank   *solitary* – sociable/gregarious   *sullen* – cheerful
touchy – easygoing

NOTE: *imaginative*, *perceptive* and *talkative* are distractors, which are not
antonyms of any words listed.

3.9 Two short poems   Reading

A The two poems are recorded on the cassette.

B Suggested answers (These are suggestions – your interpretation
may differ slightly or considerably.)
1 He drowned, presumably
2 'I was much further out than you thought and not waving but drowning.'
    'Oh, no no no, it was too cold always, I was much too far out all my life
    and not waving but drowning.'
3 'Poor chap, he always loved larking and now he's dead – it must have
    been too cold for him. His heart gave way.'
4 Having fun, playing pranks
5 line 7: the water   line 9: life
6 line 11: out of control, in despair   line 12: unable to cope
7 Not having fun, enjoying himself
8 He had more interests
9 Not at all
10 Because he has much better ideas (a penny for a shilling is a twelve-fold
    improvement)
11 Because he has been in contact with her carefree spirit
12 Perhaps he foresees no further improvements in his life and no new joys
    in his old age?

C Suggested adjectives

1 lonely   unappreciated   unhappy   solitary   unnoticed   doomed
   unlucky
2 desperate   discontented   morose   sad   sorrowful   glum   pessimistic

➡ Follow-up discussion   If you or your students have any favourite poems which you/they wish to share with the class, this might be an ideal time to do this.

3.10   It takes all sorts ...   Composition

A   Suggested adjectives

elderly woman – *dour   experienced   miserable   morose   patient perceptive   sad   stoical   suspicious   tough   wise   worried   wry*

laughing woman – *active   cheerful   contented   easygoing   energetic extroverted   happy   optimistic   outgoing   outdoor-type   pleased practical   sociable   sporty*

young man – *charming   cheerful   easygoing   good-humoured   humorous jaunty   jolly   lighthearted   nonchalant   relaxed*

young woman – *calm   determined   elegant   good-looking   intelligent patient   perceptive   pleasant   sincere   stylish   successful*

brother – *annoying   cheeky   cheerful   irrepressible   mischievous   naughty obstinate   teasing*

& sister – *brainy   long-suffering   pretty   reserved   sensitive serious-looking   solemn   talented*

man in suit – *arrogant   assured   authoritative   complacent   conventional decisive   fastidious   pretentious   sardonic   self-assured   self-confident self-satisfied*

Students may need some help with suitable descriptive phrases. If so, some of the following vocabulary could be written on the board:

Clothes: *anorak   business suit   casual clothes   crew neck   V-neck polo neck   jumper/pullover   open-necked shirt   smart clothes   tracksuit*

Age: *a teenager   elderly   in his/her early/late forties   in his/her mid-twenties   middle-aged   thirtyish   thirtysomething*

Hair: *balding   black   curly   fair   fringe   grey-haired parted in the middle/on the left   parting   she wears her hair up shoulder length   sleeked-back   straight   unkempt   wavy*

B   Remind students to leave a wide margin on either side of their work and leave a line or two between each paragraph. This will leave them room to add extra ideas, and even to rewrite complete sentences later if necessary. There's also more space for you to add comments.

4 Communication

A Suggested descriptions

He looks dangerous – intimidating and threatening.
Now look here, if you do that again you're going to regret it.
– Don't talk to me like that! or *I think you're overreacting.*

She looks delighted and triumphant – very pleased with herself.
I've done it! I've passed!
– Congratulations! Well done! I knew you'd do well.

He looks downhearted and depressed, very much down in the dumps.
Oh God, I don't know what I'm going to do.
– Cheer up! It's not as bad as all that. Try to look on the bright side.

B Answers

2 mumbling   muttering   whispering ✓
3 jot   note   scribble ✓
4 glance at   scan   skim ✓
5 chuckling   grinning   sniggering
6 frown   scowl   sneer
7 scream   shriek   yell
8 imply   intimate   suggest
9 attitude   expression   tone ✓
10 expression   phrase   idiom

A   If students are asked to prepare the text before the lesson, these questions could be 'points to think about' before reading the passage.

B Answers

TRUE: 1   6
FALSE: 2   3   4   5   7

C   Answers

TRUE: 1   3   5   6   7
FALSE: 2   4

D   Answers

¶ 1 *objective* – impartial   *prejudice* – bias   *instructive* – revealing
¶ 2 *exhilarating* – stimulating   *euphoria* – happiness   *mitigated* – moderated
¶ 3 *associations* – connotations   *formulate* – devise   *aesthetic* – artistic
   pet – favourite
¶ 4 *derisive* – contemptuous   *badge* – emblem   *intrinsic* – inherent
   the men – workers   *excite* – arouse

E   Follow-up discussion   These points will be taken up further in 4.9
Accents and dialects.

4.3   *–ing* and *to* —   Grammar review

A   Meanings

1   We stopped to take photos, but . . .
   – *We were walking along and then stopped in order to take photos.*
   We stopped taking photos, but . . .
   – *We were taking photos and then we stopped taking them.*

2   Did you remember to send the fax or . . . ?
   – *You were supposed to do it: did you in fact do it?*
   Do you remember sending the fax or . . . ?
   – *Just think back for a moment: can you remember whether you did it
   or not?*

3   I can't help you to feel better, but . . . – *I'm unable to assist you.*
   I can't help feeling better, but . . . – *I'm unable to stop myself from
   feeling better.*

4   I'm not used to using a typewriter, but . . . – *I'm not accustomed to
   using one.*
   I used to use a typewriter, but . . . – *I once used a typewriter, but not now.*

5   I heard her scream, but . . . – *She screamed once.*
   I heard her screaming, but . . . – *She screamed repeatedly.*

Suggested continuations

1   We stopped to take photos, but . . . the light wasn't bright enough, so we
   went on walking.
   We stopped taking photos, but . . . we went on watching what was going on.

2 Did you remember to send the fax or . . . did you forget to send it?
Do you remember sending the fax or . . . have you forgotten all about it?

3 I can't help you to feel better, but . . . I can sit by the bed to keep you company.
I can't help feeling better, but . . . I realise I ought to stay in bed today.

4 I'm not used to using a typewriter, but . . . I'll do my best with it.
I used to use a typewriter, but . . . now I use a word processor.

5 I heard her scream, but . . . I didn't take any notice.
I heard her screaming, but . . . there was nothing I could do to help.

B   Connections

to call someone on the phone
to contact someone by phone / by post
to drop someone a line
to get through to someone on the phone
to give someone a ring
to keep in touch with someone
to reply to a letter
to tell someone a story
to write someone a letter

Answers

2 in contacting them
3 to writing
4 to send them
5 tell the story
6 to reply to
7 to keeping in touch with people/calling people
8 in getting through to her
9 to drop me
10 giving me

C   Suggested answers

1 taking a taxi/going by underground if you've got a lot of luggage
2 to go there some day
3 taking any exercise/doing anything strenuous
4 staying up late/going out for the evening/staying up all night
5 trying to read the book
6 listening   to listen to Mozart/listening to jazz
7 reading the book till I got to the end
8 walking in the hope that it might stop

9   working   having a good rest/going out tonight
10 crying/screaming   to listen/to stand by and do nothing
11 doing some extra homework/committing so much time to it
12 being/feeling   to feel much better/to recover
13 to get through/to make contact
14 to buy/to have   to buy one
15 not to hear/to be deaf

4.4 This book . . . Reading

This section concentrates on style. Suggested answers are given to the
questions posed, but these are tentative rather than authoritative. A reader's
reactions to a piece of writing are personal, unpredictable and often
surprising – make sure, therefore, that everyone has understood the extracts
and hasn't got hold of the wrong end of the stick.

A   Suggested answers (very much open to discussion)

Extract 1
   a) an academic, no personal information given
   b) to provide a scholarly document
   c) experts in or students of the writer's field
Extract 2
   a) earnest, sincere poet
   b) to move, influence, inspire the reader
   c) people who will share the poet's attitudes
Extract 3
   a) an expert in his or her field
   b) to interest, entertain and educate
   c) the general reader, non–experts

B   Quotes (just a selection)

1 *face-to-face interaction   which are yet detailed enough   a comprehensive
   basis for further work in the subject   minor editorial adjustments
   footnotes   bibliographical references   journal titles   fourth edition of the
   World List of . . .*
2 *my poems shine in your eye   they look from your walls   lurk on your
   shelves   to become a weapon*
3 *a mixture   off the beaten track   a knowledgeable companion   My hope is
   that my tastes and yours will coincide   at least some of the time*

C   Follow-up discussion   Students who deal with books and articles in
their studies may find this more relevant than non-academics.

4.5 Forming adjectives   Vocabulary development

A Answers

–able	acceptable admirable advisable breakable describable forgivable obtainable predictable preventable recommendable recyclable workable
–ing	astonishing convincing dying distressing disturbing forgiving inspiring overwhelming promising upsetting working
–ive	communicative cooperative deceptive descriptive informative instructive possessive preventive productive

B Answers

–al	adjectival adverbial conventional editorial educational fictional functional intentional musical personal professional proportional seasonal secretarial sensational
–ic	diplomatic enigmatic idealistic magnetic materialistic optimistic pessimistic realistic romantic
–ous	adventurous ambitious (fictitious) malicious spacious
–ly	fortnightly quarterly weekly yearly
–ed	curly-haired experienced long-legged pale-skinned

➡ Notice also these suffixes:

–ed/–en	educated finished satisfied unknown
–ical	alphabetical historical
–ish	boyish childish snobbish stylish
–y	airy brainy draughty funny
–worthy	newsworthy noteworthy roadworthy seaworthy trustworthy

C Answers

1 poisonous 2 astonished 3 automatic 4 idealised 5 stylish
6 economical 7 heartbroken 8 satisfactory 9 legible 10 childish

D   The exercise could be written at home (alone) and then given to a partner to do in class.

➡ There is more on *–ing* and *-ed/-en* in 5.5 Position of adjectives & participles.

4.6   The Interpreter

A   Suggested attractive features

1 It contains 700 commonly used phrases
2 It can 'say' any word aloud
3 It speaks five languages
4 Instant translation
5 In 'teach' mode you can use it to help you to learn words and phrases

B   🔲 Answers

1 five
2 at the airport ☒   at the chemist's ☑   at the railway station ☒
   at the bank ☒   business ☑   camping ☒   complaining ☑
   emergencies ☑   in the post office ☒   making friends ☑
   motoring ☑   restaurants ☑   shopping ☑   sightseeing ☑
3 'How much does it cost to get in?'
   'Please call the fire brigade.'
   'Is that your best price?'
   'We are still waiting to be served.'
4 'I have lost my voice.'
5 personal earphone (and the screen)
6 screen

Transcript   (NOTE: The Voice was recorded from the *The Interpreter*
itself: its intonation and stress patterns are sometimes rather eccentric!)

Presenter: As many of us who take our two weeks' holiday abroad will know,
   communication in a foreign language is often very difficult. Well, now there's a
   new gadget on the market for the tourist or businessperson, which can help to
   communicate in five different languages. It's called *The Interpreter* and it speaks
   those languages. All you do is press the right buttons to find a word or phrase in,
   say, Spanish and it'll say aloud the same word or phrase in English or, if you
   prefer, German, French or Italian. Sarah Watts has been trying it out for us.

Sarah: The Interpreter has quite a wide vocabulary: over 13,000 words. It can say
   them all aloud and it can say them in phrases too. This means that all you have to
   do is press a button and either imitate what it says or just let the Interpreter speak
   to people on your behalf.

Voice: Hello.

Sarah: Oh, hello, how are you?

Voice: I'm fine, thank you.

Sarah: Good. Now there are many situations that a traveller, whether he or she is on
   business or travelling for pleasure, may find themselves . . .

Voice: Excuse me.

Sarah: Yes?

Voice: Please speak more slowly. I do not understand. I'm sorry.

Sarah: Oh dear. I'm sorry too. *(as herself again)* Well, let's take for example, the situation of someone alone in a foreign city, wanting to strike up an acquaintance with someone in a bar, for example. Let's see what opening gambits the Interpreter can suggest.

Voice: I am on holiday here.

Sarah (responding): Oh really?

Voice: Are you alone?

Sarah: Yes . . .

Voice: Would you like a drink?

Sarah: Thanks, I'll have an orange juice please.

Voice: Do you mind if I smoke?

Sarah: No, go ahead.

Voice: What is your name?

Sarah: Sarah. What's yours?

Voice: My name is . . .

Sarah (as herself again): But then the conversation might start to get rather more personal:

Voice: Are you married? Do you have any children? Are you busy tomorrow? Would you like to go out with me? Please.

Sarah (responding): Er, no thanks. But, perhaps if you have a free afternoon you would like to do some sightseeing?

Voice: What is there to see here?

Sarah: Oh, lots of things. There's a wonderful art gallery, and . . .

Voice: How much does it cost to get in? Is there a guided tour? How long does the tour take? Is there a reduction for children?

Sarah (as herself again): So much for culture. Of course the Interpreter's repertoire of phrases covers all eventualities, such as emergencies:

Voice: Please help me. I have been robbed. Get the police. Where is the nearest hospital? My child is missing. Please call the fire brigade.

Sarah: Very polite! And shopping. Let's suppose you want to buy something unusual . . .

Voice: Where can I buy a bed?

Sarah: Yes, that *is* unusual. Anyway, you go to a store and ask the assistant:

Voice: Have you got a bed? Show me a bed.

Sarah: Or you might ask, rather more politely:

Voice: I would like a bed. I would like to see a bed. Which bed do you recommend?

Sarah: So you select a particularly nice bed. And it might be worth checking if you can get a discount:

Voice: Is that your best price?

Sarah: There's no discount, but you still want to make your purchase:

Voice: Can I buy this, please? Do you take credit cards? May I have a receipt?

Sarah: So your brand new bed is delivered to your hotel? – no, you must have an apartment you want to furnish. But, oh dear, when you unwrap it:

Voice: The bed is broken.

Sarah: So you go back to the store and say:

Voice: Can I exchange this bed?

Sarah: This leads us on to the topic of complaints. Let's suppose you're in a restaurant where the service is rather slow:

Voice: We are still waiting to be served.

Sarah: And after your meal:

Voice: May I have the bill, please? Is service included?

Sarah: You examine the bill:

Voice: I think you have made a mistake. You have overcharged me. I want to see the manager.

Sarah: So, there we are, the Interpreter covers a wide range of social situations, as well as business situations:

Voice: I am here on business. Where can I get some photocopying done? Can I send a fax from here?

Sarah: And motoring:

Voice: My car won't start. Can you repair the car? I have run out of petrol. Where is the nearest petrol station? I have a flat tyre. Can you tow me to a garage?

Sarah: And, finally, at the chemist's:

Voice: Have you anything for insect bites? Have you anything for sunburn? I want something for a headache. I want something for toothache. I have a cough.

Sarah: Another useful one, which is not in the Interpreter's repertoire might be: *(hoarsely)* 'I have lost my voice', perhaps!

The Interpreter comes with a personal earphone, and all the phrases appear on the screen as they are spoken, which is a great help in learning them and means that you can use it in complete privacy, without any of the people around you being able to hear it.

Voice: Excuse me.

Sarah (responding): Yes?

Voice: Is it safe for children?

Sarah: Oh, yes, I think so. And you can use it any time you want to.

Voice: I am free tomorrow morning.

Sarah: Oh good. Thank you for your help, by the way.

Voice: You're welcome.

(Time: 6 minutes)

C The follow-up discussion leads in to the Communication Activity in D.

D 🏃 Student A looks at Activity 25, where there are extracts from the *Oxford Advanced Learner's Dictionary*, student B at 30 for extracts from the *Longman Dictionary of Contemporary English* and student C at 39 for extracts from the *Collins COBUILD English Language Dictionary*.

This Activity may take some time to complete – if necessary postpone it till the next lesson.

4.7 Paragraphs – 1

A Divide the class into groups of four so that one member of each group can look at a different text.

Answers

1.6 has eleven paragraphs
2.1 has thirteen paragraphs
3.4 has one paragraph in A and five in B
4.2 has four paragraphs – each over 200 words long

B You may wish to add further guidelines to the list. Deal with any queries that the class may raise.

C **Suggested answers** (You may decide to call a halt to this activity before students get to the very end.)

¶ 7 Change of 'speaker' (the writer's thoughts)
¶ 8 Time had passed, different friends' reactions
¶ 9 Prominence to last sentence of ¶ 8 and first sentence of ¶ 9
¶ 10 New speaker
¶ 11 Different speaker
¶ 12 Different speaker
¶ 13 Time has passed, contrast with previous speeches
¶ 14 New character introduced, given prominence
¶ 15 Change of 'speaker' (the writer's thoughts)
¶ 16 End of what depressed friend said. Prominence to first sentence
¶ 17 Prominence to last sentence of ¶ 16 and first sentence of ¶ 17. Return to narrative.
¶ 18 New characters introduced
¶ 19 Change of 'speaker' (the writer's thoughts)
¶ 20 Return to narrative
¶ 21 New character introduced
¶ 22 New speaker
¶ 23 Return to writer's thoughts. Prominence to first very short sentence.
¶ 24 Return to depressed friend, first mention of her for some time, we may have forgotten she was there by now
¶ 25 Change of 'speaker' (the writer's thoughts). Contrast between last sentence of ¶ 24 and first sentence of ¶ 25
¶ 26 Change of 'speaker' (the writer's thoughts) again – repetition for effect of writer's thoughts in ¶ 19
¶ 27 Time has passed, new arrival

D   Refer back to the original article for the 'answers'. Your students may have further ideas for paragraph breaks – for example between . . . *loneliness* and *In such a remote* . . . .

4.8   *Wh–* clauses   Advanced grammar

▲ This section doesn't cover relative clauses, which are dealt with in 16.3.

B   Suggested continuations

2 One thing I like is . . . sitting at home with my feet up.
3 What I feel like doing . . . now is having a rest.
4 There's nothing I enjoy more than . . . going for a long walk in the country.
5 Something that often surprises me is . . . the way some people find it hard to learn a foreign language.
6 All I want is . . . something cool and refreshing to drink.
7 What we need now . . . is an expert's advice.
8 I just don't want . . . to upset him by raising the subject of work.
9 What I want to do right now is . . . have lunch.

C   Matched sentences

2 Whatever you do, don't tell everyone. ⌐⌐Tell anyone anything you like.
   Make sure you don't tell everyone. ⌐⌐Tell anyone whatever you want.

3 Whoever did you give it to? ——— Who in the world did you give it to?
   To whom* did you give it? ——— Who did you give it to?

4 Why ever don't you phone her? ⤬ Why do you never phone her?
   Why don't you ever phone her? ⤬ Why on earth don't you phone her?

5 All these sentences mean the same as each other!

*To whom . . . ? would sound very old-fashioned in present-day English.

D   Answers

1 Wherever he goes, he takes a phrasebook with him.
2 You can arrive whenever you like.
3 All I did was stick out my tongue at her.
4 What you did was very rude.
5 All she needs is someone to tell her troubles to.
6 I don't mind where you put it.
7 Whether you write or phone doesn't really matter/is immaterial.

8 Whenever you arrive, get in touch.
9 What he said was very impressive/made a big impression on me/everyone.
10 What astonished me was her confidence.

4.9 Accents and dialects

➡ Before playing the recording, ask the class which British and American accents they can recognise. Which do they find most pleasant to listen to?

A 📼 Answers

TRUE: 1   3   4   6   8   9   11
FALSE: 2   5   7   10   12

B Allow plenty of time for this discussion, as some questions might be quite provocative.

C, D, E & F Follow the steps suggested in the Student's Book.

Transcript

Jackie: . . . Now, do you think, Tim, that regional accents are dying out now?
Tim: No, I don't think so. I think, if anything, they're becoming stronger and certainly they're much more... er... tolerated than they used to be.
Jackie: What about you, Mike? Do you think that?
Mike: Well, in the States you still find that the... the newscasters are all sort of mid-Western but... er... you know, people move around so much over there that the accents tend to even out. There's not nearly so much regional variation. Like... like here, I mean, like fifty... fifty miles up the road there's a different accent. That's what I find fascinating. It's so great to hear these accents.
Tim: I always think it's interesting that there's a... such a similarity between... um... US accents and... er... the accents we get in the West of England, Scotland and Ireland. You know the... particularly the R, you know, in words like... er... *hard* and *car*, for example, you know.
Jackie: Mm, yes, as you say in Ireland, I mean, you... the Irish people always pronounce the Rs in *hard* and *car*.
Mike: Yeah, it... that's the first thing you notice when you... when you come over here, listening to the various accents. But I will say that most of... my American friends who come over here, they can't really tell the difference between, like, an Englishman or... and an Australian: an Australian to them sounds like a Londoner.
Jackie: Really?
Mike: Yeah. Yeah.
Tim: But we c... I mean, we can tell the difference in America, f... mainly from

movies and things, I mean, you've got your Southern accent, and the New York, New England, Canadian and so on, they're very . . .

Mike: Well, Canadian's very similar... er... er... I... the only thing I notice about Canadians is they say *eh* all the time, you know?

Jackie: I haven't noticed that.

Mike: Oh yeah, well, the real Canadians do: 'You're going down the store, eh?'

Jackie: But you know, in... in America, for instance, when I was over there, I think that most people there assume that everyone in Great Britain – that includes England, Ireland, Scotland, Wales – all talk with a... a BBC accent. And only 5% – did you know that? – 5% of people in Britain have what they call, you know, a sort of standard English accent.

Tim: It... it's... it's... it's incredible that... w... I always think, wh... when I was in the States, you know, people say 'Hey, gee, you're British!', you know... and they'd want you to speak to them just so that they could listen, and they'd get a... half their family over to... and you'd find yourself speaking to ten people in the supermarket!

Mike: Yeah, my wife gets that as well, yeah, 'cause she's English and she gets the same deal. But, you know, what surprises me is you go and you... you hear people being taught English over here, you know, foreigners who don't speak any English and yet that's the accent they... they learn, you know the... the...

Jackie: What, the BBC accent?

Mike: Yeah, the... the... what do they... I don't understand that at all...

Jackie: I suppose you have to have something to teach...

Tim: I mean, RP is... it's... it's...

Mike: What's that?

Tim: ... which is Received Pronunciation...

Jackie: It's like BBC.

Tim: ... It's really a social accent, I mean, you know... i... in some circles, speaking like I do people would think I was stuck-up or superior or something, and that's... er... but... er... but there needs to be some kind of... er... sort of standard English... er . . .

Mike: You think so?

Jackie: Yes, w... I think there... there has to be a way of... of teaching people a language. There has to be a standard form of pronunciation, but...

Tim: I mean, for instance...

Jackie: But, well, no, it's just that in the old days when you... when we were at school, for instance, when I was at school in England, we were... they... people tried to teach us to lose our accents. Now they don't do that now. I mean, there's... it really doesn't matter what accent you have at all.

Mike: Yeah, well, I think it's more a matter of grammar and... and vocabulary rather. I think an accent's fine.

Tim: That's right, that's right. But I mean, there's g... for instance... um... you've... there's got to be a standard form... for instance... er... er... a phrase like *I haven't got any* is ac... quite acceptable, but you wouldn't say *I ain't got none*. I mean you wouldn't teach somebody who's learning English...

Mike: No, grammar. Yes, but that's grammar, right? Rather than accent.

Tim: Yes, yes, that is rather... yes, it is.

Mike: So... I think... I think accents are great. I... what... what bugs me is that

when... when... er... because I'm originally from the South. I don't have a
Southern accent now, but when I did when I was a kid, and... I'd meet kids from
the North, they'd always make fun of me as if I was some kind of farmer from...
from, you know, some kind of hick. They always think that people who have a
Southern accent are really ill-educated. But, you know, the Southerners are really
suspicious of Yankees: anybody who has not got a Southern accent is
automatically 'out to get them', or trick them.

Jackie: I think that's the same in England. I mean, a... a lot of people who live in the
West Country are thought, you know, are thought of as 'thick' and certainly I
know a lot of English people, who shall remain nameless, think that the Irish are
stupid because of our accents – but of course we're not!

Tim: I think there's less stigma now. I mean... you... you... you're not so likely now
not to get a job because of the way you speak, I would have thought, than... than
twenty years ago.

Mike: You think so?

Jackie: Well, I would hope so, I don't know whether that's . . .

Mike: I don't know. I... it's hard to say. I... when you s... and yet, the regional
accents you see on the TV here are just very slowly creeping in and, I mean,
there's one or two . . .

Jackie: Mm.

Mike: People still make fun of that Irish guy who commentates for the BBC on
politics . . .

Tim: Oh, John Cole.

Jackie: Yes, I think he's wonderful.

Mike: John Cole... all the comedians take him off. I do too. I think it's a great
accent.

Jackie: And I used to love it when we... we had the Welsh-speaking programmes,
you know, they were networked. Because they were just gorgeous... even though
I didn't understand a word of it . . .

(Time: 5 minutes)

4.10 Make + do   Verbs & idioms

A   Answers

MAKE: an agreement with someone   an appointment with someone
an arrangement   an attempt   certain about something
a comment about something   an excuse   a good impression
friends with someone   a lot of money   love   a mistake   a profit or a loss
progress   a reservation   sure

DO: your best   business with someone   your duty   someone a favour
harm to someone   someone a good turn   the washing-up   wrong or right
your own thing

NOTE: *make* often refers to creative or productive processes, while *do* often
refers to the performance of a service or work.

B Answers

1 manage to understand
2 manage to see
3 criticising me
4 doomed
5 ... how this concerns you
6 move up to allow me to sit there
7 invented
8 recompense/compensate
9 afford the necessities of life
10 repay you – I am very sorry and I can't compensate you
11 getting things out of proportion
12 have an embarrassing public argument
13 show his good looks/personality well enough
14 work harder/drive faster to catch up
15 wrapped and tied up

C Answers

1 made off with
2 done   up
3 make up for
4 do without
5 made   up
6 doing up
7 done away with
8 making for
9 done out of
10 made off

5 Food and drink

A   Warm-up discussion   It may be necessary to ask everyone to specify the location of the various places, and to justify their choices, rather than just name the establishments.

B   **Suggested answers**

Fish and shellfish   oysters   mussels   prawns   shrimps   scampi
    lobster   sole   swordfish   clams   octopus   squid (calamari)   eel
Poultry   chicken   turkey   duck   goose
Game   venison   pheasant   wild boar   rabbit
Herbs   parsley   basil   rosemary   tarragon   bay leaf   marjoram
    oregano   dill   sage   thyme
Spices   cinnamon   nutmeg   allspice   pepper   ginger   paprika   cloves
Dairy products   cheese   yogurt   butter   cream   buttermilk
Nuts   hazelnuts   walnuts   chestnuts   cashews   pistachios   almonds
    Brazil nuts   pine nuts
Desserts   apple pie   chocolate mousse   profiteroles   rice pudding
    pancakes   trifle   fruit sorbet
Cakes and buns   apple strudel   carrot cake   croissants   Danish pastry
    doughnut   fruit cake   gateau   jam tarts   scones

C   If your students are interested in cooking or eating, allow plenty of time for this discussion. They may need to be reminded of different ways of preparing and cooking food:
    chop   slice   mix   weigh   knead   beat   whip
    fry   grill   roast   steam   parboil   sauté   microwave   bake   etc.

A   This is a warm-up discussion. Students with first-hand knowledge of work in the restaurant business should be encouraged to tell their partners about their experiences.

B   🔲   Students should make notes in answer to questions 1, 4 and 6.

C Before starting this follow–up discussion, ask for the class's reactions to what they heard in the interview.

Answers

1 Pancakes are suitable for a light lunch and a more substantial evening meal – they give them flexibility
2 b
3 doesn't mind spending money   enjoys eating out   communicates their wishes to the restaurant staff   eats out regularly   takes an interest in food
4 Personal service: the customers must know that the proprietors are always going to be there cooking for them and serving them
5 Susan: preparing pancake fillings   taking orders   making desserts making soups   welcoming the customers
   Stephen: cooking pancakes   making ice cream   making desserts preparing salad dressings
6 Knowing the restaurant is full of appreciative customers   Creating an atmosphere and an occasion for them

Transcript

Susan: I'm Susan Hill and I'm joint chef-proprietor of Hobbs' Pavilion in Cambridge.
Stephen: And I'm Stephen Hill and I'm the other half of the joint venture.
Susan: We're essentially a pancake restaurant and this was Stephen's idea to start with about seven years ago. We make pancakes... um... with a slightly French accent but very much in the English manner.
Stephen: We wanted something which could be... could serve as a light lunch menu but also would serve in the evenings.
Susan: Because our meals are quite cheap this means that people can come back more than once a week, they can just use us as a quick stop on the way home... um... they can just come and sit with a cup of coffee and one pancake before getting home in the evening... er... you know, but you can also have a big meal.
Stephen: Flexibility...
Susan: Yes.
Stephen: ... is what the pancakes give us. Our most recent development with the pancake has been on the dessert side. Um... right from the start we had interesting and bizarre sweet pancakes using... um... commercial sweets and confectionery – things like Smarties and Mars Bars and Cream Eggs and...
Susan: After Eight Mints.
Stephen: After Eight Mints. But I've now... um... formulated a method of making these pancakes which turns them... almost into sculpture. And... um... because of the sugar in the sweet batter, if I take the circle, the sort of disc of a flat pancake, fill it with the sweets, I can then, using my spatula and... or t... using two spatulas, I can when I take it off the hotplate before putting it onto the plate I can

twist it up into the air and it just sets almost instantly because of the sugar, and then I can fill that with cream and decorate it with more sweets. Er... these things stand nearly a foot tall and cause a lot of comment and they sell themselves because customers see one of these going to a table and they say 'What's that? I want one!'

Presenter: Is there such a thing as an ideal customer?

Stephen: Yes, I think the job description for the ideal customer is... yes... someone who is accustomed to eating out, is... is comfortable and easy with the business of eating out. Um... forthcoming: they tell you what they like and what they want and appreciate what you s... provide. Um... have a... an interest in food, I think that i... is essential...

Susan: Yes.

Stephen: ... an interest in food, an enjoyment of eating out. Er... and a willingness to spend money. But I put that last really, of course it's essential but, I mean, it makes things go so much more easily if... if there is a readiness to spend money, which is something we never take advantage of.

Susan: When you have regular customers you can afford to give them little presents here and there. That sort of thing you can afford to do if, first of all obviously business is going well, and secondly if you've got this large bank of regular customers to spoil from time to time.

Stephen: And the control which comes from... er... running this ourselves and personally.

Susan: Yes.

Stephen: The restaurant is never open when we're not here.

Susan: People need to know as regular customers that whenever they come in the door they're going to be greeted by me and that Stephen will be cooking their food, and I think that's very important to running a successful small restaurant.

Presenter: How do they divide up the work between them?

Susan: I start slightly earlier here in the morning, and I will be making the food that Stephen will then turn into pancake form when he comes in at the start of a lunchtime session. Er... we... we divide the cooking: Stephen will make wonderful dressings for the salads... um... and he also makes all our own ice cream these days – this is something which is very popular – er... and I will make soups and pancake fillings and some of the other desserts. But then as soon as it's time to open, if it's twelve lunchtime, if it's seven in the evening I will take off my chef's jacket and turn into the waitress, if you like, um... generally with one or two other people. And... er... then I will be taking orders at tables and making sure that everything's going well 'front of house'. At that point of course Stephen is in the... in the heat cooking.

Stephen: When it goes well, um... it is a very satisfying job, that is when you have, as often happens, the whole of the restaurant is filled with customers who want to be here and love the food and are appreciative. And that is... is worth a tremendous amount, I think, defin... It is creative, you're creating an atmosphere for people and creating... er... you're creating an occasion for them.

(Time: 5 minutes 40 seconds)

5.3 Everything all right, sir?

This fairly easy passage is included here to provoke discussion and as a source of examples for the Grammar review section on the passive that follows.

A Answers

TRUE: 3 4 5 7
FALSE: 1 2 6 8

B For supplementary role play on Making complaints, see *Functions of English NEW EDITION* Unit 12, particularly the Communication Activities.

➡ 🔲 On the cassette, as a bonus, there are some corny 'Waiter, waiter!' jokes to play to the class. Many of these depend on word-play.

Transcript

Presenter: Here are some traditional 'Waiter, waiter!' jokes.

Customer: Waiter, there's a fly in my soup.
Waiter: Shh, don't talk too loudly, everyone will want one.

Customer: Waiter, there's a dead fly in my soup.
Waiter: It must be the hot liquid that killed it, madam.

Customer: Waiter, there's a fly in my soup.
Waiter: Look, there's a spider on the bread, he'll catch it for you.

Customer: Waiter, what's this fly doing in my soup?
Waiter: I think it's doing the breast stroke, sir.

Customer: Waiter, there's a dead fly swimming in my soup.
Waiter: That's impossible, madam, dead flies can't swim.

Customer: Waiter, you've got your thumb in my soup.
Waiter: Don't worry, sir, it's not hot.

(Time: 1 minute)

5.4 The passive – 1

A Suggested answers

1 I'm afraid all the cakes have been eaten.
  – *Someone ate them, but I'm not saying who did.*
  I'm afraid I've eaten all the cakes. – *It was me that ate them, I confess.*

2 Arsenal beat Chelsea in the final.
   – We know both of the teams involved, no special emphasis.
   Spurs were beaten in the semi-finals.
   – We only know about the losing team, emphasis on their defeat.
   Manchester United were beaten in the quarter-finals by Southampton.
   – We know about both teams; the information about which side won is given emphasis when it is put at the end of the sentence.

3 He thinks people are plotting against him.
   He thinks he's being plotted against.
   – There is no particular difference in emphasis, but the active sentence seems easier to read.

4 The dough was rolled out and then cut into teddybear shapes.
   – This seems like a report in an impersonal style. The focus is on the action, not on who made it happen.
   We rolled out the dough and then we cut it into teddybear shapes.
   – Here it's us that did the work and it's more informal in style.

5 She doesn't think that she is being paid enough.
   – This seems the conventional way to give this information: obviously it's her employer that's underpaying her.
   She doesn't think that her employer is paying her enough.
   – This means the same, but her employer seems superfluous information.

6 There was nothing to do. *– We were at a loose end, with nothing to occupy us.*
   There was nothing to be done. *– There was no solution to the problem, no remedy for it..*

7 My wallet has been stolen!
   Someone has stolen my wallet!
   I've had my wallet stolen!
   – These mean the same: My wallet is missing and I don't know who's responsible.
   That man stole my wallet! *– I accuse that man of stealing it.*

B   Comments on the examples in the text

. . . more than 230 steak houses **owned by** Grand Metropolitan.
   – This emphasises who the owners are: the active alternative that Grand Metropolitan own *is longer and a bit clumsy.*

Nowadays if you don't like what **is provided** in your meal. . .
   – The active alternative what the restaurant provides in your meal *has to include the obvious information about who provides the meal.*

. . . diners who complain . . . have their bill **torn up**.
- *The active alternative would take many words to explain:* they don't receive the bill because the manager or another member of the staff tears it up . . .

A poll **conducted by** Berni . . .
- *Emphasis on who carried out the survey; more words required for* which Berni conducted.

. . . the scheme **was initiated** by a group of Berni managers and **tried out** in the north of England . . .
- *As the scheme is the subject of both verbs only one sentence is required and it is unneccessary to go into detail about exactly who tried out the scheme.* (other branches of the chain tried out the scheme after a group of Berni managers had initiated . . . *is clumsy.)*

Armed with this knowledge . . .
- *This can only be used in the passive with this meaning unless we say* I armed myself with this knowledge . . .

Simon Smith, the manager, told me he **had been pleasantly pleased** at . . .
- *The active alternative would be* The lack of unscrupulous diners . . . had pleasantly pleased him, *which sounds awful.*

Complaints **had** generally **been justified**.
- There had generally been justification for the complaints *sounds very clumsy.*

. . . some people who did complain **had to be persuaded** to leave the bill to him.
- *Focus on the persuasion, not on the manager who did the persuading.*

C   Suggested answers

2 I was told by a friend that you have been awarded a scholarship.
3 Both cars were badly damaged in the crash, but no one was injured.
4 After the bather had been rescued, he was taken to hospital.
5 An escaped prisoner has been seen, who is believed to be dangerous.
6 After he had been operated on, he was told to stay in bed for a week.
7 Tabasco sauce is sold all over the world.
8 Liverpool were held to a draw by Nottingham Forest.
9 The square may be crowded with thousands of demonstrators tonight.
10 The plane was scheduled to land at noon, but it has been delayed.
11 The tennis match was rained off.
12 They were flooded with requests for free samples of the new product.

➡ Point out that many of the original sentences in C are inelegant and clumsy, and that the passive rewritten ones are better, and easier to understand.

➡ See also 12.7 The passive – 2.

5.5 Position of adjectives & participles Vocabulary development

A Suggested answers

1 She has a *talking* parrot. *– a parrot that can speak*
   Have you heard her parrot *talking*? *– Have you heard it speak?*

2 She is an *old* friend. *– a friend I have had for a long time*
   My friend is quite *old*. *– not young*

3 All the people *concerned* were there. *– the people involved or who were affected*
   All the *concerned* people were there. *– the worried people*

4 It wasn't a *proper* meeting. *– only an informal meeting, no formal or binding decisions could be made*
   The meeting *proper* began at 9. *– the main part of the meeting; there had been an informal gathering before that perhaps*

5 The members of staff *present*. *– who are/were there*
   The *present* members of staff. *– current*

6 Is he the person *responsible*? *– the person who did whatever has just been mentioned or the person who is in charge*
   Is he a *responsible* person? *– someone who can be trusted*

7 I have a friend *living* in London. *– who lives in London*
   She has no *living* relatives. *– all her relatives are now dead*

8 He is a *complete* idiot. *– an utter idiot*
   The *complete* meal cost a mere £5. *– the whole meal, including drinks*

9 She has an *elder* brother. *– older than her – his exact age depends on her age*
   Her brother is *elderly*. *– old, at least 70 years old*

10 The film had a very *involved* plot. *– complicated*
   The actors *involved* were unconvincing. *– involved in the circumstances described in a previous sentence*

B Before they begin the exercise, perhaps remind students that adjectival expressions can come in three positions in a sentence:

1 Before a noun   *A very **interesting** story.*
2 After a noun   *We need the best ingredients **available**.*
3 After a verb   *She is fast **asleep**.*

Suggested completions

That was a really **tasty** meal.
The journey was an **utter** disaster.

Those buns look absolutely **delicious**!
The meal was a **complete** success.

The fire isn't **alight** yet.   Don't leave the baby **alone** all night.
Shh! The baby's **asleep** in its cot.   Her two sisters look **alike**.
The president **elect** takes office next month.
That was the most disgusting meal **imaginable**!
Work expands to take up the time **available**/the **available** time.
I love the smell of cakes (which are) **baking** in the kitchen.
The houses (which were) **damaged** in the storm have been repaired.
The survey **conducted** by Berni revealed some unexpected information.

C   Suggested answers

1 Do you have all the necessary ingredients?
2 Don't forget to follow the suggested guidelines/the guidelines
   suggested.
3 Never wake a sleeping baby.
4 I'd love a refreshing glass of lemonade.
5 She is the nicest person imaginable.
6 The meeting proper began promptly.
7 I object to his downright rudeness.
8 The people responsible have all been arrested.
9 In the sale there were bargains galore.
10 Can I try one of those delicious-looking cakes?
11 Some of the people present fell asleep.
12 It seems to me that he is an utter fool.

5.6 Compulsive eaters   Reading & summary writing

⚠ If any members of your class are unduly sensitive about their weight, it
may be best to omit the discussion phases of this section. The main bulk of
the work can be done as homework.

A   Preliminary discussion   See warning above.

B   Suggested answers

1 Compulsive eating is like an illness; compulsive eaters don't enjoy food in
   the way that greedy people do. Most people are greedy from time to time,
   but only a few people are compulsive eaters.
2 The availability of sweet foods, which are very addictive, and the way in
   which we eat to cheer ourselves up.
3 Half the world is starving, the other half has problems with their eating.
4 He believes that we may be born with a preference for sweet foods.

5 Eating the wrong sorts of food makes us even more hungry.
6 They were offered food to comfort them as babies.

C   Answers

toy with – play with   *stuff herself silly* – eat far too much   *binge* – wild, uncontrollable eating   *distended* – very fat   *fasting* – not eating anything   *gorge* – eat too much   *plays havoc* – causes damage   *stodge* – food that just fills you up   *craves* – has an uncontrollable desire for   *highly charged* – emotional   *antidote* – something to counteract the harmful effects   *moral support* – encouragement

D   Model summary

```
She encourages her patients to feel relaxed about food and
recommends to each of them a diet of sensible whole foods.
She also encourages them to discuss their problems,
offering them encouragement and support. She advises them
to avoid altogether the particular foods that induce a
craving.
```

© Cambridge University Press 1993

5.7   The Third World   Listening & discussion

A   Warm-up discussion   Here is the continuation of the passage, which mentions some of the implications.

> Our sole hope is to create a stable population by reducing the birth rate to equal the death rate. This can only be done by meeting the growing demand for education and family planning among women round the world.

B   [cassette]   The last question requires a lot of writing and students will probably need to listen to the speaker's very last answer several times to get all the information down.

Answers

1 susceptible   recover
2 bottom   priorities   'rice bowl'
3 confident   quality   life   her rights   power
4 integrated   health care   family planning services   adult literacy
   training in kitchen gardening   leadership training for women

C Follow-up discussion   This could form the basis for a composition on 'Providing aid to people in developing countries' or 'The responsibilities of developed countries towards the Third World'.

The discussion might be taken further by exploring such issues as arms sales, Western support for repressive regimes, the role of multi-national companies in the Third World, and so on.

Transcript

Presenter: We talked to Fiona Bristow, who has worked on many development projects in the Third World.

Fiona: I work for an organisation called Population Concern, which is a... a UK charity, which works towards... has two main aims: the first aim is to educate people in the UK about the world population situation and its effects on people's health, on economy, on employment, on all sorts of things, its ramifications in general. And secondly our other aim is to raise funds to support family planning and development projects in developing countries... um... in the countries with the lowest incomes, so we work in Gambia, Sierra Leone, in Ethiopia, Pakistan, India, Nepal, Bangladesh.

Presenter: We asked her about the problems of the scarcity of food in the developing countries she has worked in.

Fiona: A very large proportion of the people in developing countries are malnourished. Many many more than... than people, I think, realise. You see it in all parts of the developing countries... it's certain members of society, certain people within society who really become victims of... of malnourishment, which... it might not... they might not die from not having enough food directly, but they become very susceptible to infections such as measles, they can't spring back into good health afterwards because they continue... are continually malnourished. And it happens in a number of ways.

I've already talked about women, if they have children every year, that's a huge... that's a huge pressure to put on your... your system every year and with breast-feeding as well. So when they come to be pregnant again, for the fourth or the fifth time, their bodies just can't take it. And one of the problems within these societies is that women put themselves at the bottom of the... really the bottom of the priorities within the family. Their first priority when it comes to food and cooking is their elders and their husbands. So she comes bottom of the pile, she gets what's left in the bowl and of course you've got a fixed budget, fixed amount of income, then the bowl... the 'rice bowl' isn't always going to be big enough for the whole family. Of course they often get married very young and have children really when they shouldn't... before they should anyway, before they're fully developed physiologically. And the whole cycle carries on again.

★★★   *(Perhaps pause the tape for discussion at this point.)*

Presenter: So what role does education play?

Fiona: Well, education is one of those strange factors within the whole... within the whole thing. Ten years of education transforms a woman in a way. She comes... she becomes much more confident, she becomes... um... maybe she has a slightly wider view of the world, er... of course, many of the curricula in the Third World include health education, she'll have picked up those... the means to... er... improve the quality of her children's life. And it's not a thing that's necessarily connected with income, it may be just... it's not just that women with a higher level of education are richer, that's not... not the case at all, but it seems to... to... um... it is a very very important factor. Some... sometimes it can simply mean that a woman is more 'bolshy'*, she'll go to the health centre and she'll say, 'No, look I want you to see my... I want the doctor to see my child today' rather than being fobbed off, if you like, um... 'Come back tomorrow, come back tomorrow' and you... you've walked five kilometres to get there and you're not necessarily going to go back the next day if you're sent away. But if you've got education you just demand your rights, and then again it's power, it's giving people power to... er... seek out the things that they need in their lives.

★★★   *(The next part may need to be played several times.)*

Presenter: What then is the key to getting it right?
Fiona: The key is an integrated approach. The key is to do as many different things as you can at the same time: you provide health care, you provide family planning services, you provide adult literacy, you provide... um... you provide training in kitchen gardening, you do all these things intensively, and also you provide leadership training for women. All these things, you've got to do them all.

(Time: 5 minutes)

bolshy: argumentative

5.8 *Should* and *be*   Advanced grammar

A   Correct answers, with comments

1 is – *sounds more definite*   be – *more formal*   should be – *less definite, formal:* should *would normally be unstressed here*
2 feel – *normal, unmarked*   do feel – *emphasising the verb*   should feel – *more formal, less direct*
3 should do   ought to do – *both mean the same here, asking for advice* can do – *asking for suggested alternative courses of action*
4 should arrive – *dramatic emphasis: cf. . . .* when in walked Billy
5 am given – *straightforward unmarked form*   be given – *very formal* should be given – *quite formal*

B   Extra information

Students who have difficulty with using *be* + past participle, which is actually the **subjunctive**, should be reminded that its use is entirely optional. As long as they understand it and realise that it sounds rather formal, they may not actually need to use it.

⟫➔

In American English, the subjunctive is less restricted to formal language than it is in British English, where its use often sounds rather old-fashioned.

The subjunctive (i.e. the base form of the verb) is used in these examples:

*It is/was essential that every person **have** the same opportunities.*
*I propose/proposed that everyone **sign** this petition.*
*It's important that everyone **pay** their subscription.*
*It was suggested that they **discuss** the issues.*

The following verbs and phrases can be used with *be* + past participle or *should* (or the subjunctive):

I was ... that ...
   alarmed   amazed   amused   annoyed   astonished   disappointed   sad
   shocked   worried
   delighted   glad   happy   pleased   overjoyed   thankful
It is ... that ...
   a disgrace   a mistake   a pity   a shame   a nuisance
   awful   disgraceful   terrible   wrong

alarm   bother   disappoint   interest   intrigue   puzzle   scare   shock
upset   worry
e.g.   *It worried me that they **should feel** so upset.*
       *It was alarming that he **should be** so critical.*

And when making or reporting suggestions and recommendations:

It is ... that ...
   essential   desirable   important   vital   necessary
ask   demand   insist   prefer   propose   recommend   request   suggest

e.g.   *It is vital that the results **should be posted** on the noticeboard.*
       *It is vital that the results **be posted** on the noticeboard.*
       *It is vital that the secretary **post** the results on the noticeboard.*
       *It is vital that the secretary **should post** the results on the noticeboard.*
       *I suggested that he **gave** a talk about his experiences.*
       *I suggested that he **should give** a talk about his experiences.*
       *I suggested that he **give** a talk about his experiences.*

NOTE: The verb *to be* has two subjunctive forms:
   *I wish I **were** young and beautiful.*   (past subjunctive)
   *I insist that I **be** sent the results.*   (present subjunctive)

With all other verbs, there is no difference between the present and past subjunctive forms.

The subjunctive is also found in a number of fixed phrases and idioms:
Long live the President.
God save The Queen.
Be that as it may, . . .
Come what may . . .
Suffice it to say that . . .

C   Suggested answers (Many variations are possible – and should be encouraged in questions 6 to 9.)

1   should make notes
2   should hand in
3   be done/should be done
4   should raise
5   should have to do
6   the environment should be protected
7   the weather should be so wet today
8   my friend should have lost her handbag
9   people should be so inconsiderate to each other
10 be elected/should be elected

➡ See also 13.7 Conditional sentences – 2.

5.9   Making notes – 1   Writing skills

Background

Garrison Keillor's laconic, conversational style derives from his work as a radio performer. He is best known for his humorous stories in *Lake Wobegon Days* and *Leaving Home* about a small country town in the Mid-West of the United States called Lake Wobegon, 'where all the women are strong, all the men are good-looking . . . and all the children are above average'. His novel *Radio Romance* is about a local radio station in the days before television became popular.

A & B   The important thing to realise about this section is that it focuses on *making notes before writing a composition* – NOT making notes in the way that students might do for academic purposes while reading a textbook or while listening to a lecture.

The passages in A and C are about 300 words long, which makes them only slightly shorter than the kind of composition required in the examination.

➡ Although there are no vocabulary tasks in the Student's Book, you might like to recommend that your students highlight the following useful vocabulary from each passage:

Lutheran Pie: *from scratch   coasting   a daze of pleasure   apropos of*
Tabasco: *yucky   bland   sultry   ferment   odour   texture   residue*
    prior to

C & D   Again, the notes required aren't 'notes on the passage': students are practising making the kind of notes they should make before writing their own compositions. When marking students' work, assess their notes as well as the paragraphs which are the outcome.

5.10   Describing a process   Listening & composition

A   It might help students to separate the captions into stages in the process and the results of those stages, as well as guessing the likely sequence.
    On the other hand, you may prefer to present it as a 'particularly challenging exercise' and see how they get on with it.

B   ⌷ A difficult one! At least two playings are needed. You may need to point out that it's not necessary to understand any of the technical terms to do the exercise.

Answers

Top row:	1	14	8	6
2nd row:	11	4	3	12
3rd row:	2	5	13	10
4th row:	9	7	15	

➡ Some questions for follow-up discussion:

- Which do you normally eat: butter or margarine? Give your reasons.
- What kinds of foods are thought to be 'bad for your health'? How much notice do you take of this knowledge in your own diet?
- What can you find out by reading the small print on food labels?

C   ⏏ Arrange the class into groups of four. Students A and B look at Activity 5, C and D look at 23. Each pair has different information about the processes of brewing beer and making wine.
    After studying the information together in pairs, and making notes, the pairs split up and then recombine, as explained in the Student's Book.
    If you don't actually have 12, 16 or 20 students in your class, form one or more groups of five with two students working together as 'Student A'.

D   You may prefer to specify which of the two topics your students should choose, depending on their capabilities and interests. Perhaps don't worry about a word limit of 350 words for this exercise, and suggest that diagrams may be used in the article (though not in the exam, of course!).

The 'research' required may be no more than sitting down and thinking through a familiar process, such as writing a business letter on a word-processor, or boiling an egg. Maybe brainstorm some suitably straightforward processes with the whole class.

Transcript

Margarine, especially the kind that's made from vegetable oils like... er... sunflower seeds or corn has a very good image these days. For one thing it's supposed to be better for you than animal fats, people talk about less cholesterol, that word that's very fashionable these days, and... er... another reason is the sunny, natural taste seems attractive to people who care about their health. But just how natural is it? Well, let me explain the process step by step. All the seeds are heated firstly and then crushed to release the oil. Now this is a... a sort of crude plant oil and it still contains impure resins and gums. So, what you have to do next is to add caustic soda. This removes waste products in the form of soap. It may surprise you to know that a lot of the soap that's used is in fact derived by this method. The next step we have is to add fullers earth, now this bleaches it and so what you've got now is refined oil. Next, the oil has to be reacted with hydrogen plus a catalyst, in this case nickel, and this process hardens the oils. So, the following things have to be done: they have to be neutralised, bleached yet again, and filtered to remove any waste products. Now, at this stage there is often a very nasty smell and you take this smell away by heating the hardened oils until they melt again and then when you've mixed them with fish and animal oils you've got blended oils ready to make margarine. But there are more essential ingredients to be added. You must add some water, skimmed milk, some salt and you also have to put some flavour, artificial flavour, into this tasteless mixture and make it a nice yellow colour and put in some vitamins. But you're still not quite ready, even after this lengthy process – the ingredients won't blend until they're emulsified. Now this is done by adding lecithin and monoglyceride and cooling it and mixing it all together. Now, at last, finally, it's ready to be extruded into a plastic tub and a lid with pretty sunflowers is plonked on the top. So, that's your margarine. Butter, on the other hand, is simply made by churning cream. It's pure, it's natural and it's delicious too.

(Time: 2 minutes 50 seconds)

6 Travel and transport

A Warm-up discussion The follow-up discussion in D covers place names and nationality words too.

B Answers

Seatown is a small fishing port lying at the centre of a sheltered **bay**, which forms a natural **harbour**. The town lies in the south-east corner of a fertile **plain** separated from the north coast by a **range of hills**. On the north coast, to the east of the **woodland**, is a freshwater **lake** enclosed by a **sandbank** and surrounded by **marshes**. To the east is an impressive **headland** with high **cliffs** where seabirds nest. The River Trent, at whose **mouth** Seatown lies, is fed by many small **streams** which rise in the hills to the north, but its **source** is over 100 miles to the west. To the south of the town across the river the **coastline** is rocky and it is possible to walk across to an offshore island at **low tide**, though at **high tide** the crossing should not be attempted as there are strong **currents**. For those who enjoy coastal **scenery** it is well worth climbing to the **summit** of the hill to the north of Seatown: there is a breathtaking **view** from there when the **visibility** is good.

Seatown is a popular holiday **resort**: it has a particularly mild **climate** and is renowned for the quality of its fresh **seafood**.

➡ Get everyone to write a similar description of their own region, using a dictionary to find suitable words.

C Answers

1 holidaymakers pilgrims travellers
2 courteous easygoing hospitable
3 off the beaten track out of the way secluded
4 drive journey trip
5 abroad away from home out of the country

➡ Get everyone to look at the words they didn't choose, and explain why they didn't choose them. What situations would they use those words in?

D   Although this section may look deceptively easy, even advanced students have difficulty in using English place names and nationality words, particularly when they are spelt similarly in their own language. Take the names of some of the principal cities in Italy, for example, in other languages:

Italian: Roma, Milano, Firenze, Venezia, Napoli, Genova
English: Rome, Milan, Florence, Venice, Naples, Genoa
German: Rom, Mailand, Florenz, Venedig, Neapel, Genua
French: Rome, Milan, Florence, Venise, Naples, Gênes

6.2   Learning the language   Reading

Background
Rose Macaulay's best-known novel *The Towers of Trebizond* (1956) is an amusing account of a young woman's travels in Turkey accompanying an eccentric aunt. Her other novels include *Dangerous Ages* and *Keeping Up Appearances*.

A   Suggested answers
1 They repeated things and spoke more loudly, believing that everyone can speak Turkish
2 Because she didn't expect them to ask questions when she said she didn't understand Turkish
3 Because a Mr Yorum had come to stay at the hotel
4 Because she had sent for him, he was saying 'I'm the person you sent for'
5 She thought he might be offering to act as her interpreter
6 There was nothing to be done: there seemed to be so much confusion in Turkey that it didn't seem to matter

B & C   After discussing how the story might continue, students read the continuation of the passage in Communication Activities 4 and 19. Encourage everyone to use their own words, rather than read the paragraphs aloud.

6.3 The future

A Suggested answers

1 I'll phone him after work.
   – *Promise or offer: I undertake to phone him (maybe on your behalf, or because you want me to).*
   I'm going to phone him after work.
   – *I intend to do it then – the normal 'uncoloured' future form.*
   I'm phoning him after work.
   – *This is what I'm planning to do, I've set aside time to do it.*
   I'll be phoning him after work.
   – *Reassurance: I'm going to phone him (so don't worry) OR (While something else is going on, at the same time) I'm going phone him, and it may be a long call.*

2 It's still raining in Scotland.
   – *According to the weather report, the rain is still falling there.*
   It will still be raining in Scotland.
   – *(When you get there) the rain won't have stopped.*
   It's still going to rain in Scotland.
   – *According to the forecast, rain is expected once again in Scotland.*
   It still rains in Scotland.
   – *The Scottish climate hasn't changed, it still tends to be quite rainy there.*

3 I think I'm going to scream.
   – *I won't be able to stop myself from screaming (if I don't get out of here soon).*
   I think I'll scream.
   – *It might be a good idea for me to scream (it might attract someone's attention).*

4 When are we having lunch?
   When are we going to have lunch?
   – *What time is lunch?*
   When do we have lunch?
   – *What is the planned, arranged time for lunch?*
   When shall we have lunch?
   – *When would you like to eat?*

5 I'll work hard tonight.
   – *I promise to work hard.*
   I'll be working hard tonight.
   – *(Please don't phone me because) I'm planning to spend the evening working and I'll be busy working.*

6 Will you be going shopping today?
   Are you going shopping today?
   Are you going to go shopping today?
   – Is this one of the things you're planning to do today?
   Do you go shopping today?
   – Is today your regular day for shopping?
   Will you go shopping today?
   – Request: I want you to go shopping.

B Suggested answers

1   'm going to   Will/Could/Can
2   Will you be   are in/go to/visit
3   Are you going to go   (are you going to) take/catch
4   breaks down   will you   – OR   broke down   would you
5   to land   will be/is going to be/might be
6   lands   will have been
7   to reading   have
8   is going to be/is likely to be
9   are away on   'll be/ 'm going to be   'll send
10   'll have
11   get/receive   'll give
12   decided/discussed   are going to do
13   phones/calls/needs/wants   'll   be having
14   will/is likely to   leave/have left
15   will   be doing/feeling   'm flying
16   has in store for/will bring

➡ Make sure everyone is aware of the possible variations, and that there is little difference in meaning between them.

C   This section is crucial, especially the paragraph-writing task. It gives everyone a chance for some free practice and to find out the kinds of mistakes they make in using future forms.

6.4   What a journey!   Listening

A   Point out that more than one picture may be right for each story.

Answers

First story: Picture 3
Second story: Pictures 1 AND 2
Third story: Picture 1

Extra listening task

Note down one question you would ask each speaker to find out information that they didn't give.
For example:

- What were you doing in Norway? Why did you go off to the far north?
- What work were you and your husband doing in Egypt?
- How late were you by the time you got to Sheffield?

B Answers

making very heavy weather of it – not having an easy time
agitated – frantic
teetering – almost overbalancing
lo and behold – guess what happened next! (used in storytelling)
from the sublime to the ridiculous – it was a great contrast between this
    wonderful event and a much more mundane or silly one
bleary-eyed – still half asleep
rickety – unsteady
extricated – managed to get out of the room

C & D Follow-up discussion and writing task   To start things off, perhaps tell the class about a memorable journey *you* have had.

Transcript

Presenter: Right, first of all, David – have you had any memorable journeys?
David: Well, I've just had... I've just had quite a memorable journey, because I've
    just been to Norway. We went up into the Arctic Circle. And that was great
    because we flew to Oslo and then we... as we arrived it was snowy, and people
    walking on the frozen lakes... and that... it was quite nice... Got onto this small
    coach and drove for about eight hours up, and it got snowier and snowier and
    higher and higher and colder and colder until it got night time and then we
    suddenly found ourselves in the middle of a kind of very small parking lot, where
    there were a whole load of Norwegians all dressed up with very cold clothes on
    and driving skidoos[1] and ski... snow-cats[2] and things like that.
    So we got out of our little coach and we got into this amazing big black snow-
    cat – huge great thing. And we all piled into this thing and this maniac
    Norwegian with Yamaha jacket called Knut got into the front seat and drove off.
    It had... it was a V8 engine in it, it went off like a... We must have been doing
    about sixty within about, you know, the first two minutes, flying across these
    fields and things and we said, 'Where are we going?' and he said, 'We're take...
    We're going across this... the frozen lake' so we all went, 'Oh, bloody hell', you
    know, so this was sort of eleven o'clock at night after a long journey, we'd...
    suddenly in the middle of this... pitch black, driving across this frozen lake.
    And... um... we'd been driving for about half an hour and this thing...
    going... great speed of knots... going flying across this frozen lake, and slightly...

it seemed to be going slower and slower... so the thing was **making very heavy weather of it**, and you could see Knut up front getting more and more **agitated** and pressing buttons and pulling levers and everything and... until finally this thing stopped – completely. And there was lots of grinding and 'graunching' noises and the thing started to tilt slightly, going backwards. And he started yelling in Norwegian, which... and then somebody else translated, basically, 'Get the hell out of this, because it's sinking – in the frozen lake!' So we all leapt out and we were up to our knees in frozen water in the middle of absolutely nowhere at all – serious, serious panic. And we all got out and there was this thing halfway in... into a frozen lake, it had sort of got stuck **teetering** on the edge. And there was all our... all our bags and everything on the top. So Knut, with great aplomb, gets onto the top, gets the... gets the bags, throws them all out and they all get soaking wet, we're up to our knees in water, and... and we're surrounded by these ski-doo things and they come along, pick us up. And luckily this event happened only about sort of ten-minute ride from our... from our eventual destination, so we... we did actually get there, to cut a long story short, get there with wet clothes, fear and very wet baggage, but... er... that was fairly eventful.

Presenter: What about you, Ishia?

Ishia: Um... some time ago my... my... my husband had a job in Egypt and I really wanted to go because that's where my father comes from, and I'd never been. And we went... we went to Cairo and the work that he was doing was supposed to take him to Cairo... to Alexandria, sorry. And... er... the... the part going to Alexandria was cancelled, so I was really disappointed because that's where my father came from. So we went to a party, um... quite a smart party, and I met the British ambassador, who just happened to come from Yorkshire, which is where my mother comes from – which is where I come from. So we had a very nice chat and I told him how disappointed I was that I couldn't go to Alexandria, so he said, 'Well, that's extraordinary because I... I'm going tomorrow. Would you like a lift?' So I said, 'Well, that's very nice of you, I mean of course there's my husband here, etc.' And he said, 'No no, that's fine, I'll take you all.'

So I thought, 'Well, this is a bit extraordinary, it won't happen, I mean this is really silly.' Anyway I went down into the foyer of the hotel and, **lo and behold**, eight thirty, there was a Rolls-Royce with a flag on the front, and there was the British ambassador. So he drove us to Alexandria on the... on the desert road so that we could see what it looked like. And then he said that he'd drive us back on the delta road, which indeed he did. He then said, 'You can have my car over lunch... I mean before lunch to go and look round Alexandria, as long as you come back and have lunch with me.' So we went back and had lunch with him at the consul-general's house. So it was quite extraordinary, and apart from the fact that going round Alexandria in a Rolls-Royce which isn't yours, with people kicking the sides, then having a look at the catacombs and being asked for a tip an... and trying to explain, 'It's not really our car – we haven't got any money!' So there... there were sort of low points as well, but it was actually wonderful and coming back on the delta road was divine! It was my favourite trip, I suppose, ever. Now, Tim. Thank you. It was.

Tim: Well, I suppose you'd have to say it's **from the sublime to the ridiculous**, because my... my... my memorable journey was actually the beginning of a journey, I may be cheating a bit here, but... um... I... er... I'd been working in

Bristol and I was... had to come back to London to move... to go into a flat that I'd just moved into, and then the next day I had to go to Sheffield, get a train to Sheffield from King's Cross. And I came back very late at night, and I... everything was in a suitcase and I... I went to bed – I'd just moved into this flat and it was a... it was the middle floor of a big house in Hackney, and – the first floor that is. And my bedroom – it wasn't self-contained – and my bedroom had a... had a Yale lock on it.

So I came out of my bedroom first thing in the morning, ready to go... to set off to Sheffield, but I was rather **bleary-eyed** from the night before and I shut the door! So I was stuck in this rather short towelling dressing gown with everything that I possessed inside the room that I was in. So I decided I had... I had to get a move on, because I had to get this train to Sheffield. So I went downstairs into the garden and I found this very **rickety** old ladder, so I climbed up onto the roof, I went along the edge of the roof and got to the window, and opened the window and went in and found that I was in somebody else's bedroom . . . and that I hadn't actually... I'd gone, because I'd only just moved in, I'd gone the wrong way on the roof, I'd mis... So I quickly **extricated** myself from that thinking, 'I'm going to be... you know this semi-naked man is going to be arrested.' And ... um... found my window and managed, thank goodness, to get in.

And I just threw everything into my case from the night before, all my old dirty washing from the... that I... I'd had for weeks and everything, and my alarm clock and everything and I just ran out and I and, you know, Hackney is the worst place, it's ironic, but it's the worst place in London to get a cab. You can never get a cab in Hackney. So I then waited for about twenty minutes, and eventually got a cab, and I leapt out and I paid the cab driver and I ran into the station, I didn't have time to get my ticket so I just sort... I looked at the thing and it said Platform 2 and it was just about to go and I ran for... for the platform and I... the man said, 'Yes, all right, you can get on the train and pay on the train', so I ran down the platform and I was just about to get on and my suitcase flew open and all my clothes went all over the station and my alarm clock went off!

(Time: 6 minutes)

1 *skidoos:* small motorised vehicles that can travel over snow
2 *snow-cats:* larger snow vehicles, as illustrated in the Student's Book

---

6.5 Collocations: adverbs of degree Vocabulary development

A   Answers

(The following sentences sound right, with differences in meaning as shown.)

1 We quite enjoyed our holiday. – *It could have been better.*
   We particularly enjoyed our holiday.
   We very much enjoyed our holiday. – *We enjoyed it greatly.*

2 The weather was bitterly cold.
   The weather was extraordinarily cold.
   – Very cold indeed.
   The weather was rather cold.
   The weather was quite cold.
   – Colder than we expected, or than we were used to.

3 The food was absolutely perfect.
   The food was quite perfect.
   – It couldn't have been better.
   The food was almost perfect.
   – It could have been slightly better.

⚠ NOTE: Some of the exercises in this unit depend on the two meanings of *quite*. It means *absolutely* in these examples:

> It's quite impossible to answer.   I quite agree with what you say.
> It's quite amazing.   I quite understand.
> The meal was quite perfect.

and *somewhat* in these examples:

> I was quite pleased.   The news was quite good.
> The news was quite encouraging.   It was quite a good book.
> It's quite surprising.   I quite like historical fiction.

In American English *quite* usually means *absolutely* whenever used before an adjective.

B   Suggested answers (many variations possible)
1 I **entirely** agree with what you just said.
2 She **particularly** resented my interference.
3 I **simply** adore Chinese food.
4 We **deeply** regretted what we had done.
5 It was **totally** dark and I was **utterly** alone.
6 We **very much** prefer travelling by car.
7 I've **completely** forgotten what I was going to say.
8 I **really** appreciate what you have done.
9 You really have been **extraordinarily** kind.
10 Are you sure that you **fully** understood what they meant?

Perhaps point out that these adverbs tend to be used in more formal style:
   greatly   highly   somewhat
Whilst these adverbs are used in informal, colloquial style:
   awfully   dreadfully   incredibly   simply   terribly   utterly   pretty

C To make this exercise even more challenging, you could encourage students only to use adverbs they didn't use in B.

Suggested answers (Many variations are possible. Suggested qualifying adverbs are on the right.)

1 I was **terribly** sorry for what I had done.   rather
2 We decided to approach the problem **altogether** differently.   slightly
3 This work has been done **incredibly** well.   quite
4 She is a(n) **awfully** nice person, but he is a **thoroughly** nasty character. rather   pretty   – quite a nice/nasty
5 It was a(n) **extremely** unusual restaurant.   rather
6 Have you **quite** finished?   nearly
7 He was driving **dreadfully** dangerously.   pretty
8 It was a(n) **remarkably** interesting story.   rather   – quite an interesting
9 I was **absolutely** certain I had met them before.   almost
10 We were **bitterly** disappointed when the show was called off.   somewhat

D   Suggested answers (many variations possible)

1 It sounds as though you had a(n) **absolutely marvellous/really appalling** time on holiday.
2 We stayed in a(n) **really splendid/quite terrible** hotel.
3 We had a(n) **quite delightful/really awful** journey.
4 It was **absolutely vital/essential** to change our holiday booking at the last minute.
5 She is a(n) **really excellent/quite brilliant** musician, but she's terribly temperamental.
6 Her performance was **quite appalling/really hopeless/absolutely perfect**.

E   Follow -up discussion   Perhaps, at the very end, ask everyone to write down some sentences that came up in their discussion.

6.6   The friendly sky   Reading

Background

Jonathan Raban's travel writing includes *Coasting*, an account of a journey by sea around the coast of Britain, *Old Glory* about a journey down the Mississippi River, and *Arabia through the Looking Glass* about a journey in the Arabian peninsula. In *Hunting Mr Heartbreak* he tries to 'settle' in various parts of the United States, ending up in Seattle where he feels most at home. His novel *Foreign Land* is about an old man who returns to Britain after a lifetime spent overseas.

A & B   The passage should ideally be read at home before the lesson.

NOTE: There are deliberately no laborious vocabulary exercises or tricky comprehension questions here. The emphasis is on enjoying the passage, and letting the sense carry the reader through despite the unfamiliar vocabulary and the 1,200-odd words.

C   Answers
TRUE: 2   3   10   FALSE: all the rest

D   Highlight some parts that amused *you*, so that you can compare these with the students' reactions.

E   The process of highlighting useful vocabulary in *any* reading passage should by now have become routine, but this should act as a reminder. If necessary, refer everyone back to the notes on vocabulary learning in 1.2 E.

6.7   Revision and exam practice   Advanced grammar

This exercise revises some of the advanced grammar points introduced in Units 1 to 5. The questions reflect some of the *harder* questions of this type that come up in the Use of English paper.

Suggested answers
2   Luckily our tickets arrived in time.
3   At midnight we were still waiting for the plane to take off.
  We were still waiting at midnight for the plane to take off.
4   Arriving at the airport, I was told that my flight had been cancelled.
5   Never having flown before, I was very nervous.
6   What I want is to spend the rest of my life with you.
7   Not only do they go on holiday in the winter but in the summer too.
  They not only go on holiday in the winter but also in the summer.
8   Little did we realise that our hotel was right beside the airport.
9   I propose that he be sent a letter explaining the situation.
10   We were amazed that he should feel shy.
11   She never fails to get the right answers.
12   Only after writing several letters of complaint were we able to/did we get our money back.

6.8 Road safety

B Answers

in the prime of life – at the age when they are strongest and most active
equanimity – lack of concern or dismay
friction – the force that stops one surface sliding over another
pronounced – noticeable, remarkable
thought-provoking – controversial, make you stop and think
abundant – prolific, ample
contentious – controversial, debatable
misrepresent – give others the wrong impression, report falsely
wilful – deliberate (in a stubborn, childish sort of way)

C These are relatively easy questions but the difficulty is in rephrasing
the words the writer uses.

Suggested answers (These are quotes from the passage, followed by
suggested paraphrases.)

1 *Recent aircraft disasters have concentrated our minds on air safety.*
 They have made us think seriously about safety in the skies.
2 *This took place in thick fog, whereas the M6 crash was in what were
 described as near perfect driving conditions. Since nobody was killed in the
 fog crash, and 13 were killed in the other one, . . .*
 There were no fatalities in the M1 accident, which occurred in very poor
 visibility, but 13 people died in the M6 accident, which occurred in very
 good visibility.
3 *Common sense tells us that driving is more difficult when there is less
 daylight and more fog, and when there is less friction between the tyres and
 the surface of the road. Common sense also tells us to drive more carefully in
 such conditions, and therefore more safely.*
 The worse the conditions, the more care drivers take when driving.
 Careful driving is safer driving.
4 *The number of injuries was lowest in February, highest in August. The
 difference in fatalities was even more pronounced: just over 80 in February,
 nearly 200 in August.*
 More people were killed and injured on the roads during August than in
 February, despite (or because of) the better driving conditions in the
 summer.
5 *Some of them misrepresent his views in a way which, if it is not wilful, must
 come from an inability to read.*
 They have (deliberately or stupidly) failed to interpret his opinions
 correctly.

D To help students to approach the summary writing with confidence, perhaps ask the class to highlight the various points made by Dr Adams. Then, taking suggestions from the class, make notes on the board, or ask one of the students to make notes on the board.

Model summary

```
According to Dr Adams, there is no evidence that the
obligatory wearing of seat belts in cars or crash helmets
by motorcyclists has reduced injuries and accidents. He
asserts that the less protected people are (by seat belts
or crash helmets), the more slippery a road surface is, or
the worse the driving conditions, the more carefully and
slowly people drive. Driving slowly may not actually
reduce the number of accidents, but the accidents that do
occur tend to be less serious than ones that happen at
high speeds.
```

© Cambridge University Press 1993

6.9 Avoiding repetition
Writing skills

A Make sure everyone appreciates the difference between deliberate repetition for effect, and the kind of unimaginative repetition shown in the first extract.

B Suggested answers

2 Over a third of British holidaymakers take a package holiday, but fewer than one in ten German tourists take this kind of holiday.
3 When on holiday, British people spend £500 per head. Each Spanish holidaymaker spends over £200 more than that.
4 68 per cent of the Swedes take an annual holiday, compared with 64 per cent of the British and 59 per cent of the Germans.
5 The Germans spend £24 billion per year on their holidays, the British spend half as much.
6 Three million of Britain's visitors come from North America, but three times as many come from Europe.
7 Chicago is the world's busiest airport, handling 57 million passengers annually. 46 million pass through Atlanta, the second busiest, every year. In Europe, Heathrow deals with 38 million passengers each year, followed by Frankfurt Airport with 25 million. Athens and Zurich both handle a mere 10 million passengers each.
8 120 people in the USA are killed in air accidents every year, while 50,000 are killed on the roads.

C There are no model answers here, as it's a matter of opinion which of the information is most interesting.

Extra activity

Write a short article giving your views on how to improve road safety in your country – but without using any of these words more than once: *accident, car, safe, safety, careful, slow*.

6.10 The impact of tourism   Listening & composition

A   Answers

TRUE: 2   3   5   8   10   11
FALSE: 1   4   6   7   9   12

Transcript

Presenter: Fiji is a group of tropical islands in the Pacific Ocean. Tony Green has just revisited Fiji, where he worked during the early eighties. And he's noticed how the islands and islanders have changed. Tony, is Fiji the 'tropical holiday paradise' that the holiday brochures tell us about?

Tony: Well, in many ways it still is – if you can get away from the main island and the capital Suva. There are after all over 300 islands in the group, of which only one hundred are inhabited. Politically, Fiji is not a very stable nation – the main problem is that of the 670,000 people, half are ethnic Fijians and half are ethnic Indians, er… the descendants of labourers who came to work on the sugar plantations. The Indians tend to run the commercial life of the islands, they have the businesses and the shops, whereas the Fijians own the land and they are farmers and fishermen – oh, and they also dominate the government. Recently many Indians have left Fiji because life has become more difficult for them. And these racial tensions have rather destabilised the country, making it less popular than other more… more peaceful destinations.

　　Tourism started in the late sixties because flights between America and Australia had to land in Fiji to refuel. And visitors began to stop over in Fiji, to sample which was then an unspoilt, quote: 'tropical paradise', unquote. The tourists mainly came, a… and still do come, from Australia and New Zealand, um… about, I think, 200,000 go there each year.

　　Tourism's the main dollar earner of the islands – nearly half the country's income comes from tourists. However, for every dollar earned, 75 cents goes straight out of the country again to pay for what the tourists consume. The visitors eat meat and dairy products and vegetables flown in from New Zealand, they drink Australian beer, wine and orange juice. And the local farmers just haven't been able to cope with the international demands of the visitors. The islands of Fiji are very fertile but the farmers haven't adapted to the requirements of the tourist industry, which requires a reliable supply of standard quality products. It's easier for them to grow sugar cane, bananas and ginger for export than to cater for the… the whims of tourists. Consequently, it's cheaper and simpler for hoteliers to import what their guests want to eat and drink, even some of the fruit, by air.

One of the more noticeable effects of tourism on the people is that you see children playing truant from school to act as 'guides' for the tourists – local shopkeepers pay them to grab tourists and pull them into their gift shops. Ironically, many of the souvenirs they buy are not made locally at all, they're imported from places like Taiwan and Hong Kong.

Presenter: Oh dear.

Tony: Er… the Fijians used to be known for their friendliness and hospitality. This is something I noticed particularly when I was there before, but now you're beginning to see a sullenness creep into their character. People seem to resent the visitors and 'friendly Fiji', as advertised in the holiday brochures, is no longer so apparent, I'm afraid. Yeah, these slogans have devalued a… well a complex situation. I suppose you can't expect everyone to welcome foreigners into their community without the foreigners treating the locals with respect too. I mean, you can't buy smiles with dollars, or deutschmarks or whatever.

Presenter: Yeah, I see. They do say that travel broadens the mind, is that your experience?

Tony: Mm, quite the opposite, I'd say. Every international hotel looks very much like another: there are no local styles, and the services they offer are similar too. In fact, if you look at the visitors in those hotels, they're all starting to look alike! They dress the same and behave the same, they talk about the same things, they share the same opinions, they eat the same food, drink the same drinks. They never learn a word of the local language or find out about the local customs – oh, apart from the folklore evenings laid on for them at the hotels. They find themselves buying the same Hong Kong-made souvenirs all over the world.

But what is saddest of all is that they are totally unaware of the local people and their aspirations, of their problems and their interests. The only local people they speak to are waiters, shopkeepers, chambermaids, you know? Tourism in fact is not conducive to mutual understanding – in some cases it even gives rise to mutual contempt, I think. The only difference for the tourist being at home and being on holiday is that the weather is warmer, on holiday they have people to do the cooking and serve the food, and… and do the washing-up afterwards!

Presenter: Hm, I see. So, how do you see the future of Fiji?

Tony: Well, um… despite what I've said, I'm optimistic. Fiji can't revert to how it was in the past, that's just too much to ask, you can't put the clock back. But the airport on Fiji is no longer an essential refuelling stop – long-range jets cross the Pacific non-stop now – which means that the tourists who go to Fiji now aren't people who are just stopping over for a night or two, but people who have *chosen* to stay there for one or two weeks or whatever. And Fiji doesn't depend too heavily on tourism for its income. And recently important reserves of copper have been found which will improve the balance of payments. I think the number of tourists is likely to stabilise at an acceptable level.

And it looks likely that the relationship between the natives and visitors will develop – as it has in Spain or Greece, for example – into a mature, sensible, businesslike one.

(Time: 6 minutes)

6.11   Come + go   Verbs & idioms

A   Suggested answers
1 accepted (with difficulty)
2 happen in the expected way   didn't succeed
3 made her conceited (*also:* made her drunk)
4 attacked
5 progressing   accompany
6 stopped liking   continue, complete
7 look at, discuss   occur
8 Carry on, don't hesitate   be handy later
9 eighteenth birthday (or twentieth or twenty-first, depending on the
   country)   was a great success   received a good reaction, was received
   gratefully
10 become independent   becomes successful   investigated, examined

B   Answers
1 came up with
2 coming out
3 gone up   go down (*also:* come down)
4 came apart
5 went on at   go in for
6 went down with (*also:* came down with)
7 goes off/goes in for
8 came round
9 comes up
10 come across

C   This can be done as homework, or by students working together in
pairs.

7 Consumers

A   Warm-up discussion   Encourage everyone to justify their choices, and not merely mention the names of each store.

B   Answers

2 mall   shopping centre   precinct
3 articles   goods   merchandise
4 a bargain   good value   value for money
5 manufacturer   supplier   wholesaler
6 retailer   trader   vendor
7 break   contravene   disregard
8 purchase   sale   transaction
9 in advertisements   in commercials   on posters
10 make a down payment   pay a deposit   pay cash down
11 guarantee   twelve months old   warranty
12 client   customer   purchaser
13 courteous   helpful   knowledgeable   – obsequious *and* subservient *are also possible if used lightheartedly*

C   [cassette]   Students should make notes in answer to the questions.

Answers

1 responsibility   independence   constant challenge   dealing with people (customers and her team)   unpredictability   being busy all the time
2 watching what's going on in the department   ensuring that stock is on display   supervising the staff   intervening when there is a problem
3 serving customers   operating the till   helping and advising customers   choosing goods for customers
4 hard work   standing all day   working on Saturday (not a disadvantage for Amanda herself)   working one late night every week
5 to manage a department in a larger branch   to stay in the selling side

D   [icon]   Student A looks at Activity 2, B looks at 8, C at 17, and in a group of four, D looks at 45. Each Activity contains some information about dealing with people in shops and service industries and in other walks of life too. Allow a few moments for everyone to read through the information and absorb it, before they share it with each other.

Transcript

Presenter: Amanda Hooper is twenty-six and is a department manager in a well-known department store. What does she enjoy about her job?

Amanda: I think it's the responsibility that knowing that it's my department and that I can basically do what I like that, you know, that I think needs to be done to improve sales or to... um... have a more efficient team or to make my department look better and that's a constant challenge. Also you're always dealing with people, either customers or your own team, and people are very unpredictable, so one day is never the same as the next, it's always something different happening. And I like that, I like to be busy all the time.

Presenter: How much contact does she personally have with the customers?

Amanda: Well, I mean I'm on the floor quite a lot because that's part of my job, to have a look at what's going on... um... see that stock's out, to see that everybody's doing what they should be. Um... but I don't actually serve customers as much as the sales assistants would do, I... I don't really go on the till and that's... sales assistants that's their job, and also to help and advise customers because they're the ones with the in-depth knowledge... um... you know, they know the ins and outs,what they can offer the customer, and they're better... perhaps better placed on a day-to-day basis to help a customer or choose something for them. Um... so... but I mean you do have to be on the floor, you have to hear what's going on, you have to check that they are being served correctly, that nobody's got a problem. So if you're about and there seems to be a situation developing, then you... you would go in and see everything was all right. But... um... my job isn't to stand around all day and help customers, that's... that's not what a manager's job is.

Presenter: What are the disadvantages of working in retailing?

Amanda: It's hard work. You stand up all day, you don't sit down, as I've said. Um... it's hot, especially in this sort of weather. Sometimes some people would call the hours unsociable, I don't because I've never valued having a Saturday but I work a Tuesday to Saturday week and my days off are Sunday and Monday. So if I was a great sport fanatic like my husband, who likes to watch the rugby, I couldn't... I can't. But that doesn't worry me because I hate sport anyway. Um... also we work a late night till half past seven on Wednesday... um... and that's... basically you should expect to work one every week.

Presenter: What are Amanda's ambitions?

Amanda: Well, I've got one of the larger departments at the moment that... and that I look after and I'm responsible for, so really I'd probably be looking to move to a larger branch, still as a department manager... um... but perhaps with a more... bigger team and larger turnover... um... and also probably the extra pressures that working in a large branch brings. Um... but I think I always want to stay in the selling side... um... because that's, as far as I'm concerned, in retailing where it's at, retailing's all about selling... um... and without the selling side of it you can't do anything.

(Time: 3 minutes)

7.2 West Edmonton Mall

A   Recommend that everyone concentrates on getting the gist of the passage and absorbing its atmosphere, rather than getting bogged down with unfamiliar words. Discussion of reactions to the piece can take place before doing the questions, but you may prefer to postpone this till later if it suits the pace and tastes of your class better.

B   Answers

TRUE: 4   8   11   12   FALSE: all the others

C   Answers

parlance – jargon   *avalanche* – plethora   *barmy* – crazy   *mock-up* – replica
meandered – wander   *critical faculties* – ability to judge objectively
oasis – refuge   *blithely* – in a carefree manner   *coughing up* – spend
state-of-the-art – ultra-modern   *banal* – repetitious and dull
proceeds – profits   *pleasure dome* – palace of delights   *glorified* – seeming
more important than reality   *gratifyingly* – agreeably

1 oasis   2 proceeds   3 gratifyingly   banal   critical faculties
4 blithely   barmy   5 cough up   6 parlance   7 avalanche   glorified
8 mock-up   9 state-of-the-art   10 meandered

7.3 Past and present

A   Suggested answers

1 I didn't have time to read the paper this morning.
  – *The morning is over, it's now afternoon or evening (maybe I read it later in the day, or could read it later).*
  I haven't had time to read the paper this morning.
  – *It's still morning, so theoretically there's still time to read it this morning.*

2 I had tea when Pam came in.
  – *I waited for her to come before starting.*
  I was having tea when Pam came in.
  – *I started before she turned up.*

3 By the time we had had lunch it was 2.30.
  – *We finished lunch at half past two.*
  By the time we had lunch it was 2.30.
  – *We started lunch at about two thirty.*

4 Where has Steve gone for his holiday?
  – He's on holiday now, which place has he gone to?
  Where is Steve going for his holiday?
  – Where does he plan to go (in the future)?
  Where has Steve been going for his holiday?
  – In recent years which place has he usually visited?
  Where does Steve go for his holiday?
  – Generally or usually, what is his holiday destination?
  Where did Steve go for his holiday?
  – His holiday is over now OR possibly, he's on holiday still.

5 I had hoped you would invite me. *– I'm disappointed because you haven't invited me.*
  I did hope you would invite me. *– . . . but you didn't.*
  I was hoping you would invite me.
  – I was looking forward to the invitation you have now given me and I'm glad you have invited me at last OR I'm disappointed because you haven't invited me.
  I hoped you would invite me.
  – I was looking forward to the invitation you have now given me OR . . . but you're not going to invite me/haven't invited me.

6 What are you doing?
  – What are you up to at the moment? OR What is your current job?
  What have you done ?
  – I know/suspect you've done something wrong or foolish.
  What do you do?
  – What is your profession or job? OR What action do you take (in a situation already or about to be described)?
  What have you been doing?
  – What activities have you been engaged in recently (since we last met)? OR I know/suspect you've done something wrong or foolish.

B   Suggested answers

2 did you buy   suits
3 has been   has been
4 it had   started to   decided   wouldn't/mightn't   came out
5 has   been   touch   'll get
6 went   hasn't had   since
7 have been   since   have you been   didn't   would be/were going to be
  should have/could have   left   wouldn't have missed
8 was   used to/would   haven't got such a sweet tooth/don't eat sweets any more

C Open-ended practice   Go round from group to group listening out for errors connected with the grammar in this section.

7.4 Enhancing customers' lives

A Warm-up discussion   Perhaps ask the class to suggest other factors not mentioned, and other products they are interested in.

B **Answers**

1 14
2 courses
3 comparable
4 some
5 ready to greet you as you enter their department
6 six days a week
7 customers can relate to them as people
8 each other

C **Answers**

1 lunchbox   wine   sandwiches   magazine
2 dream room for resting   video
3 counters   fresh fish   cream cakes
4 restaurants   (and snack bars, tea rooms, coffee shops, etc.)
5 beer garden   breeze   view
6 June 1   September 1
7 brochure
8 immaculate white   bow   welcome
9 10 a.m.   7 p.m.
10 railway   platform   commuter train
11 service   pleasure   range
12 customer loyalty

D Follow-up discussion   Encourage students who have experience of stores in other countries to describe them to their partners.

Transcript

Presenter: Every country has its department stores – some are luxurious and cater for the very rich, like Harrods in London or Bloomingdales in New York, some are more downmarket. But one country whose stores are unique is Japan. Bob Atkins has just returned after spending a year in Tokyo. Bob, tell us about your experiences.

Bob: Yes, Jane, Japanese department stores *are* unique. Take Mitsukoshi, said to be 'the best store in Japan' – they have fourteen branches and fourteen other associated stores in Japan and seven overseas stores... stores too, even... they've even got a small one in London. Now a... a Japanese department store, they... they don't really try and sell you the things you need every day, like... like a supermarket. What they do is they set out to 'find ways of enhancing customers' lives'. The main Mitsukoshi store has a theatre, and a cinema, a museum and an art gallery, and classrooms – it offers concerts, lectures and all kinds of classes.

Presenter: Fantastic.

Bob: Yeah. They have a Ladies' Club with lectures and lessons in the traditional arts and crafts of Japan: the painting, and flower arranging and calligraphy, and they teach languages as well. Er... they have art... art exhibitions too and... er... some lunchtime theatrical performances – and when you buy a ticket that includes a lunchbox with... er... *sushi* and wine and sandwiches and a magazine.

Presenter: What a nice way to spend a lunchtime!

Bob: It really is, it's lovely! And there are creche facilities in the form of a 'dream room for resting babies' – is what they call it.

Presenter: Lovely!

Bob: Yeah. And if you've got older children... er... they've got a video room where they can go and watch while... while you're doing your shopping. And i... er... you can even get married in some of these stores, a... and you can get married Western-style or Japanese.

Presenter: But, now Mitsukoshi must be special – I mean, other department stores can't offer the same services surely?

Bob: Well, they are supposed to be the top store, but in fact they all have very similar services, all the big department stores. They don't all have a theatre of course, but... er... most of them do have some kind of exhibition area and they run classes – they call it a 'community culture centre' – and you can go there to learn languages, for example.

Now down in the basement of most of the large stores, there is a food department, but it's not like a supermarket, it's just a huge area with... with hundreds of separate counters and they sell everything from fresh fish to cream cakes. And... er... if you need a... if you want to try whatever they're selling, they're just... they're happy as they can be to give you a taste.

Presenter: Lovely.

Bob: And then right up the top of the building there are usually several floors with a... a lot of little restaurants. And they're all kinds of restaurants: of course there are Japanese, and then there's Western ones, you can... er... have a curry in an Indian restaurant, a Chinese, then there's the tea rooms that the Japanese like, and coffee shops, or fast food – and you name it, and you can go there and have a snack.

And then in the summer you can usually go up to the very top floor and then there'll be a roof garden, you know, out in the open air with a beer garden, and there's somewhere for the children to play, and you can just sit in the open air and enjoy the breeze and the view of the city. In fact one store even has a golf school on the roof.

Presenter: Amazing.

Bob: At the end of the summer on September 1st this is closed, they're very strict –

even if the weather's still hot – and that's… because that's the official end of summer in Japan and people start wearing their winter clothes then too. And then the next summer starts on June 1st.

Presenter: Very organised. But Bob, as a non-Japanese speaker, how does one cope with these places?

Bob: Oh, it… it's really easy. Y… you walk in the main entrance and… and right there you can pick up a store directory and a brochure and it's in English. And anywhere in the store, if you ask one of the assistants 'Do you speak English?' if they don't speak English they… they just give you a smile and run off and they come back in a minute or two with somebody who does. So it's… it's… it's really easy.

Then they have a… a whole section of the staff and… whose only duty is to welcome the customers, that's all they do. And then if you go in the lift… er… usually it's a young female operator and she… she's dressed in a little uniform with a little hat and she wears these lovely immaculate white gloves and… and she bows as you enter the lift and she welcomes you to her lift, and then … er… she announces what's on each floor, like the old lift operators used to do, you know, 'Lingerie' and so on and… er… and that's just as the doors open and… and then she bows again when you go out. And when the store opens in the morning – and it opens at… er… 10 a.m. – all the staff stand at the edge of their department and they welcome you, 'Good morning, how are you' and then… and then when the store closes at 7 o'clock they go there again and they say goodbye to everybody as well.

Presenter: So it's always 10 to 7?

Bob: Yes, that's usual. And… and they're all open six days a week. They're always open on Saturdays and Sundays and… and the national holidays. They do close one day during the week, and it's usually Tuesday, Wednesday or Thursday, but the stores in the same district all close on different days. And the floors with the restaurants, I guess they're open later, usually till 10.30.

And you know some… some of the stores even have their own railways.

Presenter: Railways?

Bob: Yeah, these are stores, they're owned by one of the private railway companies that they have in Japan, they're c… they're names like… er… Odakyu, Keio, Seibu and Tobu in Tokyo, that's just for an example. And you can… you just take the lift or the escalator all the way down and the station's right at the bottom, and you just step out on the platform where your commuter train is waiting to take you home. The main store is right at the end of the line, and you know some of these companies, they actually own baseball teams as well: the Seibu Lions are… are one of the top teams in Japan.

Presenter: From what you've been saying, these stores are… are very similar to each other. How do they persuade customers that they are 'special' or that they have a distinctive image?

Bob: Well, at one store… er… the assistants wear badges, they say something like… oh… 'Flower Arranger' or 'Veteran Golfer' to show what they're interested in, their… their hobby, so that the customers can relate to them as people rather than just shop assistants. And then at another store they all wear very bright yellow fluorescent shirts, so it's easy to pick out who's the assistants and who's the customers. And… er… the point about that is that the… the stores in Japan don't compete on price, they don't try and undercut each other, they try and give better service, they compete on just the total quality of the service and how much of a pleasure it is to... to actually go to the store, and also they compete on the wide range of things they have to buy there. I mean all the stores are full of the latest gadgets, the latest fashions and accessories from all over the world.

Presenter: Hmm. Well, I wonder how these stores would go down in this country?

Bob: Well, there *are* big Japanese department stores in Singapore and Hong Kong and other Asian cities, but I'm not sure they're likely to catch on over here. The Mitsukoshi branch in London is quite small and... and many of its customers are Japanese people. The staff don't seem to mind helping... er... tourists who've lost their luggage or passports, or if they want to get in touch with their relations – it's all part of the service they offer. And it encourages customers to be loyal to Mitsukoshi when they get back home again. Customer loyalty is... is really one of the most important things.

Presenter: Mm, yes, if your customers are happy, they'll keep coming back. Well, Bob, thanks very much.

(Time: 7 minutes 20 seconds)

7.5 Compound nouns   Vocabulary development

A   These are some of the compound nouns in the first six paragraphs. If your students have missed any of these, don't waste time pointing them all out. This is intended as a quick sensitising task, not a grammar test.

1 flatlands
2 fluorescent lights? indoor plants service industries department store
3 Empire State Building jelly babies cloakroom
4 consumer seductions? eating establishments night club bingo hall
5 wave machine undersea life skating rink golf course financial service outlets
6 public relations summer environment

B   Answers

advertising agency air conditioning burglar alarm common sense drawing pin driving licence estate agent fancy dress generation gap greenhouse effect hay fever heart attack hire purchase income tax junk food mail order mother tongue nervous breakdown package tour paper clip parking meter pedestrian crossing pocket money road works shopping mall show business unemployment benefit weather forecast window shopping

C   Suggested answers (some variations possible)

air-traffic control/controller   price war/tag   one-parent family
current account/affairs   stainless steel   traveller's cheque   compact disc
(player)   exclamation mark   ten-pound note   swimming
pool/costume/trunks   skating rink   delivery van/charge   jumble sale
chain store/saw   clearance sale   wastepaper basket

D   Suggested answers

1 shopping mall/shopping centre   window shopping/bargain hunting
2 current account/bank account   credit card
3 jumble sale   clearance sale/discount store
4 mail order   delivery charge
5 bar code
6 estate agent/real estate agent   travel agent/travel agency/travel agent's
7 fancy dress   wastepaper basket
8 driving licence   traveller's cheques/pocket money

7.6   Distorting the truth?   Reading & summary writing

➡ Pre-questions, to be answered after a first read-through of the passage.

* What is the ASA?
* What are its main aims?

A   Answers

a handful – a small number of them   *weakling* – person with no strength
pledging – promising   *akin* – similar   *ditch* – small drainage channel
yardstick – standard of measurement   *breach* – break
unwittingly – without meaning to   *monitor* – watch
sceptical – disbelieving/doubtful   *levy* – small tax or compulsory payment

B   Answers

them . . . they (line 5) – advertisements   They (line 7) – unfair advertisements
us (line 20) – the ASA   it . . . it (line 46) the walk
they (line 59) – advertisers   they (line 62) – media owners
they (line 93) – the public   they (line 101) – challenged advertisers
them (line 103) – challenged advertisements   its (line 120) – the ASA's
this (line 125) – that the system of self-control worked in the public's interest

C Suggested answers

1 Five examples are given: that a body-building course could turn 'you' into a muscleman; that a cosmetic can make you younger; that plants would produce 'a riot of colour' in just a few days; if a long walk from a hotel to the beach is claimed to take five; if the ditch that a house overlooks is described as a river.

2 They ask advertisers to supply supporting evidence for any claims they make, or request that they amend the advertisement or withdraw it altogether.

3 The chairman and most of the members of the ASA's council are not allowed to have any professional involvement in advertising.

D Model summary

```
The ASA is an independent body which is financed by a levy on
advertisers. They receive complaints from members of the
public about advertisements in the press, on hoardings and
in the cinema, but they have no responsibility for
commercials on radio or TV. Their code of practice contains
500 rules and guidelines for advertisers. Advertisers can be
asked to amend or withdraw an unfair or misleading
advertisement but they have no legal obligation to do so.
```

© Cambridge University Press 1993

➡ Further questions for follow-up discussion:

• What 'research' do you carry out before making an expensive purchase?
• Do you shop around or go to the store with the widest range? Whose advice do you seek?
• What notice do you take of tests in consumer magazines? What are the advantages and shortcomings of such tests?

7.7 Further uses of *–ing*   Advanced grammar

A Suggested answers

1 receiving/dealing with/making   being/appearing
2 looking at/reading   discovering/finding out/seeing   buying
3 talking to/appealing to/speaking to
4 reading
5 closing (really!)
6 taking/enrolling for/studying on/attending   doing   reading   keeping in touch   writing
7 to meeting
8 to being

B Answers

1 their/them coming   their/them watching   their/them being/getting
   reading
2 doing/'s doing   his/him making
3 them/their smoking   them/their asking
4 Tony falling   Jane/me/my trying

C Suggested answers

1 It isn't worth travelling to London to do your shopping.
2 Your not consulting me beforehand was inconsiderate.
   Your failure to consult me beforehand . . .
3 We were upset about his forgetting to inform us.
4 Instead of spending your money, it might be a better idea to save it.
5 Besides being a champion athlete, she speaks four languages fluently.
6 As well as having a job in an office, he works in a shop at weekends.
7 Without phoning them, you won't/can't find out if they're open.
8 While opening the door, I heard a strange noise.
9 Ever since first seeing her, he has been in love with her.
10 Shall we do something exciting, like taking up windsurfing?

7.8 Sequencing ideas   Writing skills

➡ Begin by discussing the points made in the opening paragraph in the
Student's Book, pointing out that the guidelines given are not definitive.

A   Activity 44 contains the orginal passage, embodying just one possible
arrangement of the points.

Sequence in passage (not necessarily 'the best possible sequence')

7 People increasingly concerned about what they consume
5 Concern about effects on our own health
4 Concern about effects on environment: locally & globally
6 Concern about effects on Third World
3 Advertising creates false 'plastic' needs, often forcing out real needs
2 More and more consumers want to buy responsible products
8 Green Consumers demanding more information about environmental
   performance of products & animal testing & implications for Third World
9 People want to know what additives their food & drink contains
1 We must mobilise consumer power to defend not only our own health but
   the health of the planet

B Model summary

```
Green Consumers refuse to buy products which have a
detrimental effect on anyone's health, and which harm the
environment or use up too much energy. They also avoid
products which generate excessive waste or containing
materials derived from threatened species or environments.
All products which cause any harm to animals or to Third
World countries are also avoided.
```

© Cambridge University Press 1993

7.9 Knowing your rights   Listening

A 🔲 Answers

1 contract
2 a) merchantable   secondhand   fall apart
  b) purpose   seller
  c) described   large   juicy   tiny
3 Recommended: a) b) c)
4 obvious fault
  fault
  ignored   suitability
  ignored   expert
  change your mind
  received   gift
5 If he's mistakenly priced an item too low; or if he doesn't want to disturb a
  window display
6 As evidence of purchase and date of purchase (if you need to return the
  item)
7 Citizens' Advice Bureau   Trading Standards Office
8 Too costly for seller – cheaper to give you your money back

Transcript

Presenter: Many consumers are unaware of their rights in buying goods from shops
  and stores. Dave Watts of the Office of Fair Trading is here to explain exactly
  what your rights are under English law. Dave, first of all, what are the Acts that
  give the buyer rights?

Dave: Well, Sandy, there are two Acts: there's the Sale of Goods Act and the Trades
  Descriptions Act and both cover the rights of a buyer in contracts that he or she
  enters into with traders.

Presenter: And... um... who are the 'traders' exactly?

Dave: Well, 'traders' means any shop, doorstep salesman, street market stall or mail
  order firm.

Presenter: And so what is a 'contract' then in... in this respect?

Dave: Well, if you buy anything from a trader you have in fact entered into a contract with him.

Presenter: And do traders have obligations?

Dave: Yes, they have three main obligations. The first one is that the goods are 'of merchantable quality'...

Presenter: Er... hang on, what does 'merchantable' mean?

Dave: Well, that means 'fit for the purpose', bearing in mind the price that you've paid for it, the nature of the goods and how they're described. For example, a pair of shoes which fall apart after two weeks' normal wear are not of merchantable quality. Very cheap or secondhand goods needn't be top quality but they must still fulfil this obligation. And the second obligation is that the goods are 'fit for any particular purpose made known to the seller'.

Presenter: Oh just a minute, could you give me an example of that?

Dave: Well, if you've asked the seller if the kitchen mixer you're being shown will be powerful enough to, say, knead bread dough and he says it will, then he's entered into a contract, and if it breaks under the strain of your bread-making, you're entitled to a refund. And the third one is that the goods are 'as described'.

Presenter: 'As described'?

Dave: Yes, on the package or as illustrated or described on a display sign, or verbally by the seller himself. For example, a packet of frozen prawns which shows large juicy prawns on the outside and the ones inside are tiny, then you have cause for complaint. Or if the label says the blanket is pink and it turns out to be blue, then again you have a cause for complaint.

Presenter: And... um... if you think you have cause for complaint, what should you do?

Dave: Well, you must take the item back to the shop, unless it's too large or fragile to move, in which case the trader must collect it from you. And you'll be entitled to all or part of your money back, a cash refund, plus compensation for any loss or personal injury.

Presenter: I see. Um... I've sometimes been offered a credit note by the trader in that sort of situation.

Dave: Well, no, the buyer is under no obligation to accept a credit note but he or she may accept the offer of a replacement or a repair to the item, or you can insist on a refund according to the law.

Presenter: Instead of taking it back to the shop, would it be a good idea to send it to the manufacturer?

Dave: No, definitely not. It's the retailer's responsibility. But you could sue the manufacturer if you've suffered personal injury, say.

Presenter: And are there any exceptions to the requirement that the retailer should refund your money?

Dave: Yes, there are a few. You can't get your money back if you've examined the goods before you bought them and failed to notice any obvious fault. And also if you were told about any specific fault by the salesperson at the time of purchase. And also if you ignored the seller's advice on the suitability of the product – if you were told that the mixer wasn't suitable for bread dough, for example, and it breaks down while you're doing that, you can't take it back. And also if you ignored the seller's claim that he wasn't expert enough to offer advice – I... I mean, if he said he didn't know whether the glue you're buying would be suitable for sticking metal to plastic, say, you can't blame him if it doesn't stick metal to plastic.

Presenter: I see, um... yeah, but what happens if you buy something and then you just simply change your mind about it?

Dave: Ah, once you've bought an item you can't legally change your mind about wanting it. But in practice many shops do allow you to do this for the sake of goodwill.

Presenter: Oh, and also, if you've received something as a gift and it goes wrong?

Dave: Well, legally again the recipient of the present really has no rights, it's the buyer who has the rights. Again, though, shops may not be too strict about this and the manufacturer's guarantee may cover you anyway.

Presenter: Can a shopkeeper refuse to sell you something? Er... I mean, are there any circumstances in which that could happen?

Dave: Oh yes, yes. Shops aren't obliged to sell you anything. If a retailer has made a mistake and priced an item too low or... or doesn't wish to disturb a window display you can't insist on purchasing that article.

Presenter: I see. Oh, and what about receipts – should you keep them or doesn't it matter if you throw them away?

Dave: Well, the purpose of keeping receipts is so that you have some evidence of your purchase and also of the date of the purchase, which sometimes is very important. But the retailer's not within his rights to say 'No refunds without a receipt'.

Presenter: Suppose a retailer refuses to give a refund for faulty goods, even when he legally has to?

Dave: Well, in that case you should go to your local Citizens' Advice Bureau or to the Trading Standards Office, sometimes called the 'Consumer Advice Centre'.

Presenter: And how can I find out where these places are?

Dave: You can find the addresses i... in the phone book.

Presenter: Oh, I see. And if the worst comes to the worst?

Dave: Well, you may have to go to court and sue the seller for your money or for compensation. But that's very rare, I'm glad to say, as it's more costly for the retailer to defend themselves in court than it is to give you your money back.

Presenter: Dave, thank you very much.

Dave: Thank you.

(Time: 6 minutes 10 seconds)

7.10 Prepositions

Answers

1 for   2 by   3 with   4 for   5 in
6 by   7 with   8 to   9 as*   10 of
11 as*   12 in   13 about/during/after   14 in   15 to
16 in   17 with   18 of   19 of   20 of
21 for   22 through   23 for   24 of   25 to   26 of

* *as* is a preposition here

7.11 Advertising

➡ Before the lesson, remind everyone to collect some advertisements from magazines or newspapers for discussion in class.

If they can't be relied upon to do this, make your own collection for use in class. The most provocative ads could be mounted on card for use another time.

A   The purpose of the reading passage is to provoke discussion. It is not intended as a model for the composition in B.

B & C   Discussion about which points to omit and possible sequences could take place in class – or these decisions could be made by students working alone at home.

Perhaps revoke the word limit suggested in the Student's Book if this is a topic that your students wish to write an extended essay about, particularly if they have a lot of examples up their sleeves.

8 The press

A   Discussion   Part or all of this might be postponed until after section C.

B   Answers

article – report   *circulation* – number of copies sold   *editorial* – leader
issue – number   *magazines* – monthlies & weeklies
main story – lead story   *newsreader* – newscaster   *the papers* – the dailies
reporter – journalist   *reviewer* – critic

Further useful vocabulary: *column   columnist   correspondent   cover story
scoop*

C   Suggested answers

1   The number of **victims/casualties** of the **earthquake** has risen.
2   Someone says that the **Conservative** party is **very likely/probably going** to win the forthcoming by-election. – *The inverted commas indicate that this is what someone has said or what someone predicts – the article itself would state who the speaker is.*
3   The **Prime Minister** says that (s)he **supports** the **attempts** to reconcile both sides in the port workers' dispute.
4   The police have revealed the **identity** of the **organiser** of the robberies.
5   **Over** 3 million people are now **unemployed/out of work**. The Opposition will be asking the **Prime Minister** some difficult questions in **Parliament/the House of Commons**.
6   A prominent **Member of Parliament** has been **arrested** because he is alleged to have **accepted/received** bribes.
7   The **American/United States** government have **increased** their defence budget.
8   Customs officers at Heathrow Airport have **confiscated/seized** drugs **worth/valued at** £3 million.
9   **Head** teachers are **protesting/angry** because spending on schools is to be **reduced/decreased/cut**. Some teachers are going to lose **their jobs**.
10   **Discussions** between EC **agriculture** ministers are to be **held** in Brussels.

➡ Here are five more genuine newspaper headlines. Write them on the board for the class to decipher:

- **Office death plunge probe** – There is to be an inquest after someone died after falling from a window in an office block.
- **Runaway couple vow to wed** – A young couple who have run away from their parents say that they intend to get married.
- **Premier set to visit Britain** – The prime minister of somewhere is expected to make an official visit to Britain.
- **Girls plump for new university** – More female students (than males, or than expected) have applied for places at a new university.
- **Nurses sit in over cuts** – A group of nurses have protested about reductions in pay or government support by 'sitting in' (sitting down and refusing to move).

8.2 End of an era   Reading

No apologies for the fact that this is old news. In fact, the less your students know about the events described, the more they will have to find out by reading the passages.

B   Correct sequence (according to the *Economist* extracts)

1   The deputy prime minister resigned.
2   The PM defended her stand on her European policy.
3   Mr Heseltine denied that he would stand for election as party leader.
4   Mr Heseltine announced that he would stand for election as party leader.
5   The PM announced her intention to stand her ground.
6   Geoffrey Howe made a public attack on the party leader.
7   The first ballot of Tory MPs was held.
8   The PM got more votes than Mr Heseltine, who was standing against her.
9   The PM announced her intention to stand again.
10   The PM announced that she would stand down.
11   Messrs Hurd and Major decided to stand against Mr Heseltine.
12   A second ballot of Tory MPs was held.
13   Mr Major became PM when Messrs Hurd and Heseltine stood down.
14   The ex-PM announced that she was standing behind the new PM.
15   Mr Heseltine became environment secretary in the cabinet.

C   A little background information might help students to appreciate the passage:
- Mr Major was Chancellor of the Exchequer (finance minister) in Mrs Thatcher's cabinet. As such he resided at No 11 Downing Street, next door to the PM's residence at No 10.
- Mr Heseltine is well known for his flamboyant hair style.
- Mr Major's father was a music hall performer (not exactly a circus entertainer).
- 'eating three shredded wheat' is a reference to an advertisement for a breakfast cereal. Only a superman can manage to eat three, as they are so filling.

Suggested answers

1 By saying he was excited – but not by his tone of voice or expression
2 By announcing how many shredded wheat he had eaten for breakfast
3 Totally – until they have had enough of him
4 They reeled with astonishment at the new PM's obscurity and lack of experience
5 His family worked in a circus (allegedly)
6 Accountancy
7 Grey
8 Very ironic and rather malicious – if the people involved weren't politicians and consequently 'fair game' it might be considered sarcastic and malevolent. The writer wants to poke fun at all the politicians mentioned, who take themselves too seriously.

D   Answers

1 inherit his parents' property and wealth
2 childbirth
3 the American President
4 mother   young child
5 turn on them/do harm to someone you have previously trusted
6 a circus
7 evidence or proof
8 future generations
9 we know we are going to lose but want to appear courageous
10 bravely or heroically
11 sits in the rear seat of a car criticising the driver and telling him/her what to do next
12 comfort or relief to help you to get over a disappointment

E   Follow-up discussion   If politics is a touchy subject for your students, it might be best to concentrate on international leaders here.

8.3 Modal verbs

A   Suggested answers

1 Could you finish the article?
   – Please finish reading or writing it.
   Were you able to finish the article?
   – Did you manage to finish reading or writing it?

2 Can you carry this box?
   – Are you strong enough to carry it? OR Please carry it for me.
   Can you help me to carry this box?
   – Please carry it with me: we'll do it together.

3 You can't leave yet.
   – You're not allowed to leave / I won't allow you to leave.
   You needn't leave yet.
   – You're not obliged to leave (but you can if you want).

4 I don't need to read the paper today.
   I don't have to read the paper today.
   I needn't read the paper today.
   I haven't got to read the paper today.
   – It isn't necessary for me to read it, I'm under no obligation to read it.
   I haven't to read the paper today.*
   I mustn't read the paper today.
   – I'm not allowed to read it, I've been ordered not to read it (so I won't do so).
   I haven't read the paper today.
   – So far today I've had no chance to read it (but I may do later).
   I shouldn't read the paper today.
   – It's wrong for me to read it, I'm not supposed to read it (but I may do so).

5 There could be an election this year.
   – It's possible that there will be one.
   There should be an election this year.
   – It's likely that there will be one OR There is supposed to be one, but it may not actually happen.
   There has to be an election this year.
   – This is the year when (by law) an election is held OR The government are under a moral obligation to call an election.
   There will be an election this year.
   – An election is going to be held this year, that's certain.

* Note that *haven't to* . . . is not much used these days. Students should be able to recognise and understand its meaning, but not use it.

6 That could be Tony at the door.
   That might be Tony at the door.
   – It's possible that it's him at the door.
   That will be Tony at the door.
   That must be Tony at the door.
   – I'm sure that he's at the door: no one else is expected.
   That can't be Tony at the door.
   – Someone is at the door but I'm sure that it's not Tony.
   That should be Tony at the door.
   – I'm fairly sure it's Tony.

B Suggested answers

1 *Example: make sure everyone knows what they are supposed to do.*
2 She said that they might be able to help me.
   She said that it was possible that they could help me.
3 He told me that I couldn't/mustn't use a dictionary in the exam.
   He told me that I wasn't allowed/permitted to use a dictionary in the exam.
4 She asked me if I had to leave so soon.
   She asked me if it was necessary for me to leave so soon.
5 He told us that we mustn't /shouldn't believe everything we read in the newspapers.
   He told us that it was unwise to believe everything . . .
   He told us not to believe everything . . .
6 She told us that she didn't dare to dive into the swimming pool.
   She told us that she didn't have the courage to dive . . .
7 He told us that we needed to book a table.
   He told us that it was necessary to book a table.
8 She wondered what time she had to arrive there.
   She wondered what time it was necessary for her to arrive there.

C Suggested answers (many variations possible)

1 The socialists should win the election.
   The socialists are likely to win the election.
2 Patrons/People mustn't smoke in a cinema.
   Smoking is not allowed/permitted in cinemas.
3 Passengers (will) have to wear a seat belt in the rear seat of a car.
   Wearing seat belts in rear seats is (going) to be compulsory.
4 Drivers will no longer have to keep to 70 mph.
   Drivers will be able/allowed to drive over 70 mph.
5 Thousands of people had to leave their homes after the earthquake.
6 There may well be another recession.
   Another recession is likely in the near future.

7 The minister for sports said that fewer people can swim than in the past.
  The sports minister has said that more people are unable to swim than in
  the past.
8 Many commuters couldn't get home because of a railway strike.
  A railway strike has prevented many commuters from getting home.

Extra information on *dare*

Some students find *dare* a tricky verb to use, as it can function both as a
modal verb and a normal verb, as in these examples:
  I *daren't* jump.
  I didn't *dare (to)* jump.
  Dare you jump?
  Do you *dare to* jump?
  Don't you *dare* speak to me like that again.
Notice also the use of *I daresay*:
  I daresay (that) the Conservatives will win the election.

8.4 Working as a journalist   Listening

➡ Before they listen to the recording, get the class to discuss these lead-in
questions:

• What are the responsibilities of a journalist?
• How do journalists spend their working day, do you think?

A Answers

How does she get her stories?
– From regular contacts, usually on the phone
– Talking to trade union officials and press officers

Why doesn't she spend more time travelling?
– Not enough time

What does she dislike about her work?
– Having to make routine phone calls to keep abreast of the news, e.g. to
  companies (on the local paper to the police and ambulance stations)

What does she enjoy about her work?
– Going out and meeting people
– Writing – she even seems to relish the pressure of writing 400 words in
  half an hour, interrupted by a phone call halfway through!
– You get paid to ask people about their lives

What attracted her to journalism?
- Being interested in other people – she is very nosy (curious)
- Wanting to know how other people see the world

What kind of tensions have there been between her personal feelings and doing her job?
- Interviewing members of the public who were distressed, asking intrusive questions and asking for photographs
- Now she deals with professionals, many of whom are paid a lot of money to deal with the press, so she doesn't worry if they cause themselves embarrassment

B Follow-up discussion Encourage students to talk about the positive and negative aspects of journalism, including TV news coverage. Can they think of recent stories that have been handled badly? How much credence do they give to information that's reported in the papers?

Transcript

Presenter: Lisa Wood is a labour correspondent on the *Financial Times*, writing reports on labour relations and trade union affairs. First of all we asked her how she gets her stories – does she go around the country with a spiral-bound notebook, asking people embarrassing questions?

Lisa: Well, I used to work on a... on a local newspaper and that was much more the... the case, I would be writing sort of a lot of human interest stories, going off... pehaps doing vox pops in the streets, asking people what they thought about this or that but on the *Financial Times*... um... there's less actual sort of inter... interface with... er... the general public, and we're mainly dealing with trade union officials... um... press officers. I do a lot of my work on the telephone. I do like getting out, I do like talking to people and... um... one finds that, you know, you're very welcome and you get many many more stories if you actually go out and... and meet people. But there are pressures on time. If I want to go away for the day to Birmingham, you know, it's two hours on the train, two hours back, um... a... and we have a much sort of tougher discipline in terms of time. So one can't roam perhaps as one used to.

Um... so I'll spend perhaps... mm... half my day on the telephone, talking to people, talking to regular contacts. Um... and an important part of j... being a journalist on the *Financial Times* is actually building up a strong repertoire of good contacts, people who you trust, they trust you, um... obviously sometimes you... you have to push them perhaps further than they'd like to go so, you know, relationships are sometimes stretched. Er... one of my colleagues yesterday wrote a story which she said that the organisation wouldn't like because it was embarrassing to them, but it was true. Er... so one, you know, has those sort of er... constraints... um... and then perhaps ten per cent of the time I'll go out and talk to people... um... but that is... actually sort of the nice bit of the job.

Presenter: So that's the nice part of the job, what's the worst part?

Lisa: The worst part of the job is... is sort of routine... er... the routine calls that...

um... today I have to make four routine calls on stories that... um... you know might happen this week, next week or in two weeks' time, but because one has to be abreast of the news one has to sort of make very regular sort of calls just to make sure that you're covered. If you're working on a local newspaper you'd have to do the same with the police: every four hours you ring up all the police stations on your 'beat', you ring up the ambulance stations, you know, to check that you've actually got you know a brief of what's happening. Here we do have sort of similar calls but they're not obviously to the police or the ambulance... um... but it's... it's to companies just to check that things that they said that were going to happen haven't happened.

But... um... writing is an enjoyable part. I mean it can be very stressful, if a story breaks –i.e. that is the information comes in to you at 5.30 and you have a deadline of 6. And if you have a deadline of 6 that means that your story has to be in at 6 o'clock and to write 400 carefully honed* words i... in half an hour can be... um... you know quite difficult, particularly as the telephone'll go halfway through and somebody will demand to speak to you about another story and you say, 'I'm dreadfully sorry, I'm on a deadline, can you ring me tomorrow?' They then get very offended because they think that their story is the most important in the world so you have to break off, talk to them for ten minutes and then, you know, type a... at some... er... considerable... er... speed.

But it rarely happens that people can't write a story: I can't think of one instance either in my own case or anybody else here, who basically has said, 'I can't write it', you know, that their brain seizes up or... or... or whatever. I mean, we always make it. I don't know how, it must be fear, total terror! Er... but one is trained to an extent that you perform, and if you have to write the words, you write them. And if somebody comes in at quarter to six and says, you know, 'I want a story on... er... the pickle market', er... and you've got quarter of an hour to do it, you'll do it, I don't know how but it gets done!

Presenter: What was it that attracted Lisa to journalism in the first place?

Lisa: I was always interested in other people, um... I am by nature nosy... um... and I think that's a... an important qualification for a journalist. When I was a child, Cinderella was one of my favourite stories and if I'd had three wishes I'd have been three different people, you know, if I'd had a fairy godmother because I... I always want to see how other people see the world.

Presenter: On emotional issues, are there sometimes tensions between doing the job and personal feelings?

Lisa: There are tensions and they have occurred to me in previous occupations. I worked on a... on a local newspaper where I had to go often on accidents and interview people whose children or husband or wife had died, and often when I asked . . . I remember in one instance a child had died and – a wall had dropped on this child and it was a local authority-owned wall. My news editor wanted me to talk to the family at a time when they'd just been told that their child had died about negligence, whose fault it was, etc. And I knew what I'd got to get from this family, I'd been told what to ask, etc. And when people are very upset they say things sometimes that on reflection they wouldn't say, and the next day, or perhaps the day after, the lady rang me up and said, 'I don't remember saying that' and I said, 'Well, I have a note, and you did say it.'

And I was never very proud of myself sometimes in those instances, because you had to push people, you had to prod them, you had to ask for pictures, that sort of thing. And I found that personally very difficult and also sometimes intrusive. And if I'd been those people I'd have slammed the door and said, 'Go away!' but my job was to get through the door. So I don't like that sort of 'peek-a-boo' journalism.

The great thing about the FT is that you are generally dealing with professionals, so if I press... push a chairman of a company and he says something which is perhaps... causes him embarrassment later, at least I say to myself, 'You know, that person is paid £100,000 a year just to sort of fend off questions like that.'

Presenter: What is it then that Lisa enjoys most about being a journalist?

Lisa: It gives one the most amazing sort of access into... into life. I can talk to anybody: you know, street cleaner, I can talk to the company chairman, and if there's a story there I can write about it. I think it just, I mean, it comes back to being nosy. It gives you a licence and it pays you to enquire from people about their lives, and I think it's endlessly fascinating.

(Time: 7 minutes)

* *honed:* sharpened and polished

8.5 Prefixes Vocabulary development

A Answers

anti- anti–American anti–computer anti–federal anti–school?
anti–strike anti–union

pro- pro–American pro–computer pro–federal pro–school
pro–strike pro–union

pre- pre-cooked pre-packed pre-school pre-test

super- supercomputer super-intelligent superstar superstore

half- half–American half–brother half–cooked half–expect
half–holiday half–time half–truth halfway

B Answers

re- reappear rebuild recapture re-estimate refasten refillable
reload renumber reprint reunited reusable revalue

un- unblock unfasten unload unusable

over- overbuild? overestimate overload overprint? oversimplify
overvalue overwork

under- underestimate undervalue

out- outbuild outgrow outnumber outvote

Point out that used 'actively' we can say, for example:
Once something is printed you can't unprint it.
This area has been overbuilt (= there has been too much building).

C Answers

self-   self-defeating self-educated self-employed
            self-explanatory self-governing self-preservation
            self-sufficient
co-   co-director co-exist co-owner co-president?
counter- counter-measure
ex-   ex-boxer ex-director ex-official ex-owner ex-police officer
            ex-president
semi-   semi-automatic semi-circular semi-educated
            semi-employed? semi-official
sub-   subheading substandard subtitle

D Answers

1 oversimplification
2 overestimating/underestimating
3 pro-strike outvoted
4 counter-productive over-react
5 subtitles
6 super-rich superstars outsell
7 self-explanatory
8 half-expected ex-wife pre-Christmas
9 counter-attack pre-arranged
10 reappeared half-frozen

➡ Here are some more prefixes which you might like to remind your students about:

ante- (before)   ante-natal anteroom
auto- (by itself)   auto-record auto-reverse auto-timer
fore- (before)   forewarned is forearmed foretaste
post- (after)   postgraduate post-war
mega- (large/great) megadollars megastar
mono- (one/single) monochrome monosyllabic
bi- (two/double)   bi-annual bicentenary bilateral bilingual
                  bisexual
tri- (three/triple) trilateral trilogy triplet

8.6 The world's most wonderful job

Background

Michael Buerk is well-known in Britain as a presenter of the Nine o'clock News on BBC 1. It was his startling on–the-spot reports of the famine in Ethiopia in 1984 which alerted the world to the situation there.

A   Suggested answers

1   *shuffling on the landing* – noise of moving feet outside the room
    insouciance – lack of concern   *itchy feet* – wanting to travel
    fronting – being the presenter   *dovetail* – fit neatly together
2   Because of the noise of the men queuing outside in the corridor
3   There was plenty of wine and amusing reading matter to keep the men happy
4   He spent all night looking for a scorpion
5   He is paid to go all over the world to see the most interesting and important events happen
6   He likes being recognised and treated as 'important'
7   Twelve times . . .   It gives the effect of dramatic pauses in speech; maybe it seems a little overdone in print

B   See Activity 6 in the Student's Book.

C   Follow-up discussion   Perhaps also ask the students to compare Michael Buerk's job as foreign correspondent with his work as TV newsreader – and with Lisa Wood's work, as described in 8.4.

8.7   *There . . .*

A   Suggested answers

1   There is someone waiting outside to see you.
2   There are no easy answers to most political problems.
3   There's no point in trying to explain the problem to them.
4   There is more coverage given to sport in some papers than others.
5   Luckily for us there was a telephone box nearby.
6   There's no need to shout, I can hear you perfectly well.
7   There are 14 branches of Mitsukoshi in Japan – and (there are) 14 associate stores too.
8   Come quickly! There's been an accident! There may be some people hurt!
9   There he stood in the doorway with a sheepish grin on his face.
10   There were fifteen of us waiting in the lecture hall.

B   Suggested answers

1 will be/to be	5 is just one
2 must be no	6 denying
3 comes	7 being
4 is a lot of	8 seems

C   Suggested answers

1   The police say that there were fewer than 5,000 people in the peace demonstration.
2   The forecasters say that there will be more sunshine next week.
3   The England soccer manager says that there is no doubt that the team will win in tonight's international match.
4   Environmentalists say that there are too many cars, causing pollution and accidents.
5   According to the newspaper there could/might be a general election this year.
6   There have been attempts to reconcile both sides in the teachers' strike/dispute.
7   There have been fewer road accidents this year.
8   There were 150 people killed in the ferry disaster.

⚠ Some students confuse *There* . . . with *It* . . . in sentences like these:

It's a shame/pity you couldn't come.
It's difficult to know who is in the right.
It gets dark earlier in the winter.
It's Susan who is responsible.
It was a good thing you warned me.

D   Student A looks at Activity 24, B at 36 and C at 38. Each student has a short news item to tell their partners about in their own words, using *There* . . .

8.8   Here is the news . . .   Listening

A   Answers

TRUE: 1   2   3   6   13   14   16   18
FALSE: 4   5   7   8 (according to the report at the very end)   9   10   11
    12   15   17   19

B & C   Follow the development of a news story day by day on the radio news and in the papers with the class, discussing what is likely to happen next.

Transcript

Brian (Presenter): ... and it's just coming up to 8 o'clock and it's time for the news. First the headlines: an air traffic controllers' dispute is hitting holidaymakers – many flights are being delayed or cancelled. Storms during the night have caused widespread damage in the western half of the country. Japan has been hit by a severe typhoon. There's to be an economic summit meeting next month.
   Here's Fiona MacMillan with the details.

Newsreader: The strike of air traffic controllers at Heathrow and Gatwick, which began at midnight last night is already causing chaos for travellers. Scores of flights have been cancelled or diverted. The Association of Air Traffic Controllers called out its members last night when talks with the management reached deadlock. Discussions have been going on all week over the Civil Aviation Authority's plans to rationalise the shift working system. Managers and supervisors (who are not members of the union) are working double shifts in an attempt to minimise the disruption. A report from Larry Harrison at Heathrow.

Harrison: The latest from here is that there will inevitably be further cancellations and delays today and the situation is almost certain to deteriorate during the course of the day. British Airways say that they hope to get up to half of their flights away but that there will delays of at least an hour to many departures and to arrivals. Their advice to passengers is to turn up on time for their flights because some flights will be getting away on time. Many incoming flights have been diverted to Bournemouth, Stansted and Birmingham. If you're meeting someone on an inbound flight, you're advised to phone the airport before setting out. According to a spokesman for the AATC the differences between the management and the union are 'irreconcilable' and there looks to be no prospect of a resumption of normality for at least 48 hours. Management are asking the union to allow the case to be put to ACAS the Advisory, Conciliation and Arbitration Service, but the union is refusing to do this.
   Gatwick seems to be less badly affected than Heathrow. No incoming flights have been affected so far and 80% of departing flights are getting away with delays of under two hours. All passengers should check in on time, according to the airlines. However, it does look as if the situation may worsen during the course of the day. This is Larry Harrison at Heathrow Airport.

Newsreader: The numbers to ring for flight information are 081 759 4321 for Heathrow and 0293 28822 for Gatwick, or the airline concerned. Information is also available on BBC Ceefax page 140.
   Storms yesterday in the West Country have caused extensive damage and flooding. A report from Jenny Dawson of Radio Devon.

Dawson: After the worst storms of the year, damage running into millions of pounds is reported to buildings throughout the South-West. Twenty-nine football supporters were taken to hospital at Barnstaple after the coach they were travelling in was hit by a falling tree on the A39. None of them are said to be seriously injured. A family of six had a lucky escape when their house caught fire after being struck by lightning in Appledore – they had left home only five minutes earlier on their way to the cinema. Elsewhere flooding has cut many major routes in Somerset, Devon and Dorset. The whole of the M5 between Wellington and Exeter has just reopened after being closed since 9 o'clock last night due to flooding, and the A30 and A303 are still closed. Police say that motorists should only travel if their journeys are really necessary, and they should check locally on road conditions before setting out.

Newsreader: Overseas, the weather has also been causing problems. The southern Japanese island of Kyushu has been hit by a severe typhoon, the worst for 20 years. At least 30 people died near Kumamoto when a landslide carried a train into a river. Services on the high-speed bullet train have been suspended for the first time since 1986. The typhoon is now moving across the Inland Sea towards the densely populated areas of Kobe and Osaka, and is showing no sign of abating.

Plans were announced late last night for an economic summit meeting to be held on the Greek island of Rhodes next month. A report from our economics editor, Simon Greenlees.

Greenlees: The announcement of a meeting between the leaders of the United States, Japan, Britain, France, Italy, Germany and Canada comes as a complete surprise. It's believed to come at the request of France and Italy, whose currencies have come under heavy attack from the dollar recently. Meetings of this kind are normally planned many months in advance, and an emergency meeting would generally only be called in time of crisis. Moreover, meetings are not generally held in a non-participating country. The only explanation seems to be that the leaders of Canada, Germany and Britain are all due to be holidaying in the Eastern Mediterranean next month.

Newreader: News is just coming in of a late development in the air traffic controllers' dispute. Over again to Larry Harrison at Heathrow. Larry, what's the situation now?

Harrison: Well, Fiona, it's just been announced that controllers at Heathrow have agreed to allow their case to be taken to arbitration and they've called off their action with effect from midnight tonight. So that means that flights today are still subject to cancellation and delay and are not likely to be back to normal till tomorrow or even the day after. Gatwick controllers have yet to announce their decision.

Newsreader: That report from Larry Harrison. Finally, the weather. Western areas of England after yesterday's heavy rain and strong winds should be mainly dry today with scattered showers towards evening. Central and eastern parts will have heavy rain at first with some thunderstorms, but by the evening brighter, drier weather will reach these areas. In the North and in Scotland and Northern Ireland, temperatures will be below normal but some sunshine can be expected. The outlook for tomorrow and the weekend: continuing unsettled, but clearer weather spreading across from the West on Sunday. That's all from me in the news room, now back to Brian.

(Time: 5 minutes 50 seconds)

8.9   Paragraphs – 2 Writing skills

A   Suggested answers

1 As we rush . . .   – *Striking, attention-catching opening sentence*
2 One of the liabilities . . .   – *Change of topic*
3 The new breed . . .   – *Further information given extra emphasis or prominence by being at start of new paragraph*
4 We have already . . .   – *Further information given extra emphasis, at beginning of very short paragraph*
5 Now the time has come . . .   – *Conclusion starts*

B   Preferably allow students to decide for themselves on the total number of paragraphs they think appropriate. However, you could specify that three or four paragraphs are generally desirable in a passage of this length (about 230 words).

Suggested paragraph openings

1 New Yorkers are escalating . . .
2 The most popular gecko is . . .
3 Those who fear . . .
4 In the distant future . . .

C   Be prepared to adjudicate if there are any disagreements during this discussion.

8.10   Politics Interview practice

A   This could be done in pairs, or as a whole class as a warm-up.

B & C   There is plenty of scope for discussion here. Perhaps rearrange the groups for each part, so that there are more points of view.

8.11   Two points of view Composition

A   First discuss as a class how the two points of view might differ.

B, C & D   In place of the 'story' students might substitute two points of view on a more momentous topical issue.

8.12 Bring + get

A Suggested answers

1 made me realise   raise   go unpunished for
2 caused   find a way round/find a way to manage in spite of them
3 find a way of dealing with/recover from   asking for advice or help from
4 reveals/shows everyone my worst characteristics   be friendly   making me feel depressed
5 made the whole audience laugh   understand the point of
6 criticising/poking fun at him   recovers from
7 get revenge   have my revenge on
8 Not much time is left   come to the end of
9 make them understand
10 trying to communicate
11 make him less shy
12 fall asleep   not making enough progress with   got out of bed   started   completed/accomplished

B Answers

1 get on with   2 get out of   3 got off with   got at (bribed or threatened)
4 get   down   5 getting up to   6 get on   get in with
7 get on to/bring up   8 get round   9 get round to   10 get   up
11 bring   up   12 brought about

9 Education

➡ Begin by asking the class what they understand by 'the three Rs'. Point out that this term is used frequently – even in serious discussions about education. (The 'three Rs' are reading, writing and arithmetic.)

A   Pause the tape between each speaker, to give students a chance to 'catch-up' and write their answers.

Suggested answers

1 the work was dull, she wasn't challenged, it was formal
   doing dictation and learning information for exams
   rebel (for the rest of her life)
2 broader but less deep
   hearing different viewpoints from all over the USA
3 i)   good fun/interesting
   ii) beneath contempt
   iii) utterly contemptible
   iv) relationships and friendships
4 bully
   victimised/belted   English   heard
   disapproved

B   Discussion   This draws on some of the themes raised by the speakers.

Transcript

Presenter: We asked three people to talk about their schooldays. First, Ishia, who went to a grammar school for girls.

Ishia: Um, I can't say it was a terribly happy experience, though I had lots of friends and a jolly good time but actually I just thought that the work was so dull, and I was constantly trying to get people to... to . . . challenging people I suppose because I wanted... I really did want to think and understand and try and work things out, and when I went to school it didn't seem to be what education was about. It was very much, and because it was a grammar school and very formal, it was very much about... um literally being dictated to, listening to sort of pages and pages of dictation, writing it all down and then learning it for the exams. Um... so I found it deeply boring and I think it probably... probably the good thing it did was that it... it turned me into a rebel for the rest of my life.

Presenter: Mike was educated in the United States.

Mike: I think the main difference between the way we educate children and the way you do here is that our education is so much broader, it's not nearly so deep. I mean, 'A' levels in English schools are more or less equivalent to first year university in the States, similar kind of thoroughness and depth, but most people who do A levels here take three, three is good and four is exceptional... er... whereas in my senior high school I had seven different subjects. And not all of which I studied to a great depth, but I had for instance to do physical education, I had for instance to take some kind of social studies, I had to do some kind of mathematics, which I... was my particular thing. But everybody had to do mathematics: if you couldn't do calculus you could do arithmetic, even at the highest... your last year in... in high school. So we all had a very broad education.

It's true that in America the... the quality of the educa... education varies tremendously, not only from state to state but from county to county within states. I mean, you may have a very good high school in one town: the next town is short of funds, as ever it's like here or anywhere else the main thing is... is the lack of funds. But I think the thing I got most out of my education was the different viewpoints of people from all over the country.

Presenter: Christine went to school in Scotland, where the education system has similarities to the American and European systems. What was her school like?

Christine: Well, it was a school which you went to at five and you stayed, all being well, until you were eighteen. And there were boys and girls, and it meant that you developed a really interesting view of boys, which changed as you got older. So when I was very little the boys were good fun... um... th... because I was a bit of a tomboy, they had... they did things and played with things in the classroom that I thought were much more interesting than the things the girls played with. And then we went through a phase of ignoring the boys strenuously because they were completely beneath contempt, and I suppose that was between the ages of about 10½ and about 14 or 15. And then discovering that boys were awfully interesting but not the boys in your own year group which were... who were utterly contemptible... um... because girls and boys are so different in their development, aren't they? And a 14-year-old girl can see no merits whatsoever in a 14-year-old boy. And all the girls are gazing at the 16, 17 and 18-year-old 'big boys', who are much more interesting.

And then as we got to the end of our schooling... er... what in Scotland would be the fifth and the sixth year, in England would be the lower and the upper sixth years, the last two years, of course things... the boys had caught up really and we became very good friends again all of us and so our last two years at school, um... I think we... we had lovely relationships and lovely friendships. And... er... we did lots of things together. And when we left school we had an amazingly tearful last evening, er... of... oh... nearly all fifty of us who'd been in the year group, of whom perhaps thirty had grown up together since they were five. And leaving school was actually quite hard for us because having established good relationships with the boys around us in our last two years we all had long memories.

Presenter: What were Christine's strongest memories of her schooldays?

Christine: Of hating some of it. My strongest memories are negative ones, of a period in my two last years in primary, as it would be, 11 and 12 where our class teacher... I just loathed her and so did almost everybody else in the class and she was a bully and she taught very traditionally and it was very much 'the three Rs'[1] and we were... we just had tests all the time, we were drilled in grammar.

And she also had an uncertain temper and was a great shouter, and her... the tip of her nose would go white when she was really angry and her whole face would go scarlet. And she also used the belt very freely, and I didn't approve of that, I thought it was wrong. And she used to belt[2] people for spelling mistakes. And I'll never forget, Anne Black and Alan Davidson who couldn't spell, and they used to make spelling mistakes and if by Friday you had twenty mistakes out of the hundred, twenty a day, you got the belt in front of the class and I just thought that was so wrong. And it never improved their spelling, I mean years later as sixth-formers they still couldn't spell. And Anne Black used to get it particularly badly because she was English, because her mother was English, and she used to spell as she sounded and she used to make... create the most awful offence by spelling *saw S O R* rather than *S A W: I sor it* because that's how she heard it. And she used to be victimised by Miss Rae for her English spelling, and so I... and I really didn't like her. I just thought that the way she treated people was wrong, it wasn't with respect, it was... um... I don't quite know what she was doing when she bullied people, but she was a big bully. And I grew up very firmly disapproving of that way of treating children.

(Time: 6 minutes 20 seconds)

1 *'the three Rs':* reading, writing and arithmetic
2 *belt:* beat with a leather belt on the hand

C   Make sure everyone knows what they're supposed to do: that this is intended to be an activity where students discuss the vocabulary and the relationships between the words. This is not an exam-style test and there are no 'right answers'.

Suggested answers (The words with similar meanings are connected with a dash. The odd one out is at the end, after the bullet: •.)

1   A few words of justification about the examples:
award – grant – scholarship *(all money that is given to finance someone's education)*
grant – loan *(the two most common ways of financing higher education)*
trophy – prize – award *(all honours that may be given for outstanding achievement)*
award – scholarship *(another possible combination: both are only given to the brightest or luckiest students, unlike a grant which all students are entitled to)*
• reward *(isn't connected with education, unless discussing its rewards or pleasures; unlike a prize or trophy it is simply cash to pay someone back for doing something, like finding something that has been lost)*

2 certificate – degree – diploma – doctorate   certificate – diploma
recommendation – reference – testimonial
● licence *(connected more with driving than with education, though it has something in common with a certificate)*

3 assignment – composition – essay – paper   report   dissertation – thesis
● article *(not usually written by a student, but by a journalist or academic)*

4 law school – medical school   private school – public school (in the UK, but not in the USA)   state school
● Sunday school *(religious school, only operating for a couple of hours a week)*

5 comprehensive school – grammar school – secondary school   junior school – primary school   kindergarten – nursery school
● gymnasium *(= hall where pupils do PE: physical education)*

6 further education college – technical college   university – polytechnic
training centre
● electoral college *(group of people electing a leader or Pope)*

7 BA – BSc – first degree   MA – master's – MSc   BSc – MSc
BA – MA doctorate – PhD
● bachelor *(unmarried man)*

8 grades – marks – scores   credits
● numbers *(the other words have something to do with assessment)*

9 continuous assessment – evaluation   examination – test
● questionnaire *(not a way of assessing, but a way of gathering information)*

10 class – seminar – study group   seminar – lecture   study group
● conference *(a gathering of people who attend a series of lectures and seminars)*

11 apprentice – trainee – participant   freshman – student – undergraduate
graduate – post-graduate   pupil – schoolchild
● contestant *(someone who enters a competition or game show)*

12 associate professor – lecturer – don   coach – trainer
instructor – trainer   professor   teacher – tutor
● business associate *(no connection with education)*

13 correspondence course – distance learning course
evening course – part-time course – sandwich course   degree course
● race course *(where horse races are held)*

14 academic year   half-term – holiday – vacation   semester – term
● financial year *(a term used in business)*

15 cheat – crib   practise   cram – revise – study
● rehearse *(connected with performance, rather than education)*

D **Extra task** Ask everyone to come up with some more questions that might be asked (in the exam interview) about the two photographs.

9.2 Describing your own education   Composition

This is the first of two compositions in this unit. The other one is at the end of 9.9.

A   Warm-up discussion   Make sure both partners have time to take their turn as interviewer.

B   If any of your students are Japanese, draw their attention to the footnote.

C   It may be necessary to remind students how a formal letter should be laid out. This is best done on the board in class, in collaboration with the students :

```
                                    Your address,
                                    but not your name

The name, title
and address of the person
you're writing to
                                    Date

Dear . . . ,

    Main body of letter starts

    Yours sincerely,
    Your signature
    Your name
```

Extra activity

Write your own CV, giving details of your education and including any vocational training and work experience. Compare this with a partner's and ask for suggestions on how it could be improved.

A short model CV

<u>Clare Annabel LOVEGROVE</u>

Address 44 Charminster Road, Swindon, Wiltshire SN7 8PQ

Telephone 0793 897563 (Home) 071 444 5555 (Work)

Date of birth 17 June 1970 **Marital status** single

EDUCATION

From: 1975 Kingley Primary School
To: 1981 Ashley Road, Swindon, Wiltshire

From: 1981 Wyvern Comprehensive School
To: 1988 Western Avenue, Swindon, Wiltshire
  GCSEs in English, Maths, French, German, History, Religious
  Studies, Science, Economics and Commerce (1986)
  GCE A levels in German (B), French (C) and English (C) (1988)

From: 1988 Wessex Polytechnic
To: 1990 Lansdowne Square
    Bournemouth, Dorset BH1 4ZT
  Higher National Diploma in Travel and Tourism (June 1990)

EMPLOYMENT

From: July 1990 Receptionist
To: June 1991 Bellavista Hotel
    42-50 West Cliff Road
    Poole, Dorset BH17 6RT

From: June 1991 Assistant Front Desk Manager
To: December 1992 Hotel Metropole
    Place Pépinet 4
    CH 1003 Lausanne, Switzerland

From: January 1993 Assistant Manager
To: present Palace Hotel
    100 Grosvenor Street
    London SW1E 4RP

Special skills I speak fluent German and French. I am
  proficient in word-processing and in preparing publicity
  materials.

REFEREES

Mr J.A. Fisher, Personnel Manager, Palace Hotel Group, 44 Marylebone
Road, London NW2 4YT

Ms J.P. Robinson, Senior Tutor, Wessex Polytechnic, Lansdowne Square,
Bournemouth BH1 4ZT

9.3   Question tags and negative questions   Grammar review

A   Suggested answers

1 He used to play squash, didn't he?
   Didn't he use to play squash?
   – *I'm fairly sure he did in the past.*
   He used to play squash, did he?
   – *You told me he played, but are you quite sure about that?*
   Did he use to play squash?
   – *I'd just like to know if he played in the past.*

2 Isn't this a great party!
   This is a great party, isn't it?
   What a great party!
   – *These mean the same and would be used in similar situations.*
   This is a great party!
   – *This one seems a little lukewarm in comparison, but it means the same.*

3 Didn't she do well in her exam!
   – *This is an exclamation – she really did well!!*
   She did very well in her exam.
   – *I'm telling you: she got good marks.*
   How did she do in her exam?
   Did she do well in her exam?
   – *Both mean: tell me what you know about her success.*
   Didn't she do well in her exam?
   – *This is a question: I'd be rather surprised if she did badly, which is what I have just heard, but you seem to know more than I do.*

4 Isn't it strange that everyone thinks they are experts on education?
   – *Don't you agree that it's strange (I'm encouraging you to agree).*
   It's strange that everyone thinks they are experts on education.
   – *I'm telling you this (you may or may not have an opinion on this matter).*

5 So you enjoyed my talk, did you?
   – *I know you enjoyed it, but I'd like you to say it again or tell me more.*
   So you didn't enjoy my talk?
   – *I know you didn't like it, but I'd like you to tell me why.*
   So didn't you enjoy my talk?
   – *I suspect you didn't like it, but I'd like you to confirm it or tell me I'm wrong.*
   So did you enjoy my talk?
   – *I don't know if you liked it.*

B Answers

1 hadn't we
   Hadn't we better stop work soon?
2 aren't I
   Aren't I right about this?
3 wouldn't you
   Wouldn't you rather stay in bed than get up early?
4 can't they
   Can't anyone apply for the scholarship?
5 will there
6 shall we
7 did they
8 won't you/will you
9 did he
10 oughtn't they

C Suggested answers

2 All our work will be done for us by robots and computers one day, won't it?
3 Computers couldn't be installed in every classroom, could they?
4 No robot teachers have been invented yet, have they?
5 Teachers should be paid on results, shouldn't they?
6 Students are often supported by their parents, aren't they?
7 Grants might be replaced by student loans, mightn't they?

2 Won't all our work be done for us by robots and computers one day?
3 Couldn't computers be installed in every classroom?
4 Haven't any robot teachers been invented yet?
5 Shouldn't teachers be paid on results?
6 Aren't students often supported by their parents?
7 Mightn't grants be replaced by student loans?

➡ Lead-in question   How would you expect a group of 13-year-olds to behave in class?

A Suggested answers

1 They had had no inkling that she was about to decide to give up teaching
2 She had become increasingly terrified and nervous at the prospect of teaching
3 Not particularly well
4 Thanks to the pressure of their peers and advertisements, they became bossy and noisy and had empty heads
5 Because she would have had to stay behind after school herself (supervising detention)
6 The teaching staff of the school
7 They greet her and then carry on messing about
8 Having the stamina and a liking for teaching

B Answers

beating loudly – pounding (line 18)   *incomplete* – patchy (line 34)
hungry – breakfast-less (line 49)   *tell off* – remonstrate with (line 75)
laughing disrespectfully – sniggerings (line 79)   *way of putting things right* –
redress (line 82)   *unable to take action* – incapacitated (line 89)   *exercise
control* – assert myself (line 98)   *laughing shrilly* – cackling (line 100)

C Model summary

As she knows that ten years ago she was able to manage
well enough and she is fond of children and adores her
subject, she doesn't blame herself. She believes the
problem is that children have changed for the worse over
the years. Now not only are they bored, disobedient and
badly behaved, but they are rude and they swear.

She explains that children are under pressure from
advertising and from each other: the disruptive pupils
dominate the hard-working pupils, which disturbs the whole
class. Although their parents are themselves unable to
cope, they must also take their share of the blame, for
allowing their children to stay up late watching videos
and not feeding them properly, so that when the children
come to school they are tired and hungry, and unable to
concentrate on their work.

9.5 Teachers and pupils

➡ Warm-up discussion   What are the advantages and disadvantages of teaching as a job?

A Answers

1 a   2 c   3 a   4 b   5 b   6 c   7 a   8 b

Transcript

Presenter: Christine teaches in a secondary school. What does she enjoy about being a teacher?

Christine: I enjoy the fun you have, I enjoy the… er… the unexpected, the things that c… that you can't plan for. When we were at college I think the only thing that they… they kept on about was planning lessons, and we used to have to make these lesson plans up and they always seemed to me like the great works of modern fiction, the lesson plans, because real lessons aren't like that, they don't work out the way you plan them and that's what makes it really interesting is that you just go in, thinking you're going to do thing A and it turns into thing B, depending on what the students do and say. Or if you're teaching two parallel classes, as I used to quite often for literature at 'A' level, you'd be doing the same set book, and you might even be at the same part of the book with the two groups, but it would go completely differently depending on the youngsters you had in front of you.

And they're also so funny, yeah, I mean students are terribly entertaining a… they're just a hoot. And they… they come out with all these amazing things and they tell you things. And if you're any good at it they will trust you as a person. And so what you're teaching them in English is much less important than what you're teaching them about 'the big world' and the world they're going into, and about relationships and values and things like that.

And it's quite the most unboring job in the world, and you could… if you were bored in teaching then (a) you shouldn't be there, um… but something awful would have gone wrong if you didn't find it absolutely rivetting and… er… each day interesting.

I think the only downside[1] is that it's terribly hard work and it's awfully tiring physically – and emotionally at times. But… um… children are just such nice people, and if you treat them properly then they'll do anything. You can… you can turn them into anything you want if you treat them well and you develop appropriate relationships with them. Then there's very little that they can't learn and can't do, and a good teacher can take children into a whole world which is magic and exciting.

Presenter: What changes have taken place in the relationship between teachers and pupils since she was at school?

Christine: I think that there has been a real change in the quality of relationships, I think they're much more open, more relaxed, less formal. Some people would say that implies a l… a drop in the standards, I would disagree violently with that. I think that quality relationships bring quality work. And familiarity does *not* breed contempt, care and control are not opposites. If you care for children you manage your classroom well, and it is a well-ordered classroom, it doesn't mean it is not a relaxed classroom, it's not a friendly classroom, it's not a supportive classroom.

What matters is that... that it's a... there is a good quality of relationship between the teacher and the student, and the student trusts the teacher as an individual and vice versa. And I think teachers have become more human and more open with their students and are more prepared to allow the students to know more about them as individuals. And many of the things that we've developed in the past few years, like records of children's achievement replacing school reports, have meant that there is formally built in much more dialogue now. Students are involved much more in their own progress and their own assessment, they have a voice in their programmes of study and their progress. And that voice has always been a vital voice and the teachers who failed to take that on board, who didn't listen to student feedback, were losing out on a whole valuable resource for planning and developing work: it's how the students are receiving the work.

I mean when I was at school nobody had... showed any signs of being remotely interested in what I thought of what was going on or whether I thought it could be different. Yet by the seventies and eighties it was becoming much more widely recognised that consulting with students and making decisions with them was much more positive than imposing them upon them, you know. And it isn't just a simple tension between authoritarian and democratic ways of running a classroom: it's about a partnership for learning, in which teachers and students work together. And that partnership needs to involve the family as well, so that everybody is taking part in shaping the child's learning and is paying due attention to what the child or student themself thinks and feels.

Children are wonderful at assessing their own progress. There was a lot of tosh[2] talked at the early stages about, if you invited children to comment on their own progress or to assess their performance or to set goals that they couldn't do it, they'd be unrealistic, they'd say they were brilliant. And it just... there was never any evidence for that, and a lot of work's been done since, and children are deeply self-critical. You could ask a teacher to put the children in a rank order, if you asked the children to put the children in a rank... themselves in a rank order they'd get it right. They know exactly where they are relative to other people, they always have done. Um... and they are very good judges of their own progress, they're un... unnecessarily harsh critics of their own abilities, particularly as teenagers, and they are deeply *un*self-confident.

And I think one of the big changes has been the handing over of some of the responsibility in the classrooms to children. But it does, I think, demand more skill not less. I think it's much harder to take risks with youngsters, to be open, to be relaxed. It's easy to run an authoritarian classroom, it's easy to rule using t... f... fear and punishment and threat. Anybody can do that, particularly if you've got a big system of r... sanctions behind you to put into place. But winning and earning the respect of children, and earning a... a relaxed relationship and relaxed classroom, that's much harder.

And that's why I get so cross with critics who get on their high horses about 'standards' and 'sloppiness', you know, and 'not expecting enough of the children'. A relaxed classroom isn't about low expectations, it's about purposeful quality work. And it's very very hard to achieve, it's much easier to bully them into submission and shout at them.

(Time: 6 minutes 30 seconds)

1 *downside:* disadvantage
2 *tosh:* nonsense

B 〔▱〕 The pupils' opinions are intended as lead-in to the discussion. There are no comprehension questions.

Transcript

Presenter: We asked three 12-year-olds for their views on teachers. First, Sharon explains what she thinks makes a good teacher.
Sharon: A teacher that... um... doesn't jump to conclusions.
Interviewer: What makes a bad teacher?
Sharon: A teacher that makes you work in silence.
Interviewer: Elizabeth, what about you?
Elizabeth: Well, I don't think they should be like strict all the time. I think they should sort of have a little joke, but I don't think it should last long, just... and then get back to work. But we... I don't think you should work in complete silence every lesson, it's kind of boring. But most teachers let you talk, unless it gets too loud.
Interviewer: OK. Wayne, what makes a good teacher?
Wayne: That lets you talk quietly, and strict but still like funny, though... that like if they let you speak... some... our English teacher lets you speak like quietly but if you get too loud she tells you to stop, so really it's your own fault for going over the level really.

(Time: 1 minute 10 seconds)

9.6 Abstract nouns   Vocabulary development

A Begin by getting the class to identify the verb or adjective from which the examples are derived:

– administer   cooperate   describe   destroy   detain   evaluate
  recuperate   satisfy   suspect
– astonish   enjoy   punish
– fair   happy   rude

Answers

-ation/-ion concentration   contribution   explanation   invention
                justification   negotiation   objection   opposition
                pronunciation (NB pronouncement = solemn announcement)

	qualification reception recommendation representation variation
	↑ *Careful about spelling in all of the above!*
-ment	accomplishment achievement acknowledgement amusement embarrassment encouragement management
-ness	carelessness clumsiness half-heartedness mischievousness narrow-mindedness selfishness

B   Again get the class to identify the word from which the examples are derived, or with which they are associated:

– anxious   humble   real   senior
– annoy   brilliant   insignificant   intolerant
– absent   intelligent   present   refer
– absent   national   optimistic   real
– apprentice   relate   scholar   sponsor

Answers

-ty	availability creativity eligibility equality extremity familiarity generosity honesty loyalty productivity reliability stability
-ance	extravagance relevance resistance self-assurance
-ence	diffidence incompetence inconvenience independence insistence insolence preference self-confidence
-ism	extremism favouritism professionalism symbolism
-ship	censorship companionship craftsmanship friendship leadership sportsmanship

C   Some suggestions

creation   direction   imagination   organisation   protection   realisation
replacement   requirement   retirement
aggressiveness   helplessness   mildness

informality   instability   normality
disappearance   disturbance   resemblance
disobedience   persistence   reminiscence
journalism   plagiarism   sexism
comradeship   membership   ownership

D   Answers

–dom	bored free
–th	broad filthy healthy long stealthy strong warm wealthy wide

−cy   adequate bureaucratic delicate democratic efficient fluent
         frequent inadequate inefficient redundant urgent

enthusiastic hungry hysterical proud sarcastic successful

E   If necessary, encourage students to use a dictionary to check the
meanings of the nouns they have highlighted before they join another pair.

F   Suggested answers
1 inconvenience
2 reliability/relevance/adequacy
3 enthusiasm   description
4 bureaucracy   inefficiency
5 favouritism   fairness   cooperation
6 relevance   justification   explanation
7 qualifications   negotiation
8 references   leadership
9 loyalty   professionalism   self-assurance   generosity   reliability   *etc.*
10 intolerance   incompetence   unreliability   extravagance   *etc.*

9.7   Organising your time   Reading

A   Answers
1 frightened
2 more fun
3 couldn't concentrate
4 organised himself better
5 deciding when each kind of task is best done
6 evaluating the success of your study methods

B   Rather than providing synonyms to choose between, this task gets the
students to do the work. English–English dictionaries should be used.

Answers
bluffing – deceiving by pretending to be cleverer than he really was
assiduously – painstakingly   *blotted out* – made an effort not to think about
at sea – confused   *segments* – sections   *strategically* – in a well-planned
manner   *dribble* away – gradually be lost   *dipping into* – reading short
passages, not the complete book   *glazed over* – unfocused
prime – best time for concentration, when you're on top form
swamp – overcome, inundate

C   Suggested key phrases (these are open to discussion)

organisation of time (¶ 4)
time management (¶ 4)
dividing big jobs into smaller sub-tasks (¶ 9)
'investing' time (¶ 10)
take control (¶ 12)

9.8   Reporting – 2   Advanced grammar

➡ Before starting this section, ask everyone to look again at 3.2 Reporting – 1.

A   Suggested interpretations

1 She said, 'I'll be arriving tomorrow.'
   *– Unless we know when she said this, we don't know which day she's
   going to arrive.*
   She told me that she was arriving tomorrow.
   *– Her expected day of arrival is tomorrow (she may have said this
   yesterday or on a previous day).*
   She told me that she was arriving the next day.
   *– Her expected day of arrival was the day after she spoke to me (she
   didn't say this yesterday).*

2 She said to me, 'You really should spend more time reading, shouldn't
   you?'
   *– Direct speech gives prominence to her exact words, and would
   enable the speaker to mimic the speaker's voice or her tone.*
   She advised me to spend more time reading.
   *– This is the gist of what she said and gives no special emphasis to the
   advice.*
   She urged me to spend more time reading.
   – This gives special emphasis to the speaker's insistence.

3 Everyone said, 'That's just nonsense!'
   *– Direct speech gives prominence to the exact words and implies that
   these words were spoken in chorus, or that each person used exactly
   the same words.*
   No one agreed with my idea.
   – A straightforward, uncoloured report.
   Everyone dismissed my idea as unrealistic.
   – This report gives more prominence to the reason for disagreeing.

4 We doubted whether the scheme would succeed.
   – *We were unsure about the prospects for success (slightly more formal than 'We didn't know . . . ').*
   We didn't know whether the scheme would succeed.
   – *Same meaning as 'We doubted whether . . . ' but more informal.*
   We had no doubt that the scheme would fail.
   – *We were sure that it wouldn't succeed.*

5 He said, 'If you phoned us from the airport, we could come and pick you up.'
   – *The exact words suggest that there is some doubt in the speaker's mind as to whether the call will be made, or whether the person arriving will decide not to call.*
   He said they could come and pick me up if I rang them from the airport.
   – *They offered to collect me (until more information is given we don't know if the phone call is to be made in the future or has been made already).*
   He said they could have come to collect me if I'd called them from the airport.
   – *. . . but I didn't call them, so they didn't collect me.*

B   Suggested answers (many variations possible)

2 She promised to tell me when they arrived.
3 She reminded me to hand in my work (that evening).
4 He regretted that I couldn't make it to the party (the night before).
5 She congratulated me on passing.
6 He assured me that I would manage if I remained calm.
7 She insisted that I (should) visit them at the weekend.
8 He disagreed with me (politely).
9 She warned me not to park on the/that double yellow line.
10 He reproached me for behaving in that way / for my behaviour.
11 She claimed that she'd have helped me with my work if she had more time.
12 He suggested that we (should) organise our time more efficiently.
   He suggested organising our time more efficiently.

C   Transcript with answers (The answers are in italics below – some of the interpretations are open to discussion.)

Presenter: Listen carefully to each speaker and select an appropriate adjective to describe their attitudes.
Presenter: ONE
First speaker: Could I have a word with you? Yes. Well, you see, I've been looking at *your* work and comparing it with... with what the others have been doing and well, you know what I think about *everyone else's* work, don't you? I mean, it's

improved a lot. Anyway, looking at yours in comparison I must say that you really are... I mean, yours is far and away the most . . .
 – *angry*

Presenter: TWO
Second speaker: Could I have a word? Ah . . . yes, well . . . Look... um... I've been... I've been watching your work and I've been comparing it with... er... with the others have been doing and well, I mean you know what I think about everyone else's work, I mean that's... that's improved quite a bit. But... uh... looking at yours, I... I have to say I mean you've... you've... ... you've really... you've just not... er... well, I mean, yours is just... it's just . . .
 – *disappointed* (OR *diffident?*)

Presenter: THREE
Third speaker: Could I have a word? Yes. Well, you see, I... I've been looking at your work and comparing it with... er... with what the others have been doing and... er... well, you know what I think about everyone else's work, don't you? I mean, w... it has improved a lot, but... anyway looking at yours in comparison I must say that you've really... I mean, yours is far and away the . . .
 – *impressed*

Presenter: FOUR
Fourth speaker: Could I have a word? Yes. Well, you see, I've been looking at your work and comparing it with... er... with what the others have been doing and... er... well, you know what I think about everyone else's work, don't you? I mean, *it* has improved a lot. Anyway, looking at *yours* in comparison I must say that you've really, I... I mean, yours is far and away . . .
 – *sarcastic*

Presenter: FIVE
Fifth speaker: Could I have a word? Yes, yes. Well... um... you see, I... I... I've been looking at your work and... um... comparing it with... er... with... er... with what the others have been doing and... um... well, um... you know... you know what I think about... er... everyone else's work, er... I... I know you do. I mean, er... th... that's improved quite a bit, hasn't it? Well... er... anyway, looking at yours in comparison I... I... I must say I... that you've really... er... I mean... er... yours is far and away the most . . .
 – *diffident* (OR *disappointed?*)

(Time: 3 minutes 15 seconds)

Suggested summaries

2 The second speaker regretted that my work hadn't improved in comparison with the others' work.
3 The third speaker congratulated me on my work and commented that it was much better than everyone else's.
4 The fourth speaker was unimpressed by my work and thought that everyone else's work had improved considerably.
5 The fifth speaker was unwilling to commit himself, but thought that my work had improved less than everyone else's.

9.9 Making notes – 2

⚠️ The article describes just one school. Other progressive schools in Britain are fee-paying and some are boarding schools. Make sure students don't form the impression that White Lion Free School is the only kind of progressive school.

A   Suggested answers (These are the main differences and characteristics of White Lion Free School.)

1 democratic and egalitarian
2 decisions made at open meetings
3 financed by donations and fund-raising
4 pupils take part in organising things
5 pupils encouraged to make their own decisions (if you agree with Karen about teachers influencing pupils' attitudes)

B   Answers

TRUE: 1   2   4
FALSE: all the others

C   Answers

egalitarian – treating everyone as equal
hand-to-mouth – almost broke   *fidgety* – restless
agenda – list of points to discuss   *vehemently* – violently
muck around – misbehave   *host* – numerous   *attached* – devoted

D   Follow-up discussion   It may be necessary to brainstorm some further educational practices and teaching methods that students consider to be 'progressive' or 'reactionary' before starting the discussion. Perhaps refer back to Christine's ideas in 9.5 Teachers and pupils.

E   This step should not be rushed. It takes time to analyse and discuss notes.

F & G   As preparation for the exam, it's important for students to know how long it takes them to make notes – and if necessary, try to speed up the process.

10 Nature and the environment

A After the discussion, allow time for students to note down ten vocabulary items, and for them to compare them with each other.

B Answers

1 endangered 2 wiped out 3 breeding 4 accepted 5 fossils
6 naturalist 7 worked up 8 wither 9 recycled 10 species
11 rodents 12 reptiles 13 deciduous trees 14 scavengers 15 prey
16 vermin 17 domesticated 18 claws 19 plumage 20 feelers
21 caterpillar 22 flock 23 mushrooms 24 endearing

➡ Here are some follow-up discussion questions:

• What is the strangest thing you've ever eaten (or seen someone else eat)?
• Could you kill an animal if you wanted to eat it?
• What are the different reasons that people have for being vegetarian?
• What animals are useful to humans in other ways than just being eaten?

10.2 Save the whales Listening

A Preliminary discussion This encourages students to pool their previous knowledge and ideas.

The questions are in three groups: B, C and D. Stop the tape at the places shown with ★ ★ ★ in the transcript.

Answers

B TRUE: 1 5
FALSE: 2 3 4 6

C 1 c 2 b 3 b (*or* a?) 4 a 5 c

D Ticks beside the following reasons:
he feels an inexplicable affinity with them ✓

their brains are large ✓
they can move in breathtakingly spectacular ways ✓
some whales are impressively large ✓
they are perfectly suited to living in the sea ✓

E   Follow-up discussion

Transcript

Ray: My name is Ray Gambell, and I'm the Secretary of the International Whaling Commission. That's the body made up of forty-three member governments who have responsibility for the management of the whaling industry, the regulation of that industry, and the conservation of the whale stocks throughout the world.

Presenter: Ray, who himself is a zoologist, spoke about some of the ways in which scientists conduct research into whales, and how research methods have changed recently.

Ray: Er... in recent years because of the pressures of public opinion against the over-exploitation of whales which has occurred, there is a pause in commercial whaling, a... a moratorium, and as a result of this very few whales are now being caught and so we're having to devise research techniques that don't rely on being able to get hold, literally, of your whale. You can't put your hands on the whale in the same way. We're having to develop very exciting new techniques, based on... on a more distant approach.

Some of the other research techniques that have been developed are... are really quite extraordinary. Um... you can actually recognise individual whales by certain patterns or colours or marks on them. For example, hump-backed whales, er... on the underside of their tail, each have a quite characteristic and individual colour pattern. I mean, i... it's enormously variable: all shades of... of black to white and... and streaks and all sorts of markings, but they are individually recognisable in same the way that you can recognise individual human faces. By taking photographs of the underside of the hump-backed whale tail you can recognise individual animals and we have a catalogue of about three and half thousand individually recognised whales in the North Atlantic.

And, so you go out with your boat now and you wait until the whale dives and tips its tail up, you take a picture of the underside of the tail and you can compare your photograph with a central catalogue of these photographs. And there's all kinds of... of laser technology that allows you to skim through this very large number of photographs very quickly. And you can see where that whale has been seen before, and therefore you can follow the movements from, say, the breeding grounds in the Caribbean up to the feeding grounds off Iceland or Greenland or wherever the whales may be. And so, without touching the whale at all, you can actually follow the... the migrations of the animals.

And over a sufficiently long period of time, you will be able to see for example that a female has had a calf one year, and you will then see when the next calf comes with that female, so you can work out the... the breeding interval. Um... but it's a long-term process. We got that sort of information before by killing and... or by having access to a great many whales that were killed and looking at the internal organs, looking at... er... the ovaries, and looking at the foetuses inside, and that sort of thing. And you got an instant 'snapshot'. Now we have to wait seven or ten years or whatever, but we haven't killed the whale, um… the whales are still swimming about and we're still getting the knowledge of them, and one would hope that there will be new techniques developed that will allow us for example to tell the age of the whale, that we can't do at the moment …

★★★

Presenter: So why isn't there a total world-wide ban on killing whales? Why can't whales be totally protected from being hunted?

Ray: We've had many problems in terms of management of whale stocks… er… because certain, particularly Arctic communities are very heavily dependent on the natural resources of a very severe environment. And so the Inuit people, the Eskimo peoples of Greenland and northern Canada and Alaska, have argued that they, in spite of a… a ban on commercial whaling, should be permitted to carry on catching for subsistence purposes. And so we have developed over the course of years, and… and with a great deal of heart-searching, a… a specific management regime for aboriginal subsistence whaling, which is much more heavily dependent, not on the number of whales in the ocean, but on the perceived need of the indigenous peoples who are hunting the animals. They need them for subsistence, for cultural purposes, er… social purposes. Um… many of these communities… um… feel bound together by the fact that they are hunters together. And so this has been a very important factor to build in on top of the basic biology of how many whales there are in the ocean.

And so I've had the chance of going out to… um… Alaska with the Eskimo whalers, standing on the frozen Arctic Ocean, and watching the bowhead whales swimming along the… the leads, the cracks in the ice that open up in the spring, and… and the hunters go out in their seal-skin boats and… and harpoon – hand harpoon, using the… the old traditional techniques. Er… and… and that's a very interesting experience. It's far removed from just studying whales, it's studying a whole culture.

Presenter: But this may not be what enlightened people in Europe and North America want to hear, as Ray explains.

Ray: And of course many people now in the comfortable Western world… er… have a very different view of what a whale is… is there for. The aboriginal subsistence hunter sees it as part of his total environment: he's dependent on the animal and he feels a special relationship to the animal because it does sustain his life. But to the… the Western communities… er… which are not dependent on… on flesh for food now – there's a… a general movement against eating red meat – um… there's a… a preference to see the whale as a beautiful animal, as a… an animal with a very large brain, an animal with… with great powers of being able to dive to… to great depths in the ocean and survive, and so on. Um… the whale is seen as a symbol of a… a… a life of freedom and… er… it evokes all kinds of… of non-culinary thoughts. So that the whale is… is now seen as something that has to be preserved and… and kept in respect in the ocean. And whether you go out on a whale-watching trip and see the whale for yourself or whether you just know that it's in the ocean, tha… that is what is important and… and the people who go out and hunt the whale for commercial purposes are very much seen to be… er… not the kind of people that you'd want to associate with any more.

So, the whale is no longer a renewable resource, but a... um... a figure to be seen as... as symbolising so much more for many people.

★★★

Presenter: Ray is obviously passionately involved with whales. What is it about the whale that stirs him?

Ray: They really are very exciting animals. Um... the large whales are *very* large. Er... to see a blue whale, which is the largest animal that has ever lived in the ocean... er... on... on this earth, and to see it turning and moving, twisting, so completely at home in the water, i... it's a very exciting sight. To see a... a large animal like a hump-back whale leaping right out of the ocean is a very spectacular event to... to actually see this happen. So they... they are dramatic animals in that sense. And some of them are very big, yes, a blue whale is like a couple of buses end to end, i... it's of that size, a hundred feet long, 150 tons perhaps of living, mobile animal.

And they do have very large brains. And so there is the sense that, you know, maybe they have a... a form of intelligence that... that... it's difficult enough to measure human intelligence, measuring the intelligence in... in another species altogether is... is really quite difficult. But the fact of the... the very large brain suggests that there is... um... you know, a degree of affinity with man which has the large brain use o... on land. These have been described as 'our cousins in the ocean'. There... we feel a... an affinity of some kind.

When you have the chance to... to get close to a... a dolphin – I've been in a... a rubber dinghy with a wild but sociable dolphin swimming around – when it comes and... and peers at you out of the water, it's like looking into the eye of s... your pet dog, you think, 'There must be something in there, if only I could... could make contact with it.' It's the same with the dolphin, it's the same with the whale, that... that there is some kind of... of instinctive bond that you feel. They are impressive animals in terms of size and ability, and... and there is this sense that there's... there's more than... than we can grasp at the moment. There's something more that we may find out in the future. They... they really are very exciting animals.

(Time: 9 minutes 10 seconds)

10.3 Conditional sentences – 1 — Grammar review

A Suggested answers

1 If you don't leave now, you'll be late.
Unless you leave now, you'll be late.
– You really ought to leave in case you're late.
If you left now, you wouldn't be late.
– You probably don't intend to go now, so that means you will be late.
If you leave now, you won't be late.
– You're probably going now, so that means you won't be late.
If you didn't leave now, you'd be late.
– I'm fairly sure you're going, but if you stayed, you would be late.

2 When I have time, I'll feed the cat.
  – I'll open the tin later, when I'm not busy.
  If I had time, I'd feed the ducks.
  – I'm very busy, so I can't/won't feed the ducks.
  If I'd had time, I'd have fed the dog.
  – I was very busy, so I didn't feed it.
  If I have time, I'll feed the goldfish.
  – I may be too busy, but if I have a spare moment I'll feed them.
  If I had time, I'd have fed the birds.
  – I'm very busy, so that explains why I didn't feed the birds.
  When I had time, I'd feed the rabbits.
  – I used to feed the rabbits when I wasn't too busy.

3 I feel upset when I think about the destruction of the rainforests.
  – Every time I think about them, I feel sad.
  I'd feel upset when I thought about people destroying the rainforests.
  – I used to feel sad every time I used to think about them.
  I'd feel upset if I thought about the rainforests being destroyed.
  – Sometimes I thought about them and I used to feel sad then OR If I let myself think about it I would feel upset, so I don't let myself think about it.
  I feel upset if I think about the destruction of tropical rainforests.
  – Sometimes I think about them and it makes me sad.
  I felt upset when I thought about jungles being destroyed.
  – I felt sad every time I thought about them is pretty much the same as *I'd feel upset when . . .* except that this suggests I didn't feel upset for quite so long. When *suggests a more frequent occurrence than* if *in the above examples.*

4 If you're interested I'll tell you about my dream.
  – Let me know if you're interested, and if you are, I'll tell you my dream.
  If you were interested I'd tell you about my dream.
  – I know you aren't interested, so I won't tell you.

B   Suggested answers

1 If you go too close to that dog it may/might/will bite you.
2 If I'd realised that you needed help, I would/could have given you a hand.
3 If the amount of carbon dioxide in the atmosphere is not reduced, the ozone layer will be permanently damaged.
4 If the forests hadn't been cut down, they might still cover most of Europe. If they hadn't been cut down, forests might still cover most of Europe.
5 If people were less ignorant about the effects of pollution on the environment, there might be less of it.
6 If animals could speak in their own defence, we wouldn't have/need to speak up for them.

7 If everyone drove more slowly, there would be less pollution.
8 If there wasn't/weren't any acid rain these lakes would still have fish in them.
   If it weren't for acid rain, these lakes . . .

C   Possible continuations

2 If he hadn't been so generous, **he might still have some money left.**
3 If you aren't careful, **you'll fall off the ladder and break your neck.**
4 If she doesn't phone me by Friday, **I'll have to go round and see her.**
5 If everyone cared more about the environment, **they would do more to protect it.**
6 If any species becomes extinct, **it can never be replaced.**
7 If human beings became extinct, **there would be plenty of other species to take our place**.
8 Unless the governments of the world cooperate, **there is no chance of the global environment being adequately protected.**

D   This open-ended discussion leads to paragraph writing. Actually writing the summary could be set as homework.

➡ There is more on the use of conditionals in 13.7 Conditional sentences – 2.

10.4 Changing the climate   Reading

➡ To begin with, ask everyone to read the passage through, and to jot down a description of Ibañez's scheme. Then read the passage again to answer the questions in A.

NOTE: According to the article, the daytime temperature in the desert may be as high as 70°C – this is probably more likely to be in the region of 40°C really.

A   Answers
1 c   2 a   3 d   4 a   5 c   6 a   7 b   8 c

B   Answers
deal with – fielded   *large area* – tracts   *secure* – anchor   *unvarying* – stable
use – application   *excessively* – wildly

➡ Finally, ask the class for their reactions to the scheme. How sceptical are they of its chances of success?

10.5 Different styles

This section deals with degrees of formality in vocabulary and also in grammatical structure. A 'neutral' style (one that is neither too colloquial, nor too formal) is likely to be appropriate in most types of composition that students will have to do in the exam – unless they choose to write a personal letter, for example.

A   Answers

I do like little kittens and puppies . . .   *– informal/colloquial*
I consider young kittens and puppies . . .   *– formal*
Small kittens and puppies are delightful, I think.   *– neutral*
Ibañez agrees that his idea will not function . . .   *– formal*
Ibañez agrees that his idea won't work . . .   *– neutral*
He doesn't think his idea's going to work . . .   *– informal/colloquial*

Examples of neutral style from 10.4:
They want to try Ibañez's plastic palm tree. (¶ 1)
He decided to look for a natural solution – and copy it. (¶ 2)
. . . and left to get on with it. (¶ 3)
It is not just desert areas that could benefit . . . but rainforests too. (¶ 7)

B   Suggested answers (many variations possible)

2 I hope your father has fully recovered (from his illness).
3 She was furious when she was told that she'd lost her job.
4 Organic fruit and vegetables are cultivated without the use of artificial fertiliser.
5 We were terrified when a large dog came bounding up to us.
6 Please be careful with the knife (you're using).
7 Testing cosmetics and shampoo on animals is not only pointless, it's also cruel.
8 You should have turned off the light when you left the room.
9 I think it's likely to rain fairly soon.
10 Instead of throwing your litter in the street, you ought to put it in a litter bin.

C   Suggested answers (many variations possible)

2 According to the experts, global warming is speeding up.
3 Even a small rise in temperature may have a big effect on the ice in polar regions.
4 Throwing cans and bottles away is an unnecessary waste of energy and materials. It's much better to recycle them.

5 Lunch is served from 12 o'clock.
6 Please be careful when getting off the train.
7 Who did you send the suggestion to?
8 You're not allowed to use personal stereos or musical instruments here.
9 Although no vegetarians eat meat, vegans don't eat fish or dairy products either.
10 It's a pity that the government won't offer funding for research.

D This activity may take some time. Rewriting in a neutral style could be set as homework. Alternatively, the informal writing could be set as homework to be done before the next lesson, exchanged during the next lesson, and completed after the next lesson as further homework.

10.6 Charles Darwin   Reading & summarising

Background

This passage is from a book by Sir David Attenborough which accompanied the TV series *Life on Earth*. David Attenborough is well-known as a TV presenter and enthusiastic naturalist. His other books, also accompanying TV series, include *The Living Planet*, *The First Eden: the Mediterranean World and Man* and *The Trials of Life*.

➡ Before they read the passage, perhaps ask everyone to pool their knowledge of Charles Darwin and the theory of evolution, being careful not to tread on the toes of anyone in the class who might consider a discussion of evolution to be heretical.

A Make sure everyone times themselves while doing this section – it is best done as homework.

Suggested answers

1 The main aim of the journey was to make maps, not to study plants and animals
2 Discovering so many species of a particular insect
3 they have not and will not change
4 He was a firm believer in God
5 They were similar to mainland animals, but different in certain details
6 came up again
7 The length of their necks suited the available vegetation: on dry islands they had long necks, on wet islands they had short necks
8 On rafts of vegetation carried across from South America
9 deep imaginative understanding

10 They were original and changed our view of the world
11 newly-hatched baby tortoises
12 He didn't publish it until he had put in 25 years of work on it
13 Another naturalist was about to publish a book proposing the same idea
14 They have given it new dimensions but not changed it in essence

15 **Model summary**

> According to Darwin, not only can one species change
> into another, but they change to suit their environment
> as generation succeeds generation. He maintained that
> the most efficient offspring would survive better than
> less efficient ones, giving the example of tortoises
> with long necks who survive in times of drought. The
> characteristics of the surviving, more efficient species
> will be transmitted to their offspring. He suggested
> that this was how amphibians evolved from fish millions
> of years ago, which in turn evolved into reptiles. He
> also speculated that this was how human beings might
> have evolved from apes.

© Cambridge University Press 1993

B The follow-up discussion focuses on approaches to doing Paper 3 Part B in the exam, not on the topic of the passage.

10.7 Uses of the past — Advanced grammar

A Answers

1 I wish that dog would stop barking.
  – *It's barking and I don't like hearing it, but there's nothing I can do about it.*
  I wish that dog didn't bark.
  – *Whenever the dog barks I find it annoying.*
  I wish that dog had stopped barking.
  – *It went on barking a long time (maybe all night), which was very annoying.*
  I want that dog to stop barking.
  – *It's barking and I don't like hearing it, but there's nothing I can do about it OR You must order the dog to stop barking (said threateningly to its owner, perhaps).*

2 It's time for you to do the washing-up.
  – *You asked me to remind you of the time, that time has now come.*
  It's time you did the washing-up.
  – *You offered to wash up and you should have started by now or You never wash up but you ought to do it.*

3 If only it were Friday!   – *I wish it were Friday.*
  Only if it was Friday . . .
  – *This could only happen if today was Friday or That could only happen on a Friday, not another day.*
  If it were only Friday . . .
  – *If today was Friday, not a later day, then . . . (. . . maybe the situation might be different).*
  If it's only Friday . . .
  – *As today is Friday, not a later day (we still have plenty of time left).*

4 Would you rather I didn't help you?
  Would you prefer it if I didn't help you?
  Would you prefer me not to help you?
  – *Do you want me to refrain from helping you?*
  Would you rather not help me?
  – *Do you want to do something else, rather than help me?*

5 I was going to phone her tonight.
  I intended to phone her tonight.
  I was to have phoned her tonight.
  – *I was planning to ring her this evening (but now the plans have changed – maybe it's no longer necessary or possible).*
  I am going to phone her tonight.
  – *My plan/intention is to ring her this evening.*

6 I wish I knew the answer.   – *I don't know the answer unfortunately.*
  I wish to know the answer.   – *Please tell me the answer.*

B   Suggested answers

1 wouldn't keep interrupting/disturbing
2 was done to stop/prevent
3 it if you arrived/you to arrive
4 had been more aware of
5 I was brave enough to/knew how to
6 were/was something we could do
7 were going to come
8 you played your saxophone/hifi
9 time we went/time for us to go
10 was fed/had its food

10.8 Showing your attitude

Background

Gerald Durrell runs his own zoo on the island of Jersey. He is a well-known broadcaster and zoologist. His books are mostly about his amusing encounters with animals and are full of anecdotes, notably: *The Overloaded Ark, The Bafut Beagles, The Drunken Forest, A Zoo in My Luggage.* His best-known book is *My Family and Other Animals*, the opening paragraphs of which are included in 13.2. *The Stationary Ark*, from which this extract is taken, is one of his more serious books.

A The passage is full of emotive language. Here are some examples:

I must agree with you . . . a few are excellent . . . the rest are appalling . . . zoos can and should be of value . . . I feel very strongly that . . . a great many rabid opponents . . . far worse off . . . the rolling vistas, the ancient trees . . .

It is odd how comforted people feel . . . purely to make money. No thought of science or conservation sullied their primary conception . . . unpleasant fungus, . . . disgraceful . . . appalling . . . I would like to stress that . . . totally impossible . . . rare beasts . . .

I am not against . . . I am against . . . of immense conservation value . . . animal abattoirs in a sylvan setting.

I feel therefore . . . not simply clamour . . . acumen and far-sightedness.

. . . all of us . . . already too hard pressed by our unbeatable competition . . . even the few good ones . . .

B Here students should make their own choices of phrases they want to remember – preferably ones that they don't already use in their own writing.

C Suggested answers

1 disgraceful
2 There is no doubt that
3 Quite frankly   appalling
4 am against   in spite of this
5 Clearly   absurd
6 It seems to me that   but you must agree that   absurd

D Before writing the paragraphs, students might like to exchange ideas on the topics listed. Alternatively, the written paragraphs can be shown to the other members of the group to start off a discussion.

10.9 Save the Earth

A   This is intended to be an entirely open-ended discussion. Remind students that this is a topic that may well come up in the Interview in the exam.

After a while, in order to encourage an exchange of view, the groups could be broken up into pairs consisting of students from different groups. Then each student has to summarise what his or her group has discussed so far before continuing the discussion.

➡ Here are some more quotes to write up on the board, to fuel the discussion:

'The future will either be green, or not at all.'   (Jonathon Porritt)

'Man is the only animal that blushes: or needs to.'   (Mark Twain)

'Small is beautiful.'   (E. F. Schumacher)

'Nowadays we don't think much of a man's love for an animal; we laugh at people who are attached to cats. But if we stop loving animals, aren't we bound to stop loving humans too?'   (Alexander Solzhenitsyn, *Cancer Ward*)

'No gain without pain.'

'The wounds we have inflicted on the Earth can be healed . . . But if it is to be done, it must be done now. Otherwise, it may never be done at all.'   (Jonathon Porritt)

B   Make it absolutely clear that students must make notes before writing – the difficult part about this task is likely to be restricting the essay to 350 words.

10.10   Filling the gaps

This text is also from *Life on Earth* by David Attenborough.

A   In the exam it's advisable to read the passage through for gist before filling in the gaps. (There are 20 gaps to fill in the exam.)

B   Make it clear, if necessary, that in the exam there aren't words to choose from in Paper 3 Question 1, but that they should run through the various possibilities in their minds, rather than assume that the first word that comes to mind must be the best one.

Suggested answers (The ones used in the original text are in **bold print**.)

2 come across **discover** find
3 **shining**
4 **collect** discover gather
5 **disguised**
6 **enormous** huge immense
7 **creatures** insects types
8 experts people **specialists**
9 **concerned** themselves
10 exactly **just** precisely quite
11 biggest **richest** strangest
12 **exist** remain survive
13 **forms**
14 **careful** fortunate
15 attacked **bitten** stung

10.11 Put + set

A Answers

PUT pressure on someone two and two together someone at their ease a question to someone a stop to something someone in the picture pen to paper
SET a trap for someone your teeth on edge a good example fire to something your watch the scene

B Answers

1 said something thoughtless which embarrassed her
2 cost me put an end to
3 depend on the success of one scheme or action
4 make him lose concentration and upset him
5 ascribed to discourage
6 asserted your authority
7 delayed
8 founded/started intended/aimed
9 humiliating put yourself in my place gives people an unfavourable impression of us both
10 wouldn't be surprised if/would consider him capable of

C Answers

1 put   up to
2 set up
3 putting   across/over
4 put   out   put   up
5 to set   off
6 put up with
7 put   back
8 set about
9 putting aside/putting away/setting aside
10 sets in
11 put in
12 sets out

➡ Follow-up   In pairs, students have to write their own fill-the-gaps exercise for another pair, using expressions from this section.

11 A good read

A   Although this is quite long, it will probably only need one playing. If students need time to take a break, and discuss what they have heard so far, stop the tape at the point shown with ★ ★ ★ in the Transcript, before question 11.

Answers
TRUE: 2 4 5 7 8 9 11 12 13 14
FALSE: 1 3 6 10 15

B   Follow-up discussion

Transcript
Presenter: We asked three people to talk about the kind of books they read, and what they've particularly enjoyed reading recently. First, Christine.

Christine: I love detective fiction, I have to say. And I think that to me detective fiction has been a respite, it's been a treat, from serious grown-up reading. I learned to love books as a very little girl with my dad who took me to the library twice a week, and I learned a great respect for plot... um... and for storytelling. And just love the cliff-hanger story and still love it. You know, so... er... something like P.D... .a big thick P.D. James novel is my idea of bliss and I'm not very good at self-denial, but one of my best examples was saving up a great big hardback P.D. James um... for nearly three months before reading it, wanted to take it off for a holiday and actually having it in the house and not reading it and that took enormous restraint. Because I can get quite lost in one of those and I... I'm a very fast reader, and my desire to work out who did it and what happened next is so great that it overpowers everything else and I will disappear into a book for hours and not speak to a soul. But I get that from my father who is exactly the same, my mum has never been a great reader and my dad and I drive her mad, because we will sit for hours contentedly reading when we're together and she thinks this is awfully boring and unsocial. But my dad is never not reading and that is where I got it from.

Presenter: Jilly, on the other hand, enjoys a different kind of book.

Jilly: Um... what sort of books do I really like to read? I like to read books that make me laugh, but I like to read books that make me laugh that are also what I consider well-written, where I can read a sentence and think, 'Oh gosh, that's nicely put together' and I can enjoy the turn of phrase. Um... I enjoy fiction and non-fiction. I read quite a lot of scientific books inevitably:

background f... for my work. But for... but for pleasure, I l... I like well-written humour.

Presenter: What would be examples of this 'well-written humour'?

Jilly: Well, just recently, Peter Mayle's *A Year In Provence*, a lovely diary of a year spent, the first year that he lived when he moved to the South of France, beautifully written, some lovely phrases in it. And a little bit of... older book um... books by Laurie Lee: the biog... the autobiography of Laurie Lee, *Cider With Rosie* and *As I Walked Out One Midsummer Morning*: again beautiful use of the English language, and er... but with... with a... very much a sort of a smiling view on humanity. Lovely books.

Presenter: Vince, too, prefers books which make him smile.

Vince: I still read for entertainment, really. So I don't read terribly serious things. Um... and I think there's a good tradition of literature in English um... which is amusing. If you look back through the twentieth century, perhaps further than that, you'd find that there were... there were a lot of authors who had tried to write with the aim of not only improving the listener's mind but also of making him smile. Um... an author in the present day who does that is a man called David Lodge who writes a lot about university life, which I know a little bit about. He tends to have a group of characters who recur in different places all round the world, um... not doing anything very important, but he... he... he writes with great amusement.

Another one is Malcolm Bradbury who has in... actually again about university life, has written... um... several novels that are often actually 'out loud' funny, I think, and he's an author I enjoy a lot. Um... again, going the other side of the Atlantic, an author who I enjoy reading a lot at the moment is Garrison Keillor who started *telling* stories and then was persuaded to write them down. Small town stories about life in a Minnesota... area of Minnesota I'm not familiar with at all but... um... it's a closed community and he writes about the characters within the community... um... in a way that's... er... that's quietly amusing.

★★★

Presenter: We asked the same people to explain the pleasure they get from reading. First, Vince.

Vince: It's the ability to make an imaginative leap into another country, another situation. It has the same appeal as sound radio, in that it is not too direct, it allows you to paint your own pictures. It's an escape, it's a way of learning... um... which makes it a... an activity to recommend to anybody.

Presenter: Christine.

Christine: It's another world, it's going into a world... um... that somebody makes convincing, where there are characters in that world about whom you have a concern and you want to know what happens to them, and... um... it matters to know what is going to unfold and what happens next. And it's about expanding your picture of the world. It's taking you into bits of people's experience that you haven't got for yourself. Um... but the best book is one where you find the environment and the situation and the conflict if there is one, because most literature involves some kind of conflict. Er... the resolution of that conflict, or whatever, you just desperately want to know what it is. And it's that... um... it's that commitment to the creation the author has made that keeps you reading absolutely desperately to the last page. Um... and it's about magic as well, it's about being taken into a world that just transports you and you forget the here and now, you know, I... I could quite forget to feed the pussies if they didn't jump on my head if I were really engrossed in a book. And I regret the fact that I seem to have so little time to read these days. Um... one of my resolutions every year is to make more time to do it, and one of these days I will. Because I love reading.

(Time: 7 minutes)

C   Answers

1 best-sellers   thrillers   whodunits
2 blurb   contents   dustjacket
3 dedication   foreword   preface
4 anthology   book   collection
5 complex   intricate   involved
6 get   struggle   wade
7 readable   thought-provoking   well-written
8 figuratively   metaphorically   symbolically
9 message   purpose   side
10 chapters   sections   units

D   Answers (The Latin is given for your information only.)

e.g. (Latin: *exempli gratia*)   i.e. – that is (Latin: *id est*)   cf. – compare (Latin: *conferre*)   ff. – and the following pages   pp. – pages   ibid. – from the book already mentioned (Latin: *ibidem*)   viz. – namely (Latin: *videlicet*)   sic – spelt in this way in the original work from which we are quoting (Latin)   © – copyright   N.B. – note well (Latin: *nota bene*)

The abbreviations can also be written without full stops (apart from ©):
eg   etc   ie   cf   ff   pp   ibid   viz   NB

11.2   Setting the scene . . .   Reading & discussion

Background

Barbara Vine is the pseudonym of the crime writer Ruth Rendell (b. 1930). Her books written under this name are more imaginative and strange than her more routine Inspector Wexford mysteries. She is a very accessible, stylish writer whose work dwells on life's losers and the darker side of human nature.

All of her Barbara Vine novels are highly recommendable: *A Dark-Adapted Eye, A Fatal Inversion, The House of Stairs, Gallowglass* and *King Solomon's Carpet*.

And as Ruth Rendell: *The Bridesmaid*, *The Tree of Hands* and *Going Wrong*.

A *Dark-Adapted Eye* concerns obsessive family relationships and a murder, the perpetrator of which is due to be executed as the book opens. During the rest of the book, the situation leading up to the murder slowly unfolds in flashbacks.

David Lodge (b. 1935) is a humorous writer whose work has a serious edge. Many of his works are concerned in some way with university life, and the worlds of game-playing, sexual intrigue and Catholicism.

His best-known books are: *Changing Places*, *Small World*, *Nice Work* and *Paradise News*.

The main characters of *Nice Work* are Vic Wilcox, the managing director of a struggling engineering firm, and Robyn Penrose, a feminist university lecturer. The book explores their different worlds and the developing relationship between two very different people.

William Boyd (b. 1952) is a writer whose early work deals humorously with the English abroad, but his later books are more serious and each one covers quite different themes. Boyd's books are consistently well-written and thought-provoking.

His best-known books include: *A Good Man in Africa*, *An Ice Cream War*, *The New Confessions* and *Brazzaville Beach*.

The protagonist of *Brazzaville Beach* is a woman who, against the background of civil war in an African country, is studying chimpanzees and makes the alarming discovery that they engage in warlike activities with each other, just as humans do.

➡ Here and in 11.6 we have the opening paragraphs of some well-known novels, which I hope will whet students' appetites, encouraging them to want to read more.

A   Suggested answers

1 Very little: she is going to die at exactly 8 o'clock, her home is in the country, she is probably the narrator's aunt (her father's sister). We don't know why she is going to die: it is a mystery. [The reader later discovers that she is going to be executed.]
2 Four times – not all that many, but enough to set a mood of gloom
3 They had stayed together despite their differences and the rockiness of their marriage
4 The narrator wakes up in her parents' house in a leafy suburb on a Thursday in August 30 years ago.

B   Suggested answers

1 He often wakes up early and can't go back to sleep, because of his worries at work; he works in industry in a senior position; he is married and has a son called Gary

2 She is Victor's wife: she is overweight, she takes sleeping pills, she reads in bed before going to sleep

3 Victor awakes in his bedroom very early on Monday January 13th 1986

4 Twelve: it makes us realise that he has a lot of problems – they attack him like alien spaceships in a video game. The technical terms ('fettling shop', 'core blowers', etc.) are puzzling to the reader, but they mean a lot to Victor.

5 ¶ 1 begins like a diary entry, followed by terse scene-setting sentences, and then we share Victor's thoughts and the questions in his mind.

   In ¶ 2 his worries seem like attackers in a video game.

   In ¶ 3 we are introduced to his wife – a series of actions is described, like a blow-by-blow account of a fight.

C   Suggested answers

1 She (or he) lives in a beach house somewhere in Africa, where she just happens to have landed up and is unlikely to stay for ever. She seems to be single.   [The reader discovers later that the narrator is a woman – some readers may recognise that the beach is in a Portuguese-speaking country.]

2 None (apart from 'some workmen' and 'everyone else who lives round here') – it gives a mood of isolation or self-containment

3 The narrator lives in a house on a beach: this is described in some detail in the last paragraph together with its garden – it is 'a few years' after 1964

4 Seven: four of which are in the phrase 'Brazzaville Beach', the title of the book – it seems that the beach is likely to be the main setting of the story

5 In ¶ 1 we find out where the narrator lives and we may be intrigued to know how she ended up there – the imagery of the 'spar of driftwood' to which the narrator compares herself is striking.

   In ¶ 2 we find out the origins of the name of the beach, but without understanding what *Quadros* means in Portuguese or knowing about the conference in 1964 we are none the wiser. The style is very matter-of-fact.

   In ¶ 3 the reader is introduced to the political background of the story. The questions asked stand out stylistically.

   ¶ 4 gives a detailed description of the house and its garden – the use of 'I' and 'my' emphasises that the house belongs to the narrator, and she considers it to be her home. The style makes the place sound very attractive.

   D   Follow-up discussion   Perhaps tell the class some of the information given in the Background notes above at this stage.

11.3 Conjunctions and connectors – 1

Even though students should be encouraged to use a variety of conjunctions and connectors in their compositions in the exam, *and* or *but* are often perfectly adequate to convey most meanings, especially in straightforward narratives and reports – as the task in C shows.

A   Suggested answers

2   Many blockbusters, such as James Mitchener's 'Alaska', are over 1,000 pages long.
3   She enjoys reading biographies, particularly ones about politicians.
4   Science fiction is an acquired taste – at least that's what sci-fi fans say.
5   She prefers reading non-fiction books, which means that she enjoys biographies, history books, as well as other similar books.
6   The reason why the book was a best-seller was that it contained a lot of explicit sex and violence.
7   She doesn't read much apart from thrillers.
8   Reading is not only an inexpensive hobby but it is also enjoyable.
    Not only is reading an inexpensive hobby, it is also enjoyable.

B   Suggested answers

1   apart from
2   what is more
3   in particular
4   even though   in other words
5   for example/apart from   consequently
6   nonetheless
7   at any rate
8   above all

C   Counting the *ands* and *buts* in 11.2 is best done in groups of three with one member of each group counting in a different extract.

In total there are about six *buts*; about thirteen *ands* joining sentences (but more joining nouns); *though* is used once. That's all.

➡ There is more on this topic in 15.8 Conjunctions and connectors – 2.

11.4   A good beginning . . . Writing skills

A   This is an open-ended discussion. It might be a good idea to pick out some of the useful vocabulary in the passage, which is the first part of a longer article. To do this, go through the passage with a highlighter, selecting words your students will find useful.

B   No suggested answers here: but you should choose your own favourite opening lines so that you can enter into the discussion.

C   There are no suggested answers for these tasks. The extracts are genuine students' work.

D   This is what we have been leading up to, and it's important that enough time is devoted to it.

E   📼 After checking answers, allow time for a short follow-up discussion about the content of the recording.
   We'll hear from Abdulrazak Gurnah himself in 11.8 Writing novels.

Answers

1   unsolicited   agents   published
2   recommending   rejecting   reads   treat   information
3   unpublishable   got a book inside them   very good
4   storyline   fresh   fresh   original
5   East Africa   winning/charming
6   growing up
7   English published   momentous   encapsulated   recognised/taken up
8   being able to read at your own speed ✓   being caught up in a story ✓
   being transported to another world ✓   choosing a book in a bookshop
   just holding a book ✓   re-reading passages you have enjoyed ✓
   learning information   seeing the world through other people's eyes ✓

Transcript

Karen: I'm a reader for a publishing company in London... um... and that involves reading manuscripts which are sent in to the... um... commissioning editors at the company, and these could be unsolicited manuscripts from anyone who has written a novel or a non-fiction... er... manuscript and would like to have it published and they send it to the company. Or, also more often, er... from agents who represent authors and of course I also read manuscripts by our published authors and then I read these and I write a report... um... about the manuscript, and I recommend it or reject it or suggest that... um... someone else reads it or that we should do some work on it, or it's an interesting idea.

Interviewer: So what's it like to read as a job?

Karen: Well, people always... I mean, a lot of people think, particularly people who like you enjoy fiction or whatever, they sort of think, 'Oh my god, you're so lucky, you get paid just to read. It's sort of like liking cricket and being paid to watch cricket all day!' It's not quite as simple as that because essentially you just read a lot of bad things. Um... it, you know, from my point of view it's wonderful to be able to read... um... you know, the sort of... the... new manuscript by someone I really admire... um... you know, before anybody else can, that's just like a treat. But for someone, you know, famous or whatever – not famous: established and... and good – I mean, basically you're just there just to write this report for information... um... and it's a treat for you.

Unsolicited manuscripts are something else, because I think, I'm not quite sure what the figure is now, but when I first started working at Cape in the mid-eighties, I think they got something like two to three thousand manuscripts a year, and a large bulk of those are unsolicited, maybe even the majority, and most of them, I'm afraid are really unpublishable. A lot of people write... you know, they get to retirement age and they think, 'Oh, I'm going to write a book about my childhood', and they send it in and actually, you know, it's only really of any interest to the family or personal friends and this is just not something that we would publish. I mean, you know, there's this famous saying that 'everyone's got a book inside them' but actually it doesn't mean to say it's going to be a very good one.

Interviewer: What then makes a good book?

Karen: I suppose what makes a good book for me is what I like and, I mean, that's what's hard. I mean,... you know, you have to try and be open to new writing, and try to be experimental but maybe at the end of the day I would just think, 'Oh well, you know, this has got a strong storyline, and this is what I like' – I mean it's not quite as simple as that but... I think it... what's important is that someone is trying to say something fresh, and that the style is fresh and original, but you know these are very easy things to say and I suppose it's all got to work... um... together as a whole, um... to really come off. But you really want to find someone who's saying something worth saying and that's interesting.

★★★

Interviewer: Who is the most interesting new author she has discovered?

Karen: Well... I think um... the person that immediately springs to mind is a very interesting writer called Abdulrazak Gurnah, who... um... originally comes from East Af... Africa and is now teaching English in a university here. Um... he sent in a novel unsolicited but with a rather winning letter – I mean, I must say the letter is... um... very important when you're sending in a manuscript – but anyway the letter was sort of rather charming and... you know, I suppose that inclined one to take it seriously. And... um... it was read by a number of people actually... um... at Cape and everybody thought – um... this was his first novel that we went on to publish – everyone thought it was very interesting. It was a... called *Memory of Departure* and essentially it was about his experiences growing up in East Africa in a country where... um... er... revolution, or the... the, you know, the government was in turmoil and it was very difficult to function. And . . . it was very powerful because it was terr... I mean, it was very hard, it was very squalid where he grew up, it was very slum-like, the father was violent. Um...

the... er... it was just amazing that he managed to get out of this and come to this country to study, the... the boy in... in the book. Um... and I think everyone was rather captivated by the strength of the description and, you know, the... the... this boy's plight. And so a number of people read it and found it very promising and we invited him in... um... and we talked to him and he – I think I worked with him on that book, that's right – and he just did a bit more... we talked about it and he... er... did a bit more rewriting and everyone was very happy with the end result and he... he got published.

And he writes... I mean, I think he just is able to tell a story very very well, but I think for me one of the reasons his novels work so well is that you are... you're just terribly aware that, you know, most English published novels are very, you know, what's described as of the Hampstead middle-class... er... novel where people are having affairs or, you know, talking about politics over dinner parties or whatever, and you know you realise that this person has got this incredible history that you have just not had and are... you know, and never hopefully going to have. But what's happened to him is rather momentous and that, you know, is all encapsulated in his fiction and I think that... you know, that's what... that when you ask me what makes a good novel, I mean in his case I really think he's got something interesting and important to say, about sort of the human condition, and he... but he says it with a light touch and I... and I think he's rather special and I hope he, you know, gets recognised. I mean he has had some good reviews but I think he, you know, really should be taken up a bit more than he has.

Interviewer: What is it about books that people find so pleasurable?

Karen: The immediate thing about a book is just it takes you into a different world, you can... immediately find yourself introduced to a whole set of behaviour or w... or ideas that you, you know, you wouldn't easily come across in your own life. You can just shut the door and that's it. I mean, I think it's much more . . . I mean it's much more pleasurable than television, although I'm interested in television and film as well, but you know obviously you can take it at your own pace, and you can read again and you can savour certain passages. And um... I think it's just the... the i... getting into one person's head, and sort of seeing how they see things. And just having... you know, also, as I said before about readability, being caught up in a good story. I mean, you're lost for a few hours, aren't you? You're in a different world for a few hours. And, also just the tactile pleasure of holding a book, of a book as an object. I mean, I like books as objects, I could never never throw them away ever, I could never give any... even a scrappy old paperback, I could never give it to a jumble sale.

(Time: 6 minutes 50 seconds)

11.5 Collocations: idioms

A Answers

2 pros and cons	10 thick and thin
3 facts and figures	11 wear and tear
4 life and soul	12 over and above
5 ups and downs	13 few and far between
6 swings and roundabouts	14 to and fro
7 law and order	15 bread and butter
8 spick and span	16 safe and sound
9 touch and go	

➡ Ask the class to think of further similar phrases. Here are some more examples:

airs and graces   an open and shut case   cut and dried   free and easy   part and parcel   rank and file   rough and ready   far and wide   here and there out and about   up and about

B Suggested answers

basket of fruit   bucket of water   bunch of flowers   carafe of wine/water
cup of tea   flight of stairs   flock of sheep   gust of wind   herd of cattle
item of luggage   jug of milk   loaf of bread   pack of cards   pair of
tweezers
piece of equipment /cake   pot of honey/tea   puff of smoke   range of hills
sack of potatoes   school of whales   slice of cake/bread   spoonful of
honey/sugar   spot of bother   team of helpers   tin or can of beans   tube
of toothpaste

C Suggested answers (other humorous variations are possible!)

1 a team of helpers	6 a range of hills
2 a bunch of flowers	7 a spot of bother
3 items of luggage	8 a flock of sheep/swarm of bees, etc.
4 a pack of cards	9 a flight of stairs
5 a pair of tweezers	10 gust of wind

D Answers

muscular – He's as strong as a horse/an ox.
short-sighted – She's as blind as a bat.
hard of hearing – He's as deaf as a post.
stupid – She's as thick as two short planks.
unemotional – He's as cool as a cucumber.
tough – She's as hard as nails.

self-effacing – He's as quiet as a mouse.
healthy – She's as fit as a fiddle.
crazy – He's as mad as a hatter.
attractive – She looked as pretty as a picture.
well-behaved – The children were as good as gold.
very slim – She's as light as a feather.

11.6 Three American novels — Reading

Background

John Steinbeck (1902–68) wrote about the lives of simple, ordinary people in America. His best-known books are: *Of Mice and Men, Cannery Row, Tortilla Flat* and *East of Eden* (the film of which starred James Dean).

The Grapes of Wrath is the story of farmers driven off their land in Oklahoma, who set off in search of a land of milk and honey in California.

Paul Theroux (b. 1941) is a travel writer as well as novelist. His travels have taken him all over the world and are described in such books as: *The Great Railway Bazaar: By Train through Asia, The Old Patagonian Express, The Kingdom by the Sea, Riding the Iron Rooster,* and *The Happy Isles of Oceania*.

His novels are full of imaginative detail and exotic locations, each one quite different from the other. Particularly recommendable are: *Picture Palace, The Family Arsenal, O-Zone* and *My Secret History*, the first paragraphs of which are in 13.2 Family life.

The Mosquito Coast is the story of a family who abandon civilisation and go to live in the jungle of Central America, hoping to build utopia for themselves. But life becomes a nightmare. as the central character ('Father') becomes more and more obsessive. The story is told through the voice of his young son.

Ernest Hemingway (1899–1961), despite his image of being a hard-drinking, macho man of action, had a genius for evoking a time and a place in his writing, by means of a delightfully simple style. His prose is particularly accessible for foreign learners.

His best-known books include: *Fiesta (The Sun Also Rises), For Whom the Bell Tolls, The Old Man and the Sea, Men without Women* and *To Have and Have Not*.

A Farewell to Arms is a love story set against the background of the First World War.

A If this is set for homework, students have time to do this at their leisure. The purpose of this section and the next is to encourage students to appreciate the writing.

B Suggested answers

1 Extract no. 1: *May . . . June   day after day*   the changing weather the growth of green weeds and their subsequent *fraying* and dying back
2 Extract no. 3: *Troops went by the house and down the road   the leaves fell   troops marching   troops marching under the window and guns going past*   the use of prepositions and particles: *across, along, past*, etc.
3 Extract no. 2: *savages   awfulness   dope-taking, door-locking, ulcerated danger-zone of rabid scavengers . . .*   a piling-up of words that suggest decay and violence
4 (see quotations above)
5 Extract no. 3 (Hemingway)
6 Extract no. 1 (Steinbeck) – or no. 3?
7 Extract no. 2 (Theroux)
8 Extract no. 1 – and no. 3?
9 (for discussion)
10 Extract no. 1 is from *The Grapes of Wrath* by John Steinbeck (1939)
Extract no. 2 is from *The Mosquito Coast* by Paul Theroux (1981)
Extract no. 3 is from *A Farewell to Arms* by Ernest Hemingway (1929)

11.7 *It . . .* constructions   Advanced grammar

A Answers

1 Did Jane Austen write Emma?
  – *Slight emphasis on the last item mentioned: the book. However, if a stress is put on different words in the sentence the emphasis and implications change:*
  Did Jane Austen write *Emma*? – *. . . I insist that you tell me.*
  Did **Jane** Austen write *Emma*? – *. . . or was it **Anne** Austen?*
  Did Jane Austen **write** *Emma*? – *. . . or did she edit it?*
  Did Jane Austen write ***Emma***? – *. . . or another book?*
  Was it Jane Austen who wrote *Emma*?
  – *More emphasis on the author's name.*
  Was Jane Austen the author who wrote *Emma*?
  – *Emphasis on the author (it seems unnecessary to use the term* author *here, and maybe* woman *might be more usual).*
  Was Jane Austen the author of *Emma*?
  – *Emphasis on the author.*
  Was *Emma* written by Jane Austen?
  – *Emphasis on the author's name.*
  Was it *Emma* that Jane Austen wrote?
  – *. . . or was it another book? Emphasis on the title, suggesting that*

this is the only book she was famous for (cf. Was it Wuthering Heights that Emily Brontë wrote?).

2 What I enjoy reading is thrillers.
   – Emphasis on thrillers (this structure helps to create suspense as we wait for the main point to be mentioned).
   Thrillers are what I enjoy reading.
   It's thrillers that I enjoy reading.
   – Emphasis on thrillers.
   I enjoy reading thrillers.
   – No special emphasis, as written. In speech we might put stress on enjoy or on thrillers.

3 It was me who borrowed your book.
   I was the one who borrowed your book.
   – Emphasis on me as the person responsible.
   I borrowed your book.
   – No special emphasis.
   It was I who borrowed your book.
   – Emphasis on me as the person responsible (this example might sound pretentious or old-fashioned in everyday conversation).

B Suggested answers

1 surprising/remarkable   get to the summit
2 lives in/went to/wrote about
3 lucky/a good job/thing   warned/told
4 is unfriendly/unlikeable   is very shy
5 long/too long   realised/discovered   we had made
6 is it   never arrive anywhere
7 'll be/will be   who answers/picks up
8 to be   who was   is/'s me who reads

C Suggested answers

1 It was because I was feeling worn out that I went to bed early.
2 It was a strange noise that woke me up in the early hours.
3 It was half past four in the morning when I heard the noise.
4 It was when I looked out of the window that I realised what had happened.
5 It was then that I found I couldn't get back to sleep.
6 It was about eight o'clock when I finally did get to sleep again.
7 It wasn't until lunchtime that I woke up.
8 It was only yesterday that she finished reading the book.
9 Is it the humour of her stories that you enjoy?
10 Was it 'Emma' or 'Persuasion' that you read recently?

11.8 Writing novels

Background

Abdulrazak Gurnah was born in 1948 in Zanzibar, Tanzania. Although his books have been critically well-received, none have yet gone into paperback.

Here are the opening paragraphs of *Pilgrim's Way*:

It was just after seven and the pub was almost empty. The only other customer apart from Daud was a thin, old man leaning over his drink at a corner of the bar. The barman was talking to him, and nodded at Daud to show that he had seen him and would presently attend to him. It was getting towards the end of the week and money was short, so Daud bought himself the cheapest half-pint of beer and sat in the alcove by the window. The beer tasted watery and sour, but he shut his eyes and gulped it.

He heard the barman chuckling softly at something that the old man had said. They both turned to look at him. The old man grinned as he leant back to stare at Daud over an angle of his shoulder, nodding as if he intended to reassure and calm him. Daud made his face as lugubrious as he could and his eyes glassy and blank, blind to the old man's antics. He thought of the grin as the one that won an empire. It was the pick-pocket's smile, given tongue in cheek and intended to distract and soothe the innocent prey while the thief helped himself to the valuables. It had travelled the seven seas, flashing at unsuspecting wogs the world over. Millions of them succumbed to it, laughing at its transparently conniving intention, and assuming that the mind behind such a ridiculous face must be as idiotic. Daud imagined how embarrassing the sight would have been: half-naked men, skins baked red by the sun, smiling with such complete insincerity. By the time the victims discovered that those bared fangs had every intention of chomping through their comic and woggish world, there was little for them to do but watch with terror as the monsters devoured them. *Never again,* Daud vowed. *Go find yourself another comedy act, you old fool.*

B 📼 **Answers**

TRUE: 3 5 7 8 9 12 13
FALSE: 1 2 4 6 10 11

Transcript (A suitable place for pausing is marked with ★★★.)

Interviewer: Abdulrazak, your first novel was about someone from Africa coming to live in England, wasn't it?

Abdulrazak: Not quite. It was about somebody leaving um… Africa and more than that perhaps it was much more about the moment of leaving. So really it was about living there, if I can put it like that. And it was called, or rather it is called *Memory of Departure*, but the departure that it tries to talk about is not so much that moment, but rather this is a memory of actually in the end leaving. So it's much more, or rather was much more really, about living there rather than leaving there.

Interviewer: And what about your second novel?

Abdulrazak: My second book was called Pilgrim's Way and was about the experience of… er… I hope again not one individual, but in the narrative it's the experience of one individual of coming to England as a student and everything going wrong. It is a story about failure but it's also a story about coping. Um… it's… I think, a funny novel. Nonetheless, through this er… apparent frivolity, he and other people that he meets talk about or confront the idea of being not… non-European, of being somebody from Africa or from Asia, living in a country like this. So to some extent I suppose it talks about attitudes of England to people like this protagonist of mine. It's also about being away from a place where one feels one belongs, so it's about 'there' as well as about here.

Interviewer: To what extent was your first book autobiographical?

Abdulrazak: I would say probably not at all, in the sense that er… none of the figures there are figures that… um… for example, the father is not my father, the young person who's the protagonist, who's the narrator, is not me, in the sense that my experiences were not like that, in precise ways of course, I mean. But probably, it's very difficult and not even desirable to say that a work doesn't contain anything of the writer. It clearly does. But there's a difference I think between something that is based or modelled on a writer's own specific experiences and specific individuals who relate to the novelist, say, in a… in the precise way that they appear in the book. Rather than to say that these… all of these things actually derive from the experience of the author. I'm quite happy with that, but… er… um… in the case of that novel anyway it certainly isn't in any important way autobiographical, although most of the experiences are ones that perhaps I witnessed or heard about or something of that kind, and some invented. I forget now which is which! But… er… not that I am trying to say, by the way, that there is anything wrong with a work being autobiographical… er… but it is very tempting, I think, to assume that… that a writer simply uses experience, and that if you don't have interesting experiences then you have nothing to write about.

★★★

Interviewer: What motivates you as a writer?

Abdulrazak: I'm not quite sure exactly what it is that makes you go through the rather, well, often difficult process of writing. I say 'difficult' because with writing you literally have to write down every word. And you agonise and worry about whether it and all the other words that you're putting down on the page actually do sit together comfortably, and so on. And it's not just a matter of putting one, as it were, foot in front of another and keeping going, but all the processes that you go through are processes that you have to consider. Er... this both sounds interesting and also sounds tedious – and it is both!

Er... Julian Barnes said that... um... making a book is not like making babies, it's not in other words something that you might just do and have fun, it's like – and he compares it to building a pyramid, and taking one stone at a time and putting it down and then... um... when the whole edifice, as it were, stands, the only use it is for is for the bourgeoisie to clamber to the top of it and for jackals to piss at the base of it. Um... so there is this kind of contradiction of labouring at something that in the end if somebody were to say to you, 'Well, what use is it?' you'd probably find yourself hard put to say, 'Well, I did it because it will make it easier to... ' – some, in other words, some fairly straightforward... er... practical use to which it can be put.

So I'm resisting, if you like, saying that it is just a matter of um... 'If you feel you have the skill, you'll do it. If you feel you have something to say, you'll do it.' But there is also another... another aspect which perhaps varies with different individuals and perhaps it's something that almost makes you feel a little... um... embarrassed to make a claim for, as if you're making a claim for something noble or something indefinable or whatever. But no doubt, no doubt – well, at least I have no doubt, that most writers have that sense of... that there is something indefinable about what I'm doing.

Interviewer: How do you go about actually writing a book? Do you wait until the inspiration comes? Do you set yourself targets?

Abdulrazak: Well, so far as inspiration, or what to write about is concerned, I'm very glad to be able to say that that has not been something that has kept me waiting. In other words, whenever I've been ready to start a new work, the new work has been waiting... er... for me to start it.

Um... when you think about a book you don't just think about the idea that you're going to explore, you think about it in the same way I think that a painter would think about a painting that he's going to make. You think about how big you're going to make it, you think about, you know, whether it's going to be colour... ful, or whether it's going to be fairly dark or gloomy or whatever. I'm simplifying of course... um... But otherwise you can't move, at least otherwise I feel I can't move, unless I have a slightly more coherent idea about what I'm going to 'make'.

When you've made decisions like that, or when you've at least projected some possibilities like that, then something else becomes obvious, that if you're going to attempt something of this nature, you estimate that it will probably take you two years, three years, whatever it might be, and that gives you something, you know, something which then provides a kind of timetable. So you do set yourself targets in this sort of way.

Interviewer: What do you enjoy about writing?

Abdulrazak: There is pleasure in having a reader, there is pleasure in the kind of response that a reader might make, most of all I think though the... the pleasure of writing is in actually being able to realise... the sense, which may develop and change as you're writing, but to be able to realise that sense and make it concrete and make it work and make it real, and that's the pleasure.

Interviewer: One last question: what for you are the pleasures of reading?

Abdulrazak: They're too complex to be able to answer easily really, honestly. Er... I mean, that I read different things and get different kinds of er... satisfaction I suppose, although not always satisfaction, but I get different things from different books or different kinds of books. Best of all is the kind of engagement with ideas, and with... with language, with... with a mind that is actually working at this, making this. And also at a very simple level, just the engagement with the story that might be going on, with the kind of tension that the writer's able to create. So there are many different levels and the beauty of the novel is that you can engage with all of these at the same time... as you read.

(Time: 8 minutes 40 seconds)

11.9 Describing a book   Interview practice & composition

A & B   Note that A and B are done in a different sequence, depending whether your students are preparing one of the prescribed texts or not.

➡ In the exam interview, if candidates elect to talk about a prescribed book, they are likely to have to deal with:
1 An illustration from the text or from its front cover to talk about
2 One or more quotations from the text to comment on
3 Questions about the text. For example, the following topics might come up, but the questions would of course refer to specific characters and ideas in the particular text:
   • The importance of certain characters in the text
   • Looking at the situations certain characters find themselves in and considering what they could have done. Or considering: what would you have done in the same situation?
   • Reasons for the text's popularity
   • Insights into life in the period the text is set in
   • Present-day relevance of the text's themes and ideas
   • Film or TV versions of the text, and how they compare to the original

C & D   If there is too much to condense into 350 words, you might ask the class to focus on certain aspects of the book, rather than all six suggested.

➡ Depending on the book your students are reading, they should be set composition questions that relate to its content and relevance. For examples of typical questions, see *Cambridge Proficiency Examination Practice Books*. Here are a few more composition questions from previous exams, just to give an idea of what students might expect:

F. Scott Fitzgerald: *The Great Gatsby*
1 Everyone went to Gatsby's parties; no one attended his funeral. How do you account for this?
2 What does this novel tell us about American life in the 1920s?

Robert Graves: *Goodbye To All That*
1 What were the advantages and disadvantages of belonging to Graves's particular regiment?
2 'The First World War was a tragic story of waste and futility.' How does *Goodbye To All That* illustrate this statement?

Margaret Drabble: *The Millstone*
1 Why is the book called 'The Millstone'?
2 Rosamund describes herself as a 'strange mixture of confidence and cowardice'. How are these two characteristics responsible for what happens to her?

12 How things work

Science and technology   Topic vocabulary

A   To settle any arguments, the photos show: the surface of a compact disc, a microchip and Velcro.

B   **Answers**

1 application   2 meteorology   3 zoology   4 anthropology
5 trial and error   6 generation   7 PhD (doctor of philosophy)
8 controlled   9 inspiration   10 setting up   11 raised   12 impractical
13 equipment   14 patent   15 think up   16 compound   17 catalyst
18 socket   19 fuse   20 microchip   21 knob   22 gauge
23 chassis [ʃæsi]   24 engineer   25 hand it to her

➡ Finish by discussing the wrong answers and considering why some of them are wrong in context.

12.2   The secret life of machines   Reading

➡ Begin by asking the class to say what kind of person they think Tim Hunkin seems, from the photo. As the article addresses the reader directly, there is no need for any more preliminary discussion, though students might want to compare their reactions to it before embarking on A and B.

A   **Answers**

somone who hates or fears machines – Luddite (a reference to workers who destroyed job-threatening machinery at the start of the Industrial Revolution in England) (¶ 1)   *give up* – admitted defeat (¶ 1)   *make less mysterious* – demystify (¶ 2)   *puzzling* – inscrutable (¶ 3)   *facade* – veneer (¶ 4)   *medical* – clinical (¶ 6)   *learn how to use* – come to grips with (¶ 6)   *derives from* – stems from (¶ 7)   *their friends' opinions* – peer group pressure (¶ 7)   *understand* – grasp (¶ 7)   *come across* – encountered (¶ 10)   *faced with* – confronted (¶ 10)   *lack of interest* – disregard (¶ 10)   *suspicion* – distrust (¶ 10)   *antagonism* – antipathy (¶ 11)   *alleviate* – assuage (¶ 12)

B   These questions are similar to the kind of questions students will have to answer in the exam.

Answers

1 b) contain so many electronic components
2 d) take decision-making away from humans
3 b) is made to feel inadequate by their colleagues
4 d) uneasy
5 demonstrations of how various machines work ✓
explanations of the basic principles underlying each machine ✓
information about inventors' lives ✓
showing the kind of problems people have with machines ✓
simple experiments ✓

C Student A looks at Activity 9, B at 26. Each has some information by Tim Hunkin about the workings of a refrigerator and a vacuum cleaner. Allow time for them to study and absorb the information before explaining it to their partner *in their own words.*

12.3 Verbs + prepositions   Grammar review

A   Answers

*combine something **with**   compare something **with**   concern yourself **with***
*contrast something **with**   deal **with**   depend **on**   dispense **with**   engage **in***
*impose something **on**   invest **in**   lean **on**   mistake it/them **for**   part **with***
*reason **with**   refer him **to**   rely **on**   separate something **from**   stem **from***

B   Suggested answers

*agree **with** someone **about** something   apologise **to** someone **for** something*
*approve **of**   bargain **with** someone **for** something   care **for/about***
*decide **on/against**   despair **of**   experiment **on**   hope **for**   insist **on***
*interfere **with/in**   intrude **on**   look **at/after/like/through**   negotiate*
***with** someone **about/for** something   object **to**   quarrel **with** someone*
over/about** something   resign **from/over**   retire **from**   smell **of/like
*struggle **with/against/for**   succeed **in**   suffer **from**   talk **to/with** someone*
about** something   vote **for/against/on**   watch **for/over**   worry **about

C   Answers

*accuse them **of**   admire him **for**   blame her **for**   borrow it **from***
*cheat them **out of**   congratulate him **on**   consult her **on/about***
*convince them **of**   cure him **of**   deliver it **to**   mention it **to**   punish him **for***
*rescue them **from**   respect her **for**   take it **from/to**   thank her **for***
*threaten them **with**   use it **for**   warn him **against/about***

E   Answers

Computers are being given elocution lessons so that they can announce the comings and goings **of** French trains **in** regional accents. Computer-controlled synthesised voices are said to be more reassuring **to/for** passengers than man-made announcements **by/from** railway staff.

According **to** a survey, travellers bristle when they hear announcements **in** the refined tones adopted **at** airports. What they like best is a deep voice **with** a touch **of** regional homeliness, even when they know it comes **from** an electronic throat. Apparently, not even the voice **of** the stationmaster can produce the effect as well as computers.

Experiments to find the perfect electronic announcer were started two years ago when the station **in/at** the Champagne town of Rheims was used **in/for** tests. Those were considered a success but **after/by** trying out the voice **at/in** other stations it was found that the reassuring effect was increased if regional accents were added.

The generalised use **of** synthetic announcers will be put **into** effect **in/during** the next few months but the reason is not entirely psychological. The synthesiser is considered more reliable and flexible. It will not depend **on** recorded messages: the announcements will be put together **on** computer keyboards just before they are needed.

In the meantime, the voices are being put **into** service elsewhere, including information offices. Already, travellers **at** Paris-Austerlitz can consult an experimental audio-visual information robot that chats away **in** four languages. Ticket offices are also to be equipped **with** automatic dispensers that respond **to** travellers' oral commands because half **of** the system's passengers are said to prefer talking **to** an inanimate object that does not answer back or go **on** strike.

But there are no statistics available **on** the train drivers' reaction **to** electronic voices. Some drivers **on** mainline services are now getting their instructions **from** robot voices, linked **to/with** centralised computers who nag them when they go too fast.

➡ See also 14.3 Word order: phrasal verbs, 15.4 Prepositions and 17.4 Adjectives + prepositions.

12.4 Ocean City   Listening & discussion

A   🔲 Before playing the recording, which students will need to hear more than once, allow everyone time to read the questions through and maybe pencil in some guesses.

Answers

1 120   18   380,000
2 300   2
3

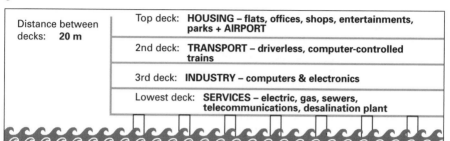

Distance between decks: **20 m**	Top deck:	**HOUSING – flats, offices, shops, entertainments, parks + AIRPORT**
	2nd deck:	**TRANSPORT – driverless, computer-controlled trains**
	3rd deck:	**INDUSTRY – computers & electronics**
	Lowest deck:	**SERVICES – electric, gas, sewers, telecommunications, desalination plant**

4 10,000   50   floating
5 water   adjusted
6 typhoons   storms   height above sea level
7 1 taxes
   2 liner
   3 outdoor
   4 storms   rainfall
   5 earthquakes

B & C   The discussion could last quite a long time if students get really interested in doing a presentation. If so, some written follow-up describing their scheme is recommended.

Transcript

Presenter: You've probably read one of those science fiction stories where a colony is established in space to solve the over-population problems on Earth. Well, a Japanese expert has come up with a scheme that sounds similar but which is apparently perfectly feasible using existing technology. But this colony is going to be in the middle of the ocean. Marilyn Evans has been finding out about it, haven't you?

Marilyn: Yes, one of Japan's biggest problems is, in fact, cramming its large population of something like 120 million into a very limited amount of space. Only 18% of the 380,000 square kilometres of its land can be used for living space, and in fact over three-quarters of its land area is mountainous and therefore it's uninhabitable, but now Kirohide Terai, who is Japan's leading expert on new technology, has set up a study group with some of Japan's most prominent industries. These include companies like Sony, Mitsui, Nippon Steel, NTT and Asahi, the TV and publishing group. Now, their answer is not the one that we'd imagine, a city in space. What they want to do is to build a vast steel metropolis 300 kilometres offshore in the Pacific Ocean. If it's a success, more identical cities could be built, each of which would be a completely self-contained habitat for about two million people.

Presenter: My word! And what would each of these floating cities look like?

Marilyn: Well, there'd be four decks, each five kilometres square with a gap of about twenty metres between each deck. Um…on the top deck, it's where people would live and work, there'd be housing, flats, offices, shops and entertainments, parks and…and probably an airport…er…to provide connections to the mainland, but of course y…you could go by ship.

Under that…um…on the next level down you'd have the transport system for passengers, which would be a computer-controlled driverless train system.

Er…below that would be the industrial zone, which would be lots of high-tech companies: computers and electronics and so on.

And on the lowest deck there'd be the services, there'd be electric and gas and sewers, and the telecommunications. And of course a…a desalination plant to convert the sea water into fresh water. And we'd have electricity which would be generated from…from wave power, from the movement of the waves, which would provide all the energy that the city would need. And the only thing that would need to be shipped in to support the community would be food.

The whole thing would be built on 10,000 hollow steel cylinders. They'd be 50 metres apart but in fact they…they wouldn't be resting on the ocean floor, but floating: this whole thing would be out in the warm waters of the Pacific where the sea is several kilometers deep.

Presenter: Yes, but wouldn't the…the whole thing sort of bob up and down in the waves? Every…everybody would be seasick!

Marilyn: No. No no no. Because in fact each cylinder would contain water to balance the weight of the structure, and the level of the water in each of the cylinders would be constantly adjusted by computers to keep the whole city floating in a…in a level, stable manner. In fact, there'd be no feeling of floating at all. It wouldn't be affected either by typhoons or storms because of its enormous size and because of its height above sea level. They've carried out tests in fact on…on models in water tanks, simulating the worst conditions imaginable and they've shown that it works.

Presenter: Yes, but surely the cost of something like that would be absolutely astronomical?

Marilyn: Yes, it would, you're absolutely right. And to build it would require 60 million tonnes of steel, which in fact is over half of Japan's annual production. The scheme would be financed by an offshore fund which…which offered tax benefits to investors. There'd be no tax to pay and the idea is that Ocean City would become a tax haven and a financial centre for the Pacific Region. I mean it would probably even replace Hong Kong.

Presenter: Yes, but who would want to live there? It sounds terrible to me.

Marilyn: Well, they're trying to make it as similar to the mainland as…as they possibly can, I mean not like an ocean liner. There'd be parks and golf courses, horse riding and swimming pools. And…er…of course, lots of outdoor activities because a big attraction for people living there would be the climate: Ocean City would be to the south of Japan, where the weather is warm and pleasant. And they've chosen a spot where there are…there are…um…few storms and not very much rainfall. Oh yes, and it…of course it would have one distinct advantage over living on the mainland in Japan.

Presenter: Oh really, what's that?

Marilyn: Well, there wouldn't be any earthquakes.

Presenter: I guess not, no! Well, thank you very much, Marilyn.

(Time: 4 minutes 50 seconds)

12.5 Suffixes

Vocabulary development

A   If in doubt about the definitions of any nouns, you should consult a dictionary. If there seem to be more words than you have time to deal with, ask everyone to pick out, say, twelve pairs of words to deal with.

Answers (These are associated abstract nouns or verbs – where no abstract noun or verb exists and a phrase or an unrelated word has to be used, these are *italicised*.)

administration – dictatorship   attack – hijack
serve drinks – moneylending/lend money   commute – compute
council – counsel/*advice*   demonstrate – *watch*   design – dine
employ/employment   fortune-telling/*tell fortunes* – storytelling/*tell stories*   housebreaking/*break into a house* – heartbreaking/*break someone's heart*   owning land – *like to be alone*   message – *travel*
mine – *being under age*   moonlight/moonlighting – ghostwriting/*write for someone else who is credited as the author*   pawn – *dealing in shares*
pay/payment   persecute/persecution – prosecute/prosecution
photograph/photography – choreograph/choreography
picnic – drug-trafficking/*traffic in drugs*   plumbing – *arrive late*
occupy the position before – follow   research – search
riot – *own*/proprietorship   *own/hold shares – own a house*
synthesise/synthesis – sympathise/sympathy
solve problems/deal with trouble – make trouble

archaeology – meteorology   cartoon – humour   chauvinism – feminism
conservation – philanthropy   guitar– telephone   opportunism – humanism
pharmacy – perfection   psychology – psychiatry   science – technology

➡ Here are a few extra pairs which might be discussed as a warm-up or follow-up to A.
auctioneer – mountaineer   brewer – reviewer   burglar – gangster
forefinger – fish finger   impersonator – operator   juror – insurer
part-timer – old-timer   perpetrator – commentator
viewfinder – reminder   well-wisher – publisher

B   Answers

contextualise   deafen   emphasise   familiarise   generalise   glamorise
harden   loosen   moisten   nationalise   ripen   sharpen   straighten
strengthen   subsidise   summarise   sweeten   sympathise   synthesise
thicken   tighten   victimise   visualise   widen

C & D   These follow-up activities give students time to decide which
words to memorise, and a chance to use them in sentences of their own
devising.

12.6   Robots

Background
Sir Clive Sinclair invented the pocket calculator, and was responsible for the
popularity of home computers in Britain, before the commercial disaster of
his £399 C5 electric one-person vehicle (a description of which appeared in
the first edition of this book). Many of his inventions have been brilliant and
innovative, but not great commercial successes. One of his more recent
ventures is the Zike, an electric bicycle. This article appeared in *The
Guardian*.

➡ Before they read the article, students might like to speculate about the
title: How soon do they think everyone will have a robot slave? What would it
be able to do?

A   Suggested answers
1   *daunt* – discourage   *progenitors* – creators   *deem* – consider to be
    triggered – set off   *founts of knowledge* – sources of information and
    expertise   *falling prey* – becoming vulnerable   *surrogate* – substitute
2   They will be able to design themselves and even reproduce, once they
    surpass human intelligence
3   By means of imports and automated production (by robots)
4   The complete expertise of an experienced person transferred into the
    memory of a computer and available on call to anyone at any time
5   Computers will have more patience and knowledge – and there will be one
    'tutor' for every child (and maybe no more jobs for teachers?)

➡ Before starting B, discuss the pun in the title of the letter as well as the
references to 'ruptured syntax'. After struggling with Sir Clive's article, your
students might appreciate this more!

B   Model summary

```
We will be able to consult computers for medical advice
and use them as ever-patient all-knowing personal
teachers. There will be fewer jobs, but great improvements
in education, enabling us to use our leisure time better
and for the appreciation of art, music and science. Robots
will do our menial household tasks for us — or maybe, if
they're so clever, they'll take over and themselves live
like the ancient Greeks, leaving humans to do the menial
jobs for them.
```

© Cambridge University Press 1993

12.7   The passive – 2   Advanced grammar

➡ The passive is used for a variety of reasons, including the following:

1 to dissociate speakers or writers from an unpopular decision or announcement
2 to give an impression of objectivity – especially in scientific or technical texts and in news reports
3 to give the effect of formality
4 to arouse sympathy for the victim
5 to describe actions where the people responsible are unknown, unimportant or irrelevant – or where it is obvious who did it
6 for variety – to make a change from using the active
7 when using the passive makes the sentence easier to read and its meaning easier to understand than a clumsy or inelegant active sentence – i.e. the passive is more concise

A   Answers (with some alternatives suggested)

1 is presented/introduced/scripted   was/were invented   are made/forced
2 were started   was used
   was found/realised/discovered   was increased   were added/used/introduced
   was found/proved
   be put
   being put/brought
   being equipped
3 be used/utilised
   be affected
   be built/constructed
   be shipped/brought
   be financed   be offered

Sentences rephrased in the active: (refer to the 7 points above for the effects)

1 TIME TO CRACK THAT TIMER
   Cartoonist and engineer Tim Hunkin presents the TV series.
   . . . in a time before anyone invented electronics.
   People's colleagues sometimes make them feel inadequate.
2 ELECTRONIC ANNOUNCERS
   The SNCF started experiments to find the perfect electronic announcer
      two years ago when they used the station . . .
   After trying out the voice at other stations they found that it increased the
      reassuring effect if the voices spoke in regional accents.
   They found that the synthesiser was more reliable and flexible.
   They will put the use of synthetic announcers into effect in the next few
      months.
   In the meantime, they are putting the voices into service elsewhere.
   They are also equipping ticket offices with automatic dispensers.
3 OCEAN CITY
   The Japanese can only use 18% of their land area for living space.
   Typhoons or storms wouldn't affect/have any effect on Ocean City.
   If Ocean City is a success, they could build more similar cities.
   The only thing that they would need to ship in would be food.
   An off-shore fund would finance it and the government would offer tax
      benefits to investors.

B Make a list of some real people on the board, taking suggestions from
the class. They could be well-known people from all walks of life, including
politics and entertainment.

C Answers

1 Those old magazines will have to be got rid of.
2 She's fed up with being looked down on.
3 The children were looked after by their grandparents.
4 This matter is being dealt with by my assistant .
5 All the survivors of the accident have been accounted for.
6 All breakages must be paid for.
7 Tony can't be relied on to finish the work on time.
8 The repairs will be seen to right away.
9 Her apartment had been broken into during the night.
10 Scientists are often looked on as experts.
11 It was pointed out to me that I was wearing odd socks.
12 He might be referred to as 'technophobic'.
13 Until permission for a new runway has been granted/given the airport
    can't be expanded.
14 Some people might be intimidated by electronics, but I'm not.

12.8 Thinking about the reader

A   Before embarking on the questions, encourage students to highlight vocabulary which they want to remember in the passage.

B   **Suggested answers**

1   'Humans do not always err. But they do when the things they use are badly conceived and designed.' (line 14)
    'To me it sounds like equipment failure coupled with serious design error.' (line 42)
    'While we all blame ourselves, the real culprit – faulty design – goes undetected.' (line 50)
2   Eighteen – it makes the text very personal
3   Three *wes*   two *ourselves*
4   None
5   Only once: 'Consider the phrase . . .' (line 26)
6   Fifteen – it raises questions that the reader is encouraged to think about
7   The first five questions are answered, three of them with quotes: 'Pilot error', 'Human error', 'Human error'.
    The following questions are all unanswered, until 'Human error?' in line 41.
    The last three questions are answered with 'While we all blame ourselves, the real culprit – faulty design – goes undetected.'
8   Very well, by involving the reader in the questions to think about and by encouraging the reader to share the writer's personal experiences, as if in a diary or personal letter
9   *Perhaps:* A reader who might share his concern for accidents at nuclear power plants and the causes of airline crashes; a reader who is sympathetic to his ideas, and is not an expert or a technologist; an educated person
10 a) He doesn't presuppose any technical knowledge and gives information that can be followed by any lay person; he is trying to interest and persuade the reader to share his views and not to give information
    b) *Perhaps:* Using the first person frequently, and having so many questions, makes a direct appeal to the reader, whom he assumes to be in sympathy
    Or, perhaps? The overloading of first person pronouns and questions makes an assault on the reader, beating us into agreement

C   The paragraph could be planned in pairs in class, but written up as homework.

12.9 Airport design and convenience Listening

⚠ Both parts of this listening exercise are quite challenging, and the recording is quite long. It's advisable to pause the tape at the places marked ★★★ in the Transcript to give students time to 'catch up' and note down their answers.

A ▣ **Answers**

1

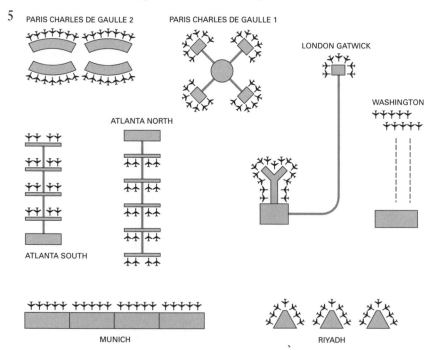

2 Congestion: sheer numbers of passengers
Transferring passengers between terminals and aircraft

3 To separate international passengers from domestic passengers

4 There are four terminals: you have to know which airlines and flights use each one – these change from time to time, too!

5

PARIS CHARLES DE GAULLE 2   PARIS CHARLES DE GAULLE 1

LONDON GATWICK

WASHINGTON

ATLANTA NORTH

ATLANTA SOUTH

MUNICH

RIYADH

B 🔲 Answers

1
Airport	Distance to city	Surface connection to city centre
Atlanta	15 km	rapid transit train *or* bus
Gatwick	45 km	direct train (30 mins)
Munich	30 km	direct train
Paris	25 km	direct coach *or* shuttle bus and train
Riyadh	35 km	taxi *or* limousine to major hotels
Tokyo (Narita)	70 km	direct train
Washington	40 km	fast bus

2 To Heathrow: the Underground stops at every station, not much room for luggage during the rush hour   To Gatwick: regular, fast trains

3 By train through the Channel Tunnel, avoiding airport delays

C   Follow-up discussion   The questions may need to be adjusted slightly if your students are frequent fliers – or if they have never even been to an airport. A good opportunity though, for those with experience to share it with the others.

Transcript

Presenter: These days aircraft technology is getting more and more sophisticated. A modern 747-400 can fly non-stop across the Pacific with only two people at the controls – it can take off and land in zero visibility and most of its operations are performed automatically. Once the flight path has been set, the computer changes course whenever necessary and can even bring the plane in to land. But we tend to forget that often more of the passengers' time is spent on the ground – at the airport.

The design of airports may not be so impressively high-tech as the aircraft, but airport design has been changing too, as Steve Farrell reports. So what do we mean by a conventional airport, Steve?

Steve: Well, Lucy, a conventional, traditional airport consists of a central terminal, usually a rectangular block with access roads for buses and cars on one side and aircraft parked the other side with gangways like tubes joining them to the terminal building. Some aircraft are parked further away and there are buses to take passengers across the tarmac to the stands further away. Most larger airports have separate floors for arrivals and departures so that incoming and outgoing passengers don't get in each other's way.

★★★

Presenter: So what kind of problems do airport architects have?

Steve: There are two big problems: the first is caused by the sheer number of people travelling by plane. You just have to go to any airport on a busy holiday weekend to see the difficulties that airports have to cope with. The numbers of flights leads to air traffic congestion, which in turn leads to delays in flights, which means that the number of passengers waiting for their flights to leave increases, and the airport has to cope with thousands of people waiting – many of whom are disgruntled and bewildered. You know what I mean?

Presenter: I certainly do!

Steve: OK, and the second problem is getting passengers between the terminal and the plane as quickly as... and as painlessly as possible. Being bussed to remote stands on the other side of the airfield is not popular with passengers and the ...

Presenter: Oh, I quite enjoy that part of it – it makes you feel as if you're really flying! Especially when you land somewhere warm and you feel the heat hit you as you walk down the steps!

Steve: Yes, but you have to remember that the principal source of airlines' income is business travellers – they want the minimum of inconvenience and they certainly don't want to get their hairdos and their suits wet if it's raining!

Presenter: Mm, I see.

★★★

Steve: Anyway, one way of solving these problems is to have two terminals: one for the time-consuming procedures involved with international flights and the other for the faster turnaround domestic flights. But a busy airport may need more than two of these, which means separating airlines into different terminals.

★★★

Heathrow, for example, has four terminals, each dealing with different airlines that operate to different destinations. It can be terribly confusing if you've forgotten which terminal to go to – especially as the airlines and destinations change from time to time. Terminal 4 is basically for British Airways intercontinental flights – but for some reason that includes BA flights to Paris, Athens and Amsterdam, but not the ones to Ankara or Tel Aviv. Oh, and Air Malta and KLM flights also leave from there.

★★★

Now, the problems I've described are solved in different ways in different countries. I went to Gatwick to meet Jane Holbrook, who is the author of *Airports of the World*, and I asked her to describe six different airports.

I began by asking her if Gatwick is a typical modern airport.

Jane: I'm not sure there is such a thing. It's untypical in that almost all flights from here are international, and both scheduled and charter flights use the same terminals. The South Terminal has its own railway station – so this means that passengers can keep on walking all the way from the train to their plane. It's connected to the more modern North Terminal, where we are now, by a driverless transit train. Passengers and their luggage – er... but no trolleys – are transported over here from the other side of the airfield. Here we are in a completely separate, self-contained concourse, with its own shopping centre, restaurants and other facilities.

Steve: Yes, it's very spacious with high ceilings and cool relaxing colours, designed to take away some of the frustration of hanging around, waiting for flight announcements, very 'user-friendly'. How does it compare with other airports around the world?

Jane: Well, similar to Gatwick is Hartsfield Airport, **Atlanta**, which is one of the busiest in the world. Here there are two huge terminals, North and South, but each has four concourses A, B, C and D for domestic flights. Oh, and the North Terminal also has an additional concourse for international flights. Here, as at Gatwick there are computer-controlled trains, but they go underground, so that the tarmac is free for planes, and these connect all the concourses together. Oh, and the design allows for more concourses to be added in the future. There's no remote parking of planes, all the aircraft are accessible from one of the concourses.

And then there's the new **Munich** Airport in Germany, which was also able to take advantage of having plenty of space at its disposal. It was built from scratch on a new site. Here there is just one enormously long linear terminal building, which is divided into four separate modules. Each of these operates independently. As in a traditional airport, you arrive on one side and the planes are all parked on the other side, each accessible directly from the terminal. Charter flights, er... domestic flights and international scheduled flights operate from different modules.

So, to take another example: Dulles Airport in **Washington**. As this airport has less traffic than the others, it can concentrate on convenience for the passenger, instead of processing huge numbers of people. Here the remote aircraft stands are serviced by 'mobile departure lounges': there's a central terminal building with a number of departure lounges adjoining it. Now, you go through the departure gate, take a seat in the departure lounge, the doors are closed and the whole lounge drives off to the other side of the airfield where your plane is parked.

Steve: Goodness!

Jane: Yes, it's pretty amazing, but of course it's only feasible at a relatively un-busy airport. Well, I mean, imagine mobile departure lounges zooming around at Heathrow . . .

Steve: Amazing.

Jane: Well, it'd just... total, total chaos!

Now next, let me mention King Khaled airport in **Riyadh**, Saudi Arabia. Here of course there's plenty of land available, and several of the terminals can be built side by side. Er... at present there are three entirely self-contained terminals, each with its own facilities and aircraft parked around it. And of course more terminals can be built alongside it if and when they're required.

So finally, **Paris** Charles de Gaulle Airport. This has two completely separate terminals. Terminal 1 is a circular central terminal surrounded by a road and this is connected by tunnels to several very remote-feeling 'satellites'– you check in in the central part and then you go off to find your plane at one of the satellites. Passengers stand on walkways which carry them down and under the road and the surrounding tarmac to the satellite, each of which has the aircraft parked around it.

Terminal 2 at Charles de Gaulle is completely different: this itself consists of four separate curved terminals: 2A, 2B, 2C and 2D, with road access on one side and planes parked on the other.

★★★

(Section B starts here.)

Steve: Mm, well, now a big question in most travellers' minds about airports is how to get from them to the city or vice versa. How long does it take, and how much time do you have to allow for traffic delays and suchlike?

Jane: Well, one factor is the actual distance from the airport to the city. But the main question in travellers' minds is: 'Is there a train?' If there is, you don't have to worry about traffic jams – and it's usually cheaper than a coach or taxi. For example, **Tokyo's** Narita Airport opened in 1978 and it's 70 kilometres from downtown Tokyo – but only since 1991 has there been a direct train connection. Before that it used to take up to four hours crawling through the traffic on the bus!

OK, well of all the places I've mentioned, **Atlanta** is the nearest – it's about 15 kilometres from the city and there's rapid transit system of trains connecting it to the city – and there are buses too. **Paris** Charles de Gaulle is only 25 kilometres from the city but the coach can take an awfully long time to get there in heavy traffic. The alternative of course is the train, but you have to get a shuttle bus to the train station, you can't just walk through to it like you can in **Munich** where there's a 30-kilometre journey to the centre and it's relatively quick and easy. **Riyadh** Airport is about 35 kilometres from the centre but there you have to take a taxi or... or there's a 'limousine' service to the major hotels – of course if your hotel isn't one of these... er . . . Now, **Washington** city is over 40 kilometres from the airport but there is a fast bus connection called the 'Washington Flyer' to take you there – again of course in heavy traffic it can get held up.

Steve: And how does **Gatwick** compare with these?

Jane: Well, although it's furthest of all from the city centre – and we are 45 kilometres from Central London – there are non-stop trains from Victoria every 15 minutes and it only takes 30 minutes to get here. And there are trains from other parts of the country too, which really means that it's very quick and very easy to get here.

★★★

Steve: And it's certainly quicker than getting to Heathrow because the Underground trains stop at every station on their way there. And I don't recommend carrying luggage on the Underground during the rush hour!

Presenter: That's right, but there's going to be a fast rail link one day soon, isn't there?

★★★

Steve: Yes. Still, if you want to get from London to Paris or Brussels, it'll still be quicker to take a train all the way, through the Channel Tunnel, than to travel out to the airport and find yourself delayed there for a couple of hours!

Presenter: Steve Farrell, thank you.

Steve: Thank you.

(Time: 11 minutes)

12.10 Modern design

➡ If possible, get everyone to do some research before the lesson, perhaps by assigning the Activities in A to each student in a previous lesson, so that A and B can be done in one go.

A ▐▐ Student A looks at Activity 11, Student B at 27 and C at 40. Each activity contains a list of questions to consider and to discuss with their partners.

B & C These are best done after a break, so that students have time to think about the issues raised in A, unless some research has been done earlier, as suggested above.

12.11 Give + take

A Answers

GIVE advice to someone   an answer   an explanation   encouragement evidence   permission   someone a kiss   someone a lift   someone a ring someone a shock   someone some help

TAKE a photograph   an interest in something   issue with someone a liking to someone or something   part in something   pity on someone pride in something   your time over something

B Suggested answers

1 assume   put up with hardships as well as easy times   start
2 be resentful   accepted it without resentment   put his side of the argument as well as I did
3 surprised   accepted
4 liked (only used in the passive)
5 deceived   revealed what was supposed to be secret
6 absorb
7 show your feelings by attacking   raise the matter
8 invite out   help you stop thinking about your problems
9 imitate/mimic   removes   has no patience left
10 raised an objection   be so familiar with him that she didn't appreciate him

C Answers

1 took   away
2 taking down
3 given over to
4 take out
5 taken on   taking   out   take   off
6 take back
7 taking over
8 have given   up   take up

D   This is probably best set as homework.

13 Relationships

A   Treat this warm-up discussion as the kind of conversation about photographs that students will encounter in the exam Interview.

B   [cassette icon] **Answers**

TRUE: 2   5   6   8   9
FALSE: 1   3   4   7   10

Transcript

Presenter: First of all we asked Anne if she had a best friend when she was younger.
Anne: Well, I had a few different best friends a... and as far as I can remember, i... it was a big moment in your life when you were at school when you decided somebody was going to be your best friend, do you remember that? And you'd... um... you'd sort of build up to it and then you'd... you'd say, 'Will you be my best friend?' – this had great significance. And then after a while you'd get fed up with them and you'd think, 'I'd rather like to be *her* best friend instead.' So you'd chuck this person, I mean, you know, really very cruelly quite often. And then you'd find somebody else and you'd say, 'You be my best friend, because I don't like *her* any more.' I think it caused an awful lot of hurt, looking back on it, people got quite upset. Um... so I had, I don't remember, maybe two or three different ones throughout my school career. And in fact there's one girl who I went through my whole school life with from the age of four till I was eighteen... um... including changing schools and we weren't best friends at all, but we now know each other and get on really well.

Presenter: Mike is from Texas. Did he have a best friend at high school?
Mike: I had a best friend at school, his name... his name was Nelson Christianson... um... but... er... understandably he insisted that everyone called him 'Buzz'. The thing about Buzz was that he was kind of ahead of all of us in a lot of ways. He... er... he wasn't much of an athlete, except at one sport... er... you may not, may or may not know, in American high schools wrestling is a big deal, and not the kind of wrestling you see on TV, this is amateur wrestling which is a very hard sport. For some reason, this very gentle guy was absolute king at this... very tough sport.

But I guess the main re... thing that Buzz was ahead of us in was politics, because we were all very conservative really but Buzz was one of the first people in my school to go out and march in a civil rights demonstration and gradually we all were pulled into that and gradually pulled into having some kind of political awareness but he was the first. And we all thought he was terribly brave, or stupid, because we thought, 'Well, jeez, what happens – suppose you get arrested, Buzz?' and he said, 'That'd be great!' Um... but I haven't seen him since high school – I have seen him once, not long after I was married – but I'd really like to see him again.

Presenter: What about Rupert? Did he use to have a best friend?

Rupert: Well, nobody really springs to mind from my school days as a best friend and I think the reason for that probably is because I came from quite a large family and I had plenty of brothers and sisters, so I didn't really feel the need to have a best friend or... I seem to get on with most people quite well but... um... I suppose my best friend, or best friends, are still my family. They were then and they are now. Um... of course there've been fights, bust-ups, like with any relationship if you care for somebody, you know, it's not all smooth sailing. But... um... yeah, my family were my best friends and they still are.

Presenter: Next we asked Elaine to tell us about her best friend.

Elaine: One of the first things that attracts you to a friend is if you share a sense of humour. I had a terrific friend when I was in the sixth form, and we'd been thrown together really because we were the only two people who'd chosen to do German 'A' level. And there was a very dishy, and very nice, German teacher, so we were sort of brought together giggling and blushing in that... in that way. But she was somebody who was always... er... very unashamedly herself, she would never change according to who she was talking to... um... she treated everybody exactly the same. I always admired her straightness, and she was also good at everything, but never conceited and just always so self-deprecating and funny. Um... the other thing that was quite odd between us is that she was very tall and blonde and I'm very small and dark, and you'd often hear people whistling the theme from Laurel and Hardy as we walked down the street! I wonder sometimes if opposites do attract in that way. She now lives in Australia and has a family but we do keep in touch. And she came over to see her family this year and she is just the same – she even looks the same as she did when she was a schoolgirl, right down to the hairstyle, she's still lovely.

Presenter: David went to boarding school, where he had two very good friends. Why was it that they got on so well together?

David: I think partially attraction of opposites, partially because they, both of them, attracted bits of me. Um... so friendship is a very complicated thing because sometimes you're friends with people who are alike you and sometimes you're friends with people who are unlike you. If you're too alike you tend to clash, so I think there are bits in other people that you enjoy that make you become friends. And sometimes, I think with friendships, together you make up qualities that neither of you have, and so together you're more of an entity than you would be if you were just er... the two of you.

Presenter: Did he have any enemies as a boy?

David: I can think of one person because he seemed so incredibly tough, almost enjoyed making other people suffer. He was an enemy then, I mean think I would be much more understanding now but he was very much an enemy then, very much an enemy, and I used to dread him coming along because it would mean there'd be some kind of warfare between us.

Presenter: And what about as an adult?

David: It's harder to say in adult life because I think one of the things I enjoy about being an adult you have a much more rounded view, and what you are trying to do is to put yourself in somebody else's position, so even if you don't agree with it, what you're actually trying to do is find out where they're coming from. So I think I've had short-term differences, but I'd be fairly pushed I think now to think of X or Y actually as an enemy... er... because I'm always hoping that... er... we could be friends – or even agree to differ.

(Time: 6 minutes 40 seconds)

C   You might like to add this extra question to the discussion – but not if any members of the class are each other's 'enemies':

• Do you have/Have you had any 'enemies'? Describe them and explain why you dislike/disliked them.

E   This part doesn't need to be done immediately after D – if it's more convenient it can be done in another lesson.

Students will probably need to hear the recording once right through to get used to the voices before they attempt the questions.

Answers

1 despondent/timid
2 jaded
3 anxious
4 businesslike/impatient
5 sarcastic/annoyed
6 timid

Transcript

Presenter: Now listen to each speaker and select a suitable adjective to describe their mood or tone.

(The Presenter gives the number before each speaker.)

Speakers: Well, good evening. Thank you both for getting here on time and for waiting so patiently. Everyone else seems to be rather late, or maybe they haven't been able to make it. Anyway, we'll make a start I think, and if any of the others do come we can always fill them in on what's happened so far, can't we. . .

(The exact words used vary slightly from speaker to speaker.)

(Time: 2 minutes 30 seconds)

13.2 Family life

Background

Ian McEwan (b. 1948) is well-known for his short stories and novels which explore the slightly sinister and bizarre world of people who are leading seemingly normal lives. Particularly recommended are *The Child in Time*, *The Comfort of Strangers*, *The Innocent* and *Black Dogs*.

The Cement Garden is a disturbing story about a brother and his sisters who, after the death of their father, keep the death of their mother secret from the neighbours, and go on living as a family.

(See p. 178 for information about Gerald Durrell, and p. 192 for information about Paul Theroux.)

A Answers

1 The first is from *My Family and Other Animals*, the second from *The Cement Garden* and the third from *My Secret History*
2 *For discussion – the second seems to be the most intriguing – but the first is more amusing*
3 They are all told in the first person ('*I*'); they are about events that happened when the narrator was young (10, 13, 15); the narrator seems to be an independent sort of child
4 The first extract is the only humorous one
   The second extract is full of foreboding and menace, with its references to killing, death and ghostly faces
   The third extract is more philosophical and the narrator is analysing his own character
5 In the first extract, the narrator was ten years old: he has a good sense of humour
   In the second extract, the narrator was thirteen years old and though still a child in his ways, wished he could be more grown-up and fit in with adult male society
   In the third extract, the narrator is a loner and an outsider, who up to the age of fifteen kept his second life concealed; he was a dreamer and, at fifteen, lonely
6 The family 'took over' the book as he wrote it – their personalities were too strong for him to control, even when sitting alone writing   They behaved strangely
7 He probably had nothing else to do and was bored   He wanted to appear older so that he could relate to the driver and his mate
8 Poor people are not regarded as full members of society – they are outsiders

9 In the first extract the narrator regards his mother and brothers* and sister as amusing characters and as his equals, even though he was considerably younger than they were at the time
In the second extract, the narrator didn't like his father (perhaps feared him), describing him as 'irascible' and 'obsessive'; we don't know if his mother was living; we don't know about his relationship with his sisters
In the third extract, no members of his family are mentioned

(* Leslie is a brother.)

B As with 13.1 D, ask the class to suggest which are the most important features from the list – and which are the least important.

13.3 As the saying goes ...   Grammar review

A These sentences contain structures that have been reviewed in previous Grammar review sections. Questions based on proverbs like these are unlikely to come up in the exam.

Suggested answers

2 Someone who helps you in a difficult situation is a true friend. (unlike a *fair weather friend*)
3 When there is a quarrel, both parties are responsible.
4 Absent friends are quickly forgotten.
5 When people are parted from each other they grow to appreciate each other more.
6 After someone has helped you, it's only fair to do something for them in return.
7 What really counts is what you do, not what you say.
8 The world is full of many different kinds of people.
9 I believe in being tolerant and allowing others to do what they want to do.
10 If you want something badly enough, you'll find a way of achieving it.
11 A remark that is made jokingly may contain hidden truth.
12 You couldn't have foreseen what would happen.
13 Family relationships are stronger than other relationships.
14 A son tends to behave in the same way as his father.
15 Sooner or later everyone falls in love, but they recover from it eventually.

B It might be interesting, particularly in a monolingual class, to compare these English proverbs with proverbs in the students' own language.

13.4 Husbands and wives   Reading

Background

Tom Sharpe (b. 1928) is well-known for his comic novels, several of which are about the technical college lecturer, Henry Wilt. Sharpe himself used to teach at 'the Tech' in Cambridge. Among his other books are *Riotous Assembly*, *Porterhouse Blue* and *Blott on the Landscape*.

   In *Wilt*, Henry Wilt is suspected of murdering his wife after she has mysteriously gone missing and he has been seen dumping a life-sized inflatable doll in a building site hole . . .

Nigel Williams (b. 1948), also a comic novelist, has also written *Jack Be Nimble*, *Witchcraft* and *They Came from SW19.*

   The Wimbledon Poisoner humorously describes a series of murders which are committed in Henry Farr's suburban road – but not by him. Mrs Farr is not one of the victims. (Edgar Lustgarten used to present a TV series about famous murders.)

B   Answers

1 Mrs Wilt
2 Clem, the dog
3 A small house (semi-detached)
4 Because he was a pedigree dog
5 Because he was not wealthy
6 He daydreamed
7 Losing his wife   becoming rich   becoming powerful and influential
8 He tended to lose them
9 He teaches (we can infer this from his wish to be Minister of Education – the Tech is the local Technical College, or college of further education)
10 A contrived accident – or murder
11 It seems to depersonalise her, making her seem less like a character in her own right, perhaps
12 It emphasises his strange-sounding name, reminding us of *wilting flowers*, perhaps

C & D   These are questions for discussion.

13.5 Underlying meanings   Vocabulary development

A   Suggested answers

yoga exercises – middle-class? women rather than men? keeping fit? dieting?

a semi (semi-detached house) – less well-off people, suburbs, not as small as a
   terrace house or a flat but smaller than a detached house
Rovers and Mercedes – better-off people? middle-class?
an itinerary – route provided by guide or travel agent, business travel,
   planned route
a pilgrimage – religion, visiting religious sites
parried – boxing, martial arts, fencing
the Tech (technical college) – further education? lower level than a
   university? students on sandwich courses? less motivated students ?
fulfil his latent promise – children or students who have so far underachieved,
   letters of reference for less able students

B   Suggested answers

cautious	*obedient*
difficult	*dreamer*
frank	*gullible*
humble	*brats*
lazy	*frivolous*
moody	*naive*
impractical	*mistake*
pessimistic	*solemn*
spy	*stubborn*
studious	*mock*

C   Students should do this quite quickly, noting the first words that come
to mind.

D   This too should be done quite quickly.

As a variation: tell everyone that their aim is to return to the original word as
quickly as possible – the first to do this wins the round! It may be necessary
to demonstrate the game first with one of the students.

13.6   The narrator   Writing skills

Background

Margaret Drabble (b. 1939) is one of Britain's best-known writers. Her
books, though touched with humour, seriously address the consequences of
social change upon families and couples. Her best-known books include: *A
Summer Bird-Cage, The Waterfall, The Needle's Eye, The Middle Ground,*
The *Radiant Way, A Natural Curiosity* and *The Gates of Ivory.*
   The Millstone is about a young woman who has an illegitimate child, a
story which is both funny and sad.

A   Suggested answers

1   She seems to be very aware of her shortcomings, and doesn't take herself seriously. She admires her own confidence and wishes she were braver.
2   ... *if I remember rightly* ... *I do remember rightly* ...
3   Humorous; self-mocking/self-deprecating; literate, educated and possibly slightly pretentious (the use of words like *au fait, ascertain, our destined hotel*, etc.)
4   She presumably signed her own name in the hotel register: a puritanical receptionist may have refused to accommodate an unmarried couple, or at least asked embarrassing questions.

    The fact that she is 'still not married' is 'a fact of some significance. The mixture of confidence and cowardice is going to play an important part in the story.

    The story is probably going to contain a series of misfortunes, described with wry humour. *Having a millstone round your neck* means having a problem that won't go away. (Rosamund has an illegitimate child.)

B   Suggested answers

Using the first person means that the narrator can legitimately be expected to know everything about her own emotions. It makes the story more personal and is rather like a confession or diary. A third-person narrator wouldn't normally be expected to know so much.

➡ Compare this version – the details at the end of the first paragraph would almost certainly be omitted in a third-person narrative:

> Rosamund's career had always been marked by a strange mixture of confidence and cowardice: almost, one might say, made by it. Take, for instance, the first time she tried spending a night with a man in a hotel. She was nineteen at the time, an age appropriate for such adventures, and needless to say she was not married. She is still not married, a fact of some significance, but more of that later. The name of the boy was Hamish ...
>
> Hamish and Rosamund had just come down from Cambridge at the end of the Christmas term: they had conceived their plan well in advance, and had each informed their parents that term ended a day later than it actually did ...

And, in 13.4, compare these rewritten versions:

> Whenever I took the dog for a walk, or, to be more accurate, when the dog took me, or to be exact, when my wife told us both to go and take ourselves out of the house so that she could do her yoga exercises, I always took the same route. In fact the dog followed the route and I followed the dog. We went down past the Post Office ...

I did not, precisely, decide to murder my wife. It was simply that I could think of no other way of prolonging her absence from me indefinitely.

I had quite often, in the past, when she was being more than usually irritating, had fantasies about her death. She hurtled over cliffs in flaming cars or was brutally murdered on her way to the dry cleaners. But I was never actually responsible for the event.

In 13.2, the use of the third person would make them sound less convincing, perhaps. It seems to be more amusing to view Wilt and Henry Farr through a third-person narrator's eyes, than to hear them speak for themselves.

C   This may be set as homework, but allow time for comparing paragraphs together in class afterwards.

13.7   Conditional sentences – 2   Advanced grammar

A   Answers

1 If it weren't for the children they would have split up by now.
   – *Fairly formal.*
   If it wasn't for the children they would have split up by now.
   – *Fairly informal.*
   Were it not for the children they would have split up by now.
   – *Very formal.*
   If they didn't have children they would have split up by now.
   – *Informal.*

2 If you should see Terry could you give him my regards?
   – *You're not very likely to see him* . . . (rather formal style)
   When you see Terry could you give him my regards?
   – *You probably will see him* . . .
   If you happen to see Terry could you give him my regards?
   – *You're not very likely to see him* . . . (informal style)
   If you see Terry could you give him my regards?
   – *You may see him* . . .
   Should you see Terry could you give him my regards?
   – *You're not very likely to see him* . . . (very formal style)

3 If you wouldn't mind waiting I'll let them know you're here.
   – *Please wait for a moment* . . . (very polite)
   If you don't mind waiting I'll let them know you're here.
   – *I know you have no objection to waiting* (maybe because you've just told me that you've got plenty of time) . . .

If you wait I'll let them know you're here.
– *You have to wait (and not be impatient)* . . . (not polite)

4 Had it not been for your help, I couldn't have done it.
– *Very formal.*
Without your help I couldn't have done it.
If it hadn't been for your help I couldn't have done it.
If you hadn't been so helpful I couldn't have done it.
– *Fairly informal.*
I'm glad you helped me, otherwise I couldn't have done it.
– *Very informal.*

➡ They would *all* be easier to understand with commas separating the clauses.

B   Suggested answers

1 If you'd like to take a seat, I'll bring you some coffee.
2 Had they not been incompatible, their relationship might not have been doomed.
3 Should I miss my connection, I'll try to call you to let you know.
4 But for their parents' objections, they might have got married.
5 If you should have time, I'd like you to come and see us.
6 Had there been less traffic, we wouldn't have been (so) late.
7 If she were to tell him she is leaving, it would upset him.
8 Were it not for their wonderful relationship, they might not have decided to get married.
9 If it weren't for her patience and loyalty, she would have left him by now.
10 Without working hard at a relationship it's not likely to last.

C   These sentences may be fictional if students don't wish to write about their personal relationships.

13.8   Points of view   Interview practice & composition

A   The complete picture is on the next page – the one in the Student's Book shows a part of this.

B   Student A looks at Activity 12, student B at 29. They have different paintings by Edward Hopper to describe.

C   And finally one of the pictures (from Activity 12 or 29 or page 202) becomes the basis for two narratives.

Edward Hopper: 'Nighthawks', 1942

14 Earning a living

A & D   Note that the questions to discuss in both these sections are rather similar. You might wish to postpone the discussion in A until after the listening exercise in C has been done.

B   **Answers** (Some other possible answers are given *in italics*, which don't appear in the list in the Student's Book.)

1 shareholders   investors   institutions   directors
2 subsidiaries   multi-national/*major*   headquarters/*head offices*
3 monopoly   competition
4 manufactured   components   assembly line
5 jargon   product   price   place   promotion
6 personnel   welfare   training   employees/*staff*
7 salary   expenses   commission
8 bankrupt/*broke/bust*   plant/*factory*   redundant

A   As this article is very long, encourage students to read it through before the lesson. Some preliminary discussion about foreign exchange dealing might be wise before discussing the questions. Finding the *first* mention of each of the women interviewed will make it much easier to make sense of the article.

B   Answers

slip through your fingers – a) *get lost*
thick-skinned – b) *not easily hurt*
fail to make the grade – a) *don't perform well enough in their work*
They don't carry passengers – a) *You have to pull your weight*
vying with each other – a) *competing with each other*
wining and dining – a) *taking them out for an expensive meal*
the gung-ho macho atmosphere – a) *warlike male-dominated atmosphere*
a tough nut to crack – b) *not easily dominated*
changed hands – a) *been bought and sold*
the modest clutch of diamonds – a) *discreet diamond necklace*

C   Answers

1 bring buyers and sellers together
2 12
3 40
4 don't need to be
5 in a few seconds
6 sometimes
7 easily get angry with each other
8 several competing banks
9 can be more charming
10 not well liked
11 she has lived among males all her life
12 Teresa

D   This discussion takes up some of the themes of the article, including making money on the stock exchange and in the money market.

E   ⚏ Student A should look at Activity 7 while B looks at 46. Each Activity contains a spoof advertisement for a get-rich-quick scheme. After reading it through they should explain the scheme to their partner and decide what its shortcomings might be.

14.3   Word order: phrasal verbs   Grammar review

A   Point out that the lists contain mostly verbs that students are already familiar with. They should highlight and look up any unfamiliar ones.

⚠ Some phrasal verbs can be transitive or intransitive, depending on their meaning:

> *I told him to **clear out**, but he refused to leave.*
> *I told him to **clear out** his room because it was so untidy.*

clear out (*go away / make tidy*)   drop off (*deliver / fall asleep*)
look up (*use reference book / raise your eyes*)   miss out (*not include / be unlucky*)   pay off (*make payment / succeed*)   pick up (*lift / improve*)
turn up (*make louder / arrive unexpectedly*)   work out (*calculate / keep fit*)

Answers

1 a) shop around
   b) had worn off
   c) spoke up

2 a) pay it back/pay you back
   b) won over
   c) had left him behind
3 a) saw them out
   b) show her around
   c) invite her/Pam out
4 a) missing out on
   b) checking up on you
5 a) came up against
   b) leading up to
6 a) look into it/the matter
   b) part with his money
   c) stands for

B Answers

1 tear it up   pay up
2 dream up   explain it away
3 hand in   talk him out of it   stay on
4 stick up for me/sort things out
5 grew out of it
6 trade it in
7 wait up for me
8 climbed down
9 cracking down on
10 caught out!

14.4 No job to go to
Questions & summary

A   This exercise concentrates on using the context to work out meaning and references. Ideally, the article should be read through at home before the lesson – exercises B and C could also be done beforehand and discussed in class.

B   Answers

din – noise, row   *suburb of a London suburb* – anonymous district
discards – throws away   *elaborate myth* – complex fictional story
season ticket – monthly (or yearly) rail ticket
fast-dwindling – becoming less and less   *dole* – unemployment benefit
a precarious triumph – an unsure, unsafe victory
simplistic attitudes – views which are easy to understand and explain
camaraderie – a feeling of friendship within a group

C   Students should put a (ring) round the pronouns in the places they occur in the passage (or highlight them in a different colour).

Answers

line 52 – the two ex-colleagues   line 54 – the two ex-colleagues
line 57 – Dick and Jean   lines 79 and 80 – the gas and electricity people
line 101 – the friends of the person he bought a drink   line 115 – passers-by
line 121 – the two women on the seat   line 125 – dogs
line 152 – the down and outs   line 179 – people who stop for a chat
line 197 – their wives   line 197 – everyone in the cinema

D   Model summary

```
Dick begins his day as if he were going to work, catching
the 8.15 train to London. After a slow walk along the
river from Waterloo Station, he sits in the park for a
while, killing time. He goes to the public library, where
he reads the day's newspapers. At lunchtime he's in a pub,
making a single half pint last as long as possible and, on
a lucky day, he might get included in being bought a round
of drinks. After lunch he eats his sandwiches on a park
bench, watching the pigeons and the people. Some days he
goes to the betting shop or to the cinema. Finally, at the
end of the day, he catches the train home to his
unsuspecting wife.
```

© Cambridge University Press 1993

E   Follow-up discussion   If this generates a lot of interest it could form the basis for a short written assignment, or even a full composition.

14.5   Collocations: verb phrases   Vocabulary development

A   Answers

waves break   traffic lights change   a boy's voice breaks [becomes deeper]
a storm breaks   the weather can break   your mood can change   day breaks

B   Answers

You can **break** . . .   a promise   a world record   an appointment (?)
crockery   someone's heart   a habit   the ice   the law
the news to someone   the silence   your leg or your arm

You can **change** . . . a promise (?) a world record (?) an appointment
a tablecloth crockery direction gear money the bed or the sheets
a habit (?) the law the subject trains your clothes or your shoes
your mind

C Answers

You can **follow** . . . an argument a line of argument a route or
directions a story a trade or profession advice or instructions
someone's example or their lead an idea a football team a football match
the fashion or a trend

You can **lose** . . . an argument control over something face heart
a football match interest in something the thread of a story
track of something weight your job your nerve your temper
your voice if you have a cold your way or bearings

D Answers

1 ask lend lifting
2 open supply
3 cancel placed changed
4 pay raise collect
5 offered resist accept lose
6 leads running strike
7 throw drawing bear
8 raised reached hold

➡ Idioms and collocations with these verbs have been dealt with in earlier
units: *keep* & *hold* (2.9) *make* & *do* (4.10) *come* & *go* (6.11) *bring* & *get*
(8.12) *put* & *set* (10.11) *give* & *take* (12.11)

14.6 A good ending   Writing skills

A Thanks to: André Meier, E.H. Limpens, Helmut Binder and Arianna
Tommasini for allowing us to use extracts from their work.

Comments

1 Not very appealing – it seems the applicant stands to get more from the
   arrangement than the employer. It's unwise to write this, even if it may be
   true.
2 Seems fine, but maybe lacks a final punch
3 This is OK, though maybe rather dull
4 This is nice, though possibly rather pushy

B   Comments

9.4   . . . And that is why I'm giving up.
– *Short and punchy, sums up the whole of the article*

9.7   . . . Once you start to think strategically, you begin to take control of your studies rather than letting them swamp you.
– *Sums up the whole article, but rather wordy perhaps*

9.9   " . . . The problem with a free school is that you get so attached to it that you don't want to leave."
– *Nice human touch, ending with interview. Ends the article on a high note*

12.2   . . . Hunkin hopes the series will help to assuage fear or ignorance of technology by looking at the frustration of ownership and the human stories of the inventors.
– *Rather lack-lustre ending: something more snappy would leave the reader feeling more satisfied or interested*

12.6   . . . The construction of a vast, man–created world in space . . . we may begin in earnest . . . the colonisation of the galaxy.
– *Terribly verbose and difficult to grasp, even though the ideas are exciting*

14.2   . . . "If you thought in millions, you'd never do this job," she adds, fingering the modest clutch of diamonds at her throat.
– *Nice contrast between millions, modest and diamonds, bringing out the huge sums of money involved and Teresa's good salary*

14.4   " . . . I'm not alone you know."
– *Splendid open-ended final sentence, leading us to imagine ourselves in the same situation, and look around us at the people in the streets with fresh awareness*

The least effective seems to me to be 12.2, but there are several contenders for 'most effective'.

C   Please make sure enough time is allowed for this part – it's the most crucial part of this section. Students should not only *discuss* improvements but *write* them.

➡ If the members of the class don't have their recent compositions with them, postpone this activity until the next lesson and impress upon them that they *must* bring them along next time.

14.7 Revision and exam practice Advanced grammar

This section revises some of the grammar points covered in Units 7 to 13.

A Answers

1 There's a chance that you might get the job you have applied for.
2 He reminded me to arrive on time for the interview the next day.
3 I wish I had known that I had to/was supposed to write my name in block capitals.
4 According to the manager, the factory is going to close down.
5 It was never explained why she was asked to leave.
6 It was only yesterday that I read about the closure of the factory.
7 Had the government not given a subsidy, the factory could not have been built.
   Had there not been a government subsidy, the factory could not have been built.
8 I wouldn't be surprised if the company made a profit this year.

B Suggested answers

1 from being   experience
2 There is   would have   if   lost
3 I would get   were inadequate/insufficient
4 tend/seem/are known   wander   risk
5 seen/regarded/looked upon   fallacy/misapprehension/myth
6 Because of/Due to   never   had lost
7 It was/It took   admitted/realised   follow   lost
8 didn't   went to

14.8 Looking for a job? Listening & composition

A [cassette icon] Before listening to the recording, it's a good idea for students to look at the questions and pencil in any answers that they can guess.

Answers

Ticks beside: 1   5   6   7   9   11   12   13   14   15   18   20

B Follow-up discussion   Note that some of the points made in the recording do *not* apply to exam interviews.

C In the Student's Book the students have a choice of which title to write – but you may wish to stipulate which one they should attempt, depending on the age and experience of your students.

Perhaps bring some English-language newspapers into class, and do the 'job-searching' in groups. Then the planning can also be done by students working together.

However, you might prefer this to be more of a challenge for your students, where they have to do all the work themselves – as in the exam.

D This role play makes the letter-writing in C1 seem much more realistic. Make sure that everyone is aware that this is going to happen before they write the letter.

Transcript

Chairman: ... and... er... we've... er... we've discussed several ideas now and... and you've all had a chance to do some role play of interviews, so I... I think it's time now for our two experts to give some final tips. Er... Kerry, let's take the application form first, because that's the first hurdle, isn't it?

Kerry: Yes, yes, that is the first hurdle. Um... now... er... my suggestion may sound silly but... er... it's not. Um... what you should do is... is actually photocopy the application form and practise filling in the copy so that you don't make any mistakes... er... when you do the final version. Um... this helps to... and also type the final version... er... this will impress whoever's reading it and... er... always use the space provided, don't... you know, don't go on, don't exceed the space that you're... you're given, now this is important as well. Um... you may not know this but 95% of applicants are rejected on the basis... on the basis of the application form alone, it's very important. You see... um... people are so overworked, the selectors don't have time to read everything. Er... there... there may be 100 applicants for... for the job that you go after. Um... so they... they often skim the form, and they look for the important things... er... and the simple things: spelling, presentation and also vagueness, lack of precision.

Ann: Mm, yes. I agree with Kerry, um... but I would also stress that it is important to use words that actually show your interest in high achievement. Um... now, I'll explain what I mean: er... words like 'success', 'promotion'... er... 'ambition', 'responsibility'. It also helps if you've got something interesting or unusual to put on your form... um... this actually makes you stand out from the rest and it gives the interviewer something to talk to you about apart from anything else. Um... for instance, an adventurous holiday, a holiday job that you've done... um... an unusual interest you've got, as long as it's not too weird, you know, that sort of thing.

Chairman: Mm, yes, I see, thanks. Now, about the interview itself... er... we've emphasised already the importance for the interviewee to ask plenty of questions, not just to sit there and be the passive partner. Um... Kerry, what do you have to say about that?

Kerry: Yes, that's... that's very true. Always be positive, don't... um... be confident, don't undersell yourself and always do lots of homework about the company that interviews you, find out about it, about... everything you can about it: it... its activities... er... its... if it has any policies... er... that differ from other companies of that sort and its subsidiaries... er... even its competitors.

Ann: Mm, and the other thing to... to really be prepared for are some surprises at the interview. I've known all sorts of things happen, I've known applicants being asked to solve *The Times* crossword or sort through today's in-tray putting letters in order of priority. Er... the other thing that's quite common nowadays are group interviews with a few other applicants. Um... y... you might find that you're expected to spend a day with the personnel manager... er... having lunch with him, possibly even assisting him.

Chairman: Another surprise technique that sometimes happens is... um... to provoke the candidate, the interviewer insults him or... or gets up starts shouting or something like that. And well wh... what should one do if that situation arises?

Kerry: Well, I mean, it... it... it's pretty obvious: just don't lose your cool. You know, just... er... be... er... if you think about it, if... if you just keep it in your mind that that might happen, you'll prob... probably be all right but with most surprise techniques it's... it's impossible to be prepared for them, you just... um... have to learn to expect the unexpected.

Ann: Yes, that's right, yes. And of course, don't panic. The... the best way to prepare yourself is just to practise being interviewed. A... and as Kerry said it's vital to present yourself positively as somebody who's socially sensitive, sparkling, has a sense of humour, adaptable and intelligent – if all those things are possible!

Kerry: But... but if... er... if in spite of all the advice we give you, you... you keep losing out... um... it's always good to try the technique of creative job searching.

Chairman: Creative job searching? That's a new one on me!

Kerry: No, well, it's quite simple and you've probably done this sort of thing already. Decide on the kind of field that you want to work in and res... research it... er... do... do plenty of research and get in touch with the companies in that field and... er... oh, do... do everything you can: talk to people who work in... in these companies... um... anything to show your interest. If you can, get them to allow you to spend a day there to see what goes on and... um... who knows, in the end. . . .

Ann: They'll give you a job to keep you quiet?!

Kerry: No, but... er... if there's an opening, you'd be surprised, you'll be the person they think of to fill it.

Chairman: Kerry and Ann, that's a great help, thanks a lot... er... I think it's about time for coffee now, don't you?

Ann: Mm, good idea.

Kerry: Mm.   (Time: 4 minutes 50 seconds)

14.9 Good & bad   Idioms

In this section, and also in 16.12, there are plenty of idioms, but no phrasal verbs.

A Suggested answers

1 That is a difficult/impossible question to answer – or one that I'm not willing to answer
2 going to last/going to be useable for
3 reluctantly/unwillingly
4 in addition/extra
5 a favour
6 permanently
7 a restless/sleepless night
8 considered to be impolite/rude
9 deteriorated even more
10 to my advantage
11 completely useless   dishonourable person
12 is valid

B Answers

1 earn good money
2 a good deal of   a good talking to
3 in good time   makes a good impression
4 as good as her word
5 bad blood
6 as good as new
7 a bad leg/ankle/knee
8 in a bad way
9 have ('ve) a good mind to
10 put in a good word for
11 gave it up as a bad job
12 while the going's good
13 in good faith
14 in his own good time
15 a good job

➡ Some more idioms which your students might find useful or interesting:

make good the loss   *bad language*
make good = succeed   *give a dog a bad name*
the good old days   *a bad debt*
a goody-goody
all in good time = there's no rush
do more harm than good

15 Arts and entertainment

Background

The passage comes from the introduction to a history of the silent movie, published to accompany a TV series. The writer is an expert on the genre and he has arranged the rescreening of many silent classics in their original versions with live orchestral accompaniment. Silent movies died with the advent of the talkies, the first of which was *The Jazz Singer* in 1926.

A The stills show Ricardo Cortez and Greta Garbo, and Harold Lloyd.

B Answers

1 Because they were magic: they had the power to draw audiences into a story, and use their imagination
2 They think them charming and exotic, they feel nostalgic for an age of innocence
3 Because rival entertainments (TV, radio, etc.) are more accessible
4 Because they were made during a period of 'dedicated viciousness', against a background of war, slaughter, misery, disease, intolerance, starvation, gangsterism, etc.
5 To escape from a harsh reality
6 Reality
7 Word of mouth
8 Like a palace and a cathedral
9 Their reading was influenced (fan magazines), they chose clothes and furniture that they saw on the screen
10 They appealed to all classes, rich and poor
11 Because of the language barrier
12 A movie-goer in the heyday of the silent movie; the effect is to encourage the reader to share this enthusiasm

C Follow-up discussion   Perhaps ask everyone to say what they have 'learnt' from the passage, and if reading it has changed their opinions about silent movies at all.

15.2 Producing a film   Listening

A   This preliminary discussion will help students who know nothing
about film-making to gain knowledge from their better-informed partners.
You might prefer to have this discussion in larger groups or as a whole class.

➡ 🔲 As this recording is rather long, it's important to pause the tape at
the places marked with ★ ★ ★ in the Transcript. It may also be advisable to
pause the tape after the answer to each of the questions in D for students to
write their answers down and 'catch up'.

Answers

B   Ticks beside: 1   3   4   5   6

C   Ticks beside: 1   3   4   5 a) b) h)

D
1 tiny   low budget
2 car chases   sex   violence
3 period   Oxford   Switzerland   gentle   Victorian
4 selling point   comedy/comic
5 leaps/changes
6 difficult   studios
7 less
8 Venice   interiors
9 score/music

E
- He enjoys the work, and meeting interesting and/or famous people. He
  finds some aspects of travelling a chore, though he realises he is lucky to
  be able to go to places like Venice.
- He wants to go on making films in Britain, provided that the scripts
  remain uncompromised and aren't Americanised.
- He would stop working in films if the only way to finance them was by
  getting involved with criminals or dirty money.

Transcript

Presenter: What's involved in producing a film? That's the first question we asked
  Steve Abbott, co-producer of *A Fish Called Wanda* and other films.
Steve: It's very difficult to explain. It... and... and you can have the easiest job in
  the world if everything goes smoothly. I mean the... the nearest analogy one can

draw is that… is that you're if you like – a film will have a budget of X million dollars and… er… or X million pounds – and if you like you can consider yourself for the intensive period while that film is being prepared… er… shot and then made and delivered, you are responsible for effectively being the managing director of a company whose turnover is X million dollars. I think that's a decent analogy to draw. Basically, you're on the line for everything… um… and you… you're responsible for engaging everyone who works on the film, you're responsible for delivering the film to your financiers, you're responsible in the first instance for finding the money to make the film, you're responsible for ensuring that… that the… everything that you've agreed to do contractually is done, um… and you obviously engage a massive crew to do most of this for you on a day to day basis, but if they… if they make any mistakes, the buck will stop with the producer. I… I have to say I've worked, in the three films I've done as a producer, I've worked with a partner in each case, which helps share the load and gives you someone to… er… bounce this off.

I've been very fortunate because I've… I've worked with, in this short career, I've worked only with… sort of… writer-directors who… who… um… and therefore the films I've worked on have not been put together, as they sometimes are, by producers who are quasi-financiers themselves who can… who will, you know, the traditional Hollywood stereotype image of a big fat man with a cigar going out and buying the option to a book or play or whatever… going out and commissioning a writer to write, going out and then hiring the actors and… and so on, and making the deal with the studio is not the way that… that I've ever experienced working.

★★★

Presenter: *A Fish Called Wanda* starred John Cleese, Michael Palin and American actors Kevin Kline and Jamie Lee Curtis. It was an auspicious start to Steve's career.

Steve: The first film um… that I acted as producer on was… um… was… has turned out to be the most successful British film of all time in dollar terms worldwide… um… which was a comedy *A Fish Called Wanda* in 1987, and for years and years, for about four years, John Cleese was working with Charles Crichton who was the director, um… getting the script as fine-tuned as possible, not spending… not taking a penny from anybody, which would have been very… it would have been very easy at any stage to go to a studio and say, 'Give us a quarter of a million while we develop this film', that would have been fine for our… you know, for our bank balances, but would have meant that that studio, wherever they were, would have owned that script and would have been able to tell John how to write, and we wouldn't have had, in my… my view very strongly, in John's view very strongly, we wouldn't have had a… as good a film, it would have probably been compromised.

So we just spent however many years, four or five years, working not only – and this is really exceptional – not only working with the director and the writer who… who happened to be one of the actors, just getting the thing in as fine a shape as possible before looking for the money to make it, but also with the major cast. Er… there were four major stars in the film, and they were all part of that process, all unpaid for many years, which is rare and I think unique – um… I've not heard of another instance of a major feature film, certainly in the English language, being done in this way.

Er... so we had the film absolutely as ready as a film could possibly be, more ready than I suspect any film that's ever been presented to a studio for financing. Normally one would present an idea... er... a book option, you know, a play, a three-page treatment, a first draft or whatever – we presented a tenth or eleventh draft with a... all the players in place and we knew exactly, we'd budgeted the film, we'd scheduled the film, we knew exactly where we were going to find our crew, where we were going to shoot it and just left the studios – it was MGM that put up the money – um... in the position of basically saying Yes or No. They said Yes very quickly.

Presenter: Why was *A Fish Called Wanda* so successful?

Steve: Well, it's impossible to say. People went to see it. We... um... we thought it would do well, we will always say, all of us that worked on the film, will always say, 'It's because of the way we prepared it, and put it together.' It's because we knew what we were doing, we knew we wanted... we knew we didn't want to be bought at an early stage, we wanted to control as much of the film as possible. It's because we weren't arrogant enough to . . . When we first took the film in a rough form to America... er... we found that the Americans laughed in different places from where the Brits and, we suspected, the Europeans might laugh. We weren't arro... arrogant enough to just imagine that we could stick our noses in the air and ignore that, so we listened to what the American audiences were telling us, er... altered the film, played around with it a lot, kept on testing it, and... er... you know, I think... I think that together with the one ingredient that I'm learning more about but I'm not particularly qualified to talk about – the marketing of films – um... just meant that it worked, and took off, and took off enormously in the States and then... – which was the nicest and biggest surprise – and then repeated the success everywhere in the world where I think we expected to do well. But otherwise I don't know. It was a good film. It was funny.

★ ★ ★

Presenter: Steve's second film was written by and starred Michael Palin.

Steve: The second film I did as a producer was a film called *American Friends* which was a, by Hollywood standards tiny, by British standards low budget... um... British-made film with... um... a British crew and a... a good solid cast, um... and was very ambitious in as much as it was a... a period film set in Victorian Oxford and Switzerland, which had to have those locations and all of it... because it wasn't a traditional block-busting film, because it didn't have car chases in, because it didn't have sex in, because it didn't have violence in, because it was just a gentle Victorian love story, and the only selling point was Michael Palin, but Michael Palin . . . You've got to understand that Hollywood and the film world is not interested in making any leaps, Hollywood and the film world is very interested in Arnold Schwarzenegger being Arnold Schwarzenegger in every film and Sylvester Stallone be... playing... being Rocky or Rambo in every film. So had... had we been trying to raise the money for Michael Palin doing a comedy, or having chips stuck up his nose, people would have been happy to give us big cheques. Trying to do something which, again Michael had spent years and years refining and working on, um... was very very difficult. And it involved not literally... um... but... but... er... but certainly knocking at... at what in the film world would be considered as every door with the exceptions of the studios, because we knew it was never going to be a studio film, in Europe, Canada, Australia. And in the end it was a consortium for this tiny amount by film standards of just over 2½ million pounds in order to raise the money for this tiny film which we made under budget and made very well and which I'm very proud of, but the f... financing couldn't have been more diff... different or more difficult than... than *Wanda* or the film I'm just... just finishing off now.

Presenter: His latest film is another comedy, called *Blame It On The Bellboy.*

Steve: We've been the production company, they've given us all the money, we've engaged our British crew, cast the film, made it here – it... it all takes place in Venice, so obviously a lot of the... um... a lot of the shoot was in Venice – but made it with a British crew, done our interiors in England. And... um... and we're just finishing it off now. The picture's all set and we... our composer is – as we speak – is beginning to compose the score for the film.

★ ★ ★

Presenter: What is it then that Steve gets from being a film producer?

Steve: Oh, I... I enjoy the work. It obviously has its... has its rewards, you can... you can meet interesting or famous people and sometimes interesting and famous people with a great facility. Um... the travel becomes a bore rather than... rather than anything attractive or glamorous, but I suppose one does... one does travel. One can... one can get access to... to be able to shoot a feature film in... be able to have permission to shoot in St Mark's Square, places like this, as we've done this year, is... you know, the travel becomes a... a chore and you... you... I was ready, which I'll regret in a couple of years, never to have to see Venice again after working there and working hard there, but you know one shouldn't overlook that. It's more interesting than getting in a suit and getting on the 7.23 every morning and coming home on the 6.28 every night.

I've never been motivated by the financial rewards in it, and if I were then there'd be no question – I'd be living full time in Los Angeles and working there. If the... if the obstacles in the way are not insurmountable, I do want to carry on making films in this country. The things that I suppose would ultimately... have me leave the industry or stop me doing this would be if it became impossible on economic grounds to... to ever get any films made in this country, unless you compromised the script completely or allowed it to be Americanised or whatever.

I suppose the only other thing that makes me consider giving up the business is that sadly... um... there are a lot of crooks in the business and... er... so far I've managed to be able to avoid having to work with them. I suppose that would stop me working in films, if there was no way other than to compromise and have to deal in crooked ways or have to work with crooked people. The film business attracts them, I guess that was... I guess that's the attraction of the glamorous side of it. It means that dirty money, mafia money, crooked money, drug-laundering money comes... comes the way of... of films or becomes attracted by the glamour of films. And... if I found there was... the only way to carry on making a living as a film producer was to... was to become involved with that sort of side of it, then I would give up.

(Time: 11 minutes 30 seconds)

15.3 Show business

This section can be treated as a series of mock exam interviews. Arrange for partners to change between each part.

In the actual exam, candidates may be shown two or three photographs or passages and asked to comment on them, or to discuss the differences between them.

Candidates will be expected to cover more weighty topics, such as 'art', as well as more mundane topics, such as 'films'.

A   **⌘** *Photographs*   Activities 16 and 33 both contain stills from silent movies: one showing Gloria Swanson and Raoul Walsh and the other Gloria Swanson and Lionel Barrymore.

B   **⌘** *Passages*   Activities 14 and 31 each contain brief descriptions of two modern films: *Midnight Run* and *Working Girl*, and *Gorillas in the Mist* and *Twins*. They are from the in-flight entertainment guide within the British Airways in-flight magazine *High Life*.

C   **⌘** *Tasks*   Activities 15 and 21 contain a variety of questions designed to explore students' tastes in entertainment and the arts.

➡ Here is some more information about assessment to share with the students.

In the examination interview, candidates are assessed on their:

Fluency   Here the examiner is assessing the speed and rhythm of the candidate's speech, and whether the amount of hesitation would demand a lot of patience from a listener.

Grammatical accuracy   Here the examiner is listening particularly for basic errors.

Pronunciation of prosodic features   Here the examiner is assessing stress-timing, rhythm, intonation, linking of phrases, and whether comprehension is easy and pleasurable for a listener.

Pronunciation of individual sounds   Here the examiner is assessing whether individual words can be clearly understood.

Interactive communication   Here the examiner is judging whether the candidate can communicate effectively, again without demanding too much patience from a listener.

Vocabulary resource   Here the examiner is looking for gaps in the candidate's vocabulary, and whether they need to paraphrase frequently to express their ideas.

⫸➔

Each aspect is given an impression mark on a six-point scale (0 to 5), ranging from 'unintelligible' up to 'native-speaker standard'. The pass mark is around 18 out of 30: this score out of 30 is adjusted to give a final score out of 40, making Paper 5 equal in weight to Papers 1, 2 and 3.

➡ For a complete marking scale and further information, see *Cambridge Proficiency Examination Practice TEACHER'S BOOKS*.

15.4 Prepositions Grammar review

A Answers
1 beside/next to/by   with/next to
2 at   in   over   below
3 in   in   over
4 by   on/in   on
5 opposite   from   from   to   on
6 on   in   in
7 in   in front of   in   in   during
8 Besides   at
9 after   in   before
10 on   for   in/during
11 in   under   in   behind/in/on top of/under/next to
12 into   in   in   by/beside/next to/under   with   on

B & C   These sections are open-ended and present students with a challenge, rather than routine exercises. Students have to explain and describe the positions of the details of each picture, using prepositions, prepositional phrases and adjectives. It may be necessary to go through the rubric in the Student's Book to make sure everyone knows what they have to do.

NOTE: these activities may look slightly intimidating, but they are very enjoyable and do force students to 'stretch' their English. There are no 'correct answers'.

➡ Written follow-up   Write paragraphs, explaining how two or three of the illusions in B are created.

15.5 Composing music

A Preliminary discussion to introduce the topic.

B 🗗 **Answers**

1 b 2 c 3 b 4 c 5 b 6 c 7 a 8 b 9 c

C Follow-up discussion The 'downside' is perhaps this: many people who work have a hobby which allows them to forget their work and use other talents and energies. He has no 'escape' from his work.

Transcript

Presenter: From Bach to the Beatles, from madrigals to Motown, there have been people who have made a living out of writing music. One such is the composer of this particular piece . . .

MUSIC

Vince: My name's Vince Cross. I'm a musician, primarily a composer. I suppose my basic skill is as a keyboard player: synthesizers, pianos, even an organ on a good day. And that has led me in the 1980s and 1990s into composing because um... keyboards have become the staple instrumentation for contemporary music, whether that's pop or whether it's more serious. And I suppose now I make a lot more of my living from composing than I do from playing keyboards... um... perhaps because I'm in the end actually better at that.

Presenter: So who does he compose music for?

Vince: Sammy Cahn, the American songwriter, m... made a joke when he was asked... um... about songwriting, whether he thought up the words or the music first, and he said, 'First comes the phone call.' And it really depends on who phones me up and says that they need music to be written. That has very often been... er... people who require music for children in the past five to seven years, um... but it equally well be... could be for TV or radio commercials... er... for small-scale films... um... and recently for a TV series.

Presenter: Does he compose in a particular style?

Vince: No, I'm again... people have different strengths. Um... I'm no Mozart or Schoenberg or . . . By that I mean that I'm not the kind of person who's going to be an incredibly original composer who's going to do something new. Um... but I'm quite a good musical thief, in the sense that I can listen to a style of music and go away and come up with a piece of music that sounds quite similar to the style that I've just heard – again, whether that's pop or classical. So recently somebody said that they wanted some baroque music for a film about the Tower of London, and I went away and did that. Um... equally well if somebody says to me they want a piece of rock'n'roll... um... I would hope to be able to manage that. And sometimes I get odd requests, like for a Mexican piece of music, or... er... next week I have to do a particularly African piece of music. And that's good fun, it's a challenge for me to come up with something in that style. It's probably got my stamp on it, but... er... er... it's good.

Presenter: What for Vince are the rewards of his work?

Vince: I'm one of those people who's lucky enough to be able to combine their favourite hobby... er... with their way of earning a living... er... and when everything is going well of course that can be a great reward. Perhaps you lose something too, but I still think it's a... it's a pretty special way of being able to... to live is to do that. Er... the downside, the... the bad things about... er... being involved in music are that sometimes one works very long hours... um... and there is, as there is for all people who are self-employed, there's the pressure that you're earning your living really from the jobs you come up with, and therefore... um... nobody is paying you. Er... and of course if you're in a paid job there may be many days when... er... you may not be working very hard but you're still being paid for it. If I'm not working very hard I don't get paid for it most of the time.

Presenter: Most of Vince's work is commissioned, which means he's working to a client's brief. Does he ever get the opportunity to compose music for his own satisfaction?

Vince: Mm, I'm a songwriter really. And that means that I will tend to write my own lyrics as well as... er... music. And yes, I do do that. Um... it's a bit of an unpredictable pastime, because there are occasions when you wake up in the morning and you have an idea for a song and you write it. There may be months when you don't write anything for your own benefit at all. Um... it's often useful also to have people you work with, singers maybe, of whom you're fond, who will tend to inspire you to... to write things with them in mind. Um... and for the future, I hope to write musical theatre, and that's something that you can only write, generally speaking, because you want to. But the problem is to make enough time... er... to do that, and... um... that requires, generally speaking, that you've made a lot of money at something else and therefore you can take a month off and... and write at your leisure... um... but yes, I write for my own pleasure too.

Presenter: What is it that he gets out of composing? What is the personal satisfaction?

Vince: That's a *very* good question, and I think it's actually quite difficult to answer. Um, there are... there are a couple of things that come to mind immediately: one is that it's a very... it's a very physical sensation, and most of my life has been spent with ideas, um... university and... and I was a teacher for a while. There is something very physical, almost like making something with your hands, about writing a song. Um... there is something that you can hear, and you can actually look at if you've written it down, at the close of that. And I find that a rather nice thing. There is also I think in a lot of musicians something a bit obsessive, um... you're trying to achieve perfection in one particular area. Um... and maybe that's what a... an instrumentalist is doing when he's practising day after day. You think, 'How can somebody just practise the piano for eight hours a day?' Well, it's trying to get something right, um... and you've got to be obsessive. You've got to be very 'grooved', I think, to want to do that, and I recognise in myself that there is a bit of my personality that's like that.

(Time: 7 minutes)

15.6 Exam practice

The questions in this section are all based on genuine exam questions. It's advisable to discuss the annotated answers to questions 1 to 5 in A and 1 to 3 in B before students attempt the remaining questions.

A Answers

6 C will   7 B in   8 B rehearsing   9 B subsidy   10 D otherwise

B Answers

4 The show is expected to be poorly attended.
5 There's no question of me/my paying for the tickets.
6 Steve Abbott's previous film, before *American Friends*, was *A Fish Called Wanda*.
7 She was a fool to turn down the offer of free tickets for the opera.
8 It had never occurred to me to take up painting as a hobby.

➡ There are more 'annotated' examination practice sections in 16.5 and 16.9.

15.7 Guernica

A   This is a difficult passage. Consider it as a yardstick of your students' ability to get to grips with abstract ideas, and cope with an uncompromisingly erudite style and a plethora of unfamiliar vocabulary. If they can manage this, they can probably cope with anything that the examiners might throw at them!

The piece is taken from a history of twentieth century art, published to accompany a series of TV programmes. Robert Hughes is art critic of *Time* magazine.

B Answers

invective – verbal attack   *motifs* – symbols   *receptacles* – containers
archaic – belonging to the past/ancient   *bereaved* – people who are mourning the death of a relative   *paraphernalia* – pieces of equipment
ephemeral – impermanent/not lasting for long

C   These questions can be considered as a preparation for D.

Suggested answers

1 They believed that people would discuss the images in their works
2 From the mass media, particularly from television
3 Because war photography could show people the full horrors of war
4 Basically as a means of investment – rich people buy works of art in the hope that their value will rise
5 As wallpaper for the walls of the powerful: it is now completely without influence

D   Model summary

```
Before 1937, artists believed that they could influence
political thought, and even change the world. The
situation had changed by the end of the Second World War:
the photographs of concentration camps that were shown
proved painting could never have the same impact.
Nowadays, with art considered mainly as a form of
investment for the rich, its political effectiveness is
negligible.
```

E   Follow-up discussion   The role of art, and the role of the critic.

➡ The exam tips here are for discussion in class – either in pairs or in groups. Pool ideas if there are any further tips that members of the class come up with.

15.8 Conjunctions and connectors – 2   Advanced grammar

A   Answers

1 Despite not knowing much about art, I know what I like.
2 Besides painting in oils, she (also) paints watercolours.
3 Unless you go to the box office today, you won't get seats for the show.
4 Due to the illness of the tenor and soprano, the performance was cancelled.
5 Except for jazz I like all kinds of music.
6 As well as missing his wife, he was missing his children (too).
7 Like you, I didn't enjoy the film.
8 But for the soloist's wonderful performance, I wouldn't have enjoyed the concert.

B   Students may need some help with the following vocabulary items before tackling the text, which is another very demanding one:
   culpable = blameworthy   onerous = demanding   pine for = long for
   devoid of = not having/without   scruffy = not smart   lure = attraction
   collective = united

Answers (The words used in the original text are given first, but the alternatives are equally good.)

1 but   however   nevertheless
2 however   though
3 after all   nevertheless   believe it or not
4 even
5 incidentally   by the way
6 unless   even if   except if
7 and   besides being
8 while   and   moreover
9 when   whenever   while   by
10 When   If (?)
11 because
12 But   However
13 since   as   because
14 for example   for instance
15 although   but   however
16 in this one case   when this programme was on   in spite of its
    popularity

C   Suggested answers

1 Some people say that modern art is overrated and **in most cases** I do agree, but **all the same I find the work of Pablo Picasso really fascinating**.
2 **It is sometimes said** that artists lead a good life: their hobby is their profession, but **they may have trouble making ends meet if they can't sell their work**.
3 **On the whole** Hollywood movies are ephemeral, **but every so often** you see one that you can't forget.
4 **To some extent** watching television is rather a waste of time, **but now and then you do see worthwhile, interesting programmes**.
5 **As a rule** politicians are honourable, dedicated people, **but there are exceptions to every rule and there are some who are corrupt or dishonest**.
6 **Many people believe that** reading is a wonderful source of pleasure, **however some books are very badly written, and may not be worth reading at all**.

7 **To a certain extent**, people work because they have to, not because they want to, **but all the same many people do get a lot of satisfaction and pleasure from their work and their contact with people at work**.

8 **Generally speaking**, I enjoy all kinds of music **except for opera**.

15.9 Styles Writing skills

A **Suggested answers**

learned, very formal –15.7
neutral, straightforward –15.1

erudite, witty, flamboyant – 15.8B
informal, journalistic – 14.4

very long paragraphs –15.7
short paragraphs – 14.4

long paragraphs – 15.8B
medium length paragraphs –15.1

long, complex sentences –15.7
short and medium length
    sentences –15.1 & 14.4

long and short sentences – 15.8B

short sentences – none

B The most suitable 'models' would be 14.4 and 15.1, undoubtedly.

▰◣ Go through the passage *you* prefer and highlight the phrases *you* think would be most useful for your students.

➡ Again the exam tips are for discussion in pairs or in groups. Pool ideas if any more good tips come up during the discussion.

Of all the advice given, the most crucial is to **answer the question**.

15.10 Writing a narrative Composition

A I leave it to you and the class to decide which of the opening lines look most promising! And to decide what the next two lines might be.

B ▭ Student A looks at Activity 18, B at 35 and C at 42. Each student has a reproduction of *Past and Present, No. 1* in 35, *Past and Present, No. 2* in 18 and *Past and Present, No. 3* in 42. They were painted in 1858 by Augustus Egg.

Together, the three pictures tell a tragic story. The pictures illustrate the fate of an unfaithful wife (the husband seems to be reading her lover's letter in one picture). The woman tells her mother, who perhaps condemns her daughter or sympathises with her. Finally she is about to drown herself in the Thames, but perhaps she will have second thoughts. There is sufficient ambiguity in the pictures to produce several different versions of the story, and the groups will need to work out what happened before and after each of the scenes.

C   You might like to specify that this is written in exam-like conditions, without using dictionaries and within a time limit of about an hour.

➡ For more information on assessing students' compositions, consult *Cambridge Proficiency Examination Practice* TEACHER'S BOOKS. These include samples of real candidates' work with the marks they were given.

16 Mind and body

A   Warm-up discussion   Remind the students to note down any useful vocabulary that comes up in their discussion. Ask them what you'd call someone who always thinks they're ill: a *hypochondriac*.

B   Answers

1 consultant GP specialist
2 flabby plump stout
3 skinny slim thin
4 stress tension worry
5 fainted lost consciousness passed out
6 ache pain twinges
7 healthy living preventive medicine vaccines
8 a pain-killer a sedative a tranquilliser
9 capsules pills tablets
10 get better get well pull through
11 inflammation rash swelling *(some people, particularly hypochondriacs, might go to the doctor about any of these problems)*
12 catching contagious infectious
13 a check-up an examination a medical
14 fractured her wrist pulled a muscle sprained her ankle
15 alternative complementary fringe

C   Answers

1 psychosomatic *NOTE: Alternatives with incorrect spellings like 1 and 2 would not appear in the exam, so maybe they're a bit unfair in this kind of exercise.*
2 anaesthetic
3 unbalanced
4 allergy
5 gynaecologist
6 threw up
7 transmitted
8 eradicated
9 stomach
10 agoraphobia

16.2 Tricks of the trade

A Answers

1 b   2 c   3 a   4 d   5 c   6 c   7 c   8 d   9 b   10 d   11 c

B Follow-up discussion   You might want to postpone discussion of alternative medicine until you have done the listening in 16.4 Homeopathy.

➡ On the cassette there is a collection of 'doctor, doctor' jokes for you to share with the class, just for fun really. In some of them the 'doctor' is a psychiatrist, one assumes.

Transcript

Presenter: Here are some 'doctor, doctor' jokes.

Patient: Doctor, doctor, I keep thinking there's two of me.
Doctor: One at a time, please.

Patient: Doctor, doctor, I've lost my memory.
Doctor: When did this happen?
Patient: When did what happen?

Patient: Doctor, doctor, my little boy's swallowed a bullet. What shall I do?
Doctor: Well, for a start, don't point him at me.

Patient: Doctor, doctor, I keep thinking I'm a pack of cards.
Doctor: Sit down. I'll deal with you later.

Patient: Doctor, doctor, I keep thinking I'm a dog.
Doctor: Lie down on the couch and I'll examine you.
Patient: I can't. I'm not allowed on the furniture.

Patient: Doctor, doctor, people keep ignoring me.
Doctor: Next please!

Patient: Doctor, doctor, I keep thinking I'm a spoon.
Doctor: Well, sit there and don't stir.

Patient: Doctor, doctor, I feel like a pair of curtains.
Doctor: Pull yourself together, man!

Patient: Doctor, doctor, my hair's coming out. Can you give me something to keep it in?
Patient: Certainly. How about a paper bag?

Patient: Doctor, doctor, my wooden leg's giving me a lot of pain.
Doctor: Why is that?
Patient: My wife keeps hitting me over the head with it.

(Time: 1 minute)

16.3 Relative clauses

A Answers

1 The person to whom I spoke on the phone said you were in a meeting.
   – *Very formal style.*
   The person I spoke to on the phone said you were in a meeting.
   – *Informal or neutral style.*

2 The doctor I spoke to yesterday told me not to worry.
   – *I've talked to other doctors about my problem, but the one I consulted*
     yesterday tried to reassure me (informal or neutral style).
   The doctor, whom I spoke to yesterday, told me not to worry.
   – *I normally consult only one doctor and when I talked to him/her*
     yesterday, I was reassured (formal style).
   The doctor, who I spoke to yesterday, told me not to worry.
   – *I normally consult only one doctor and when I talked to him/her*
     yesterday, I was reassured (informal or neutral style).
   The doctor to whom I spoke yesterday told me not to worry.
   – *I've talked to other doctors about my problem, but the one I consulted*
     yesterday tried to reassure me (formal).

3 She told us about the treatment, which made her feel better.
   – *Just telling us about the treatment improved her health, not*
     necessarily the treatment itself.
   She told us about the treatment that made her feel better.
   – *It was the treatment itself that improved her health.*

4 They operated on the first patient who was seriously ill.
   – *Several other less sick patients were not operated on: the very ill one*
     got preferential treatment.
   They operated on the first patient, who was seriously ill.
   – *Patient number one was very ill and he/she was operated on.*

B Answers (with commas added)

The Californians have come up with a device for
people **who** have their own small swimming pool,
which should transform their lives as much as
those indoor exercise bikes **which** were so
popular in the 1970s did. Swimming, **which** is
recognised to be one of the best ways of keeping
fit, is impractical in pools **that/which** are too small
for serious swimming. But the *Hydroflex* is a new
device **which/that** can keep swimmers in the same
spot and still allow them to do all the strokes. It

consists of a plastic bar **which/that** is attached to the side of the pool by two lines and to the swimmer by a waist belt. The swimmer, **whose** legs are protected from the lines by the bar, remains stationary while swimming. It sounds like an activity **that/which** is only suitable for people **whose** desire to keep in shape helps them to ignore the taunts of neighbours **who** happen to spot them in the pool.

C   Suggested answers (with commas added)

1   She's the only person I know **who runs/swims/walks** ten kilometres a day before breakfast.
2   I swam twenty lengths, **which took** me a long time.
3   He has two sisters, both **of whom are** doctors. The younger of the two, **whose name is** Jane, qualified last year. He also has two brothers, neither **of whom** know anything about medicine.
4   One of the children must have swallowed the pills **which had been/were** left in the bathroom.
5   All **of the things that/which** people say about hospitals are true.
6   She loves talking about her operation, **which makes** us all feel ill.
7   The matron is the **person who** is in overall charge of the nursing staff.
8   Taking a degree in medicine, **which takes much** longer than most other university courses, is the only method **by which/by means of which** one can become a doctor.

16.4   Homeopathy
Listening

A   [cassette] Before playing the recording, allow time for everyone to read through the questions.

Answers

1 a   2 c   3 b   4 d   5 c   6 d   7 c   8 c   9 b   10 c

11   ACONITE – a cold   SEPIA – migraine   SAND – depression   GOLD – lack of confidence + fear of failure   PETROLEUM + TOBACCO – travel sickness

Transcript

Presenter: ... Welcome back. Now, in our series on alternative medicine we've looked at chiropractic, acupuncture and herbal remedies. Today, Rachel Shaw reports on homeopathy. Now, this therapy has a relatively short history, I believe, Rachel.
Rachel: Er... compared with acupuncture, yes, I suppose it has. In fact, it was

invented by a German chemist called Samuel Hahnemann over 180 years ago. At that time it was already known that quinine, er... which is made from the bark of a tree that grows in the mountains of Central and South America, could be used to treat malaria. Well, in his first experiments, Hahnemann gave very strong doses of quinine to himself, his family and friends, who were all perfectly healthy people, and he found that they all developed exactly the same symptoms – it was as if they actually had malaria, which they didn't really, of course.

He then carried out more experiments, again using his friends and this time pupils as guinea pigs, getting them to take doses of 98 other substances, including lots of different herbs and even metals, like gold a... and sand, to find out what the effect of each one was – to find what symptoms developed. In this process of 'proving' the substances, over a period of 14 years he discovered that... er... for example, taking regular doses of arsenic caused vomiting and diarrhoea. So, in other words, he produced 'artificial' diseases.

Well, the crucial connection he made was between the cure and the illness, and this is one of the fundamental principles of homeopathy: treating like with like. He discovered that if patients suffering from the same symptoms, from natural diseases, were given minute doses of the same substance that caused the equivalent artificial disease, they actually got better. And he used the 'single blind' technique... er... whereby none of the patients knew if they were taking an inert powder or the medicine itself – only he knew.

Presenter: Now, you said 'minute' doses?

Rachel: Yes, yes the doses were very small indeed, in fact they're so small that the original substance couldn't be detected. You see, he found that by progressively diluting and shaking up the mixture its effectiveness actually increased. He added one drop of the substance, which he called the 'mother tincture' to 100 drops of water, shook it well and then added one drop of this to another 100 drops of water and shook it, and so on – each time adding one drop to 100 drops of water and shaking it till the dilution reached what's called '30C': that means a dilution of 1 over 10^{60}, that's 10 with 60 noughts. And this worked with any substance, even insoluble ones, like sand or... or gold. Er... the former is used to treat depression and the latter to treat lack of confidence or fear of failure.

Presenter: Yeah, if I could just stop you for a moment, how many molecules of the original substance would there be in this?

Rachel: Probaby none at all. In a '30C' dilution the odds are that one dose would not contain a single molecule of the original substance. You see, the effectiveness of the medicine rests on what's called 'succussion'. It's the shaking up of the diluted mixture at each stage that seems to be the crucial thing. If this isn't done, the mixture doesn't work. It's rather like a person walking across a field of snow – when the person's gone, there's nothing physical left behind except the footprints in the snow. Well, it's the 'footprints' of the molecules of the original substance that work on the body as a medicine, acting as a catalyst to the body's immune system, er... the mechanisms of the body that help it to resist and recover from diseases.

Now I know all this sounds very far-fetched but Hahnemann discovered that it worked, and other people found that it worked for them too. That's what validates it. One of the most prominent homeopaths was the American James Tyler Kent: his *Dictionary of Symptoms* is the standard work of reference that's still used today.

Presenter: So who uses homeopathy today?

Rachel: Well, there are two classes of medical practitioners: medically unqualified people, some of whom are quacks, and qualified doctors who use the same methods. With homeopathy the unqualified person can be just as effective as the doctor – there are no drugs involved and there can be no side-effects of a homeopathic medicine which only contains these 'footprints ' and no potentially harmful ingredients – homeopathic tablets are based on chalk and salt. Actually, self-medication is very effective too. The important thing is treating both the illness and the patient, because the treatment must suit the temperament of the patient as well as their symptoms.

Presenter: So what are the advantages of homeopathy over, well, more conventional forms of medicine?

Rachel: Well, first of all, for many patients it does work – it… it cures people. Secondly, as I said there are no side-effects, which makes it much safer than orthodox drugs like painkillers, tranquillisers – and certainly less harmful than drinking coffee or smoking cigarettes. And thirdly, anyone can learn how to use it – by carefully studying a person's symptoms and knowing their personality. Er…for instance, a mother can treat her children's minor ailments just as effectively as a doctor.

Presenter: But would *you* consult a homeopathic doctor?

Rachel: Oh, I do! I suffer from travel sickness sometimes in cars, planes and always on sea, and if I take drugs from the chemist they make me drowsy, and they don't often work. So I asked a homeopathic doctor, who recommended two medicines, one based on tobacco and the other on petroleum. I tried them both and as tobacco seems to suit my temperament best I always take my tobacco tablets (30C dose) when I'm travelling and I'm fine.

And I… I used to get migraine too. But now I take sepia tablets (the original substance is derived from the cuttlefish which is a kind of squid) and I find these work brilliantly – whenever I feel a migraine coming on, I take one every hour and then I don't suffer.

Presenter: OK. Well, at the moment I think that I've got a cold coming on, so what would you advise that I take?

Rachel: Well, it does depend on how your body reacts to having a cold, but one thing that works for me is aconite.

Presenter: Aconite?

Rachel: Mm, it comes from a poisonous plant called 'monkshood' – you can get the tablets from most chemists. They're cheap and all you have to do is to follow the directions on the drum. They're tiny tablets with a… a slight salty taste, very easy to swallow or you can just let them dissolve on your tongue.

Presenter: Right, I'll try some. Well, thank you, Rachel. And next week we'll be reporting on another branch of alternative medicine: hypnotherapy – that's treating illnesses by hypnosis – and that's at the same time next week.

(Time: 6 minutes 50 seconds)

16.5 Floating

A   This an exam-style exercise, with some answers 'annotated' as a guide to what is expected by the examiners in Paper 3 Part B. Students should read the passage right through before looking at the annotated answers.

B   Suggested answers

seedy – shabby and unfashionable   *seasoned* – experienced   *surge* – increase
snatches – short pieces   *vivid* – impressive, dramatic and full of detail
chemicals – drugs that change your mood   *tedium* – boredom   *bustle* –
excitement and movement

C   Suggested answers

3 It is a box into which no light or sound can penetrate, no larger than a
   small sauna; it contains salt water and loudspeakers
4 By playing them recordings of birds singing and flutes playing softly
5 They are no longer aware of time passing, they hear music and see images
6 Loud recordings of waves breaking and whales calling are played to them
7 Drugs have a detrimental effect on your body; meditation is extremely
   boring
8 Because of the contrast between the tranquillity and serenity of floating
   and the noise and commotion of going out into city streets

D   Model summary

The effects of floating were discovered by an American
scientist who was doing research into sensory deprivation.
He found that spending time in salt water in complete
darkness and silence enabled people to meditate, which
induced feelings of extreme happiness. What began as an
experiment became a craze which swept across the USA,
particularly after its appearance in a movie. In Britain,
where it is less well-established, over forty have opened
to the public in the last six years, encouraged by
recommendations from celebrities and doctors alike.

A   Answers (The endings have been rearranged in order of vividness with the most vivid one first – the order is very much open to discussion.)

1 . . . a river of sweat was pouring off him.
   . . . he was sweating like a pig. *(not very elegant-sounding)*
   . . . he felt very uncomfortable.
2 . . . I felt unwanted and unwelcome, as if I was an outsider.
   . . . I wished I had stayed at home.
   . . . I regretted having left home.
3 . . . we could hardly keep our eyes open.
   . . . we all started to nod off.
   . . . we found it hard to concentrate.
4 . . . I couldn't keep my mind on my work.
   . . . I couldn't sit still.
   . . . I was very excited.
5 . . . we soon looked like drowned rats.
   . . . we were soon soaked to the skin.
   . . . we got extremely wet.
6 . . . his heart skipped a beat every time he looked at her.
   . . . he couldn't keep his eyes off her.
   . . . he kept on looking at her.

B   Suggested answers (Ask the class to suggest alternatives: the ones given here are not definitive.)

I woke up feeling as if **I was dying**: my head was throbbing and my joints were aching so much that **I could hardly move them**. And I felt so dizzy that **the room was going round and round as if I was on a roundabout**.

I called the doctor to make an appointment. Over the phone the receptionist spoke to me as if **I was some sort of idiot** but when I walked in she treated me as if **I was a long-lost friend**.

I found a seat in the corner of the waiting room, which looked like **an airport departure lounge** . Sitting there waiting for my turn among the other patients reminded me of **the last job interview I had attended**. Looking round, my eyes came to rest on a young man smoking a cigarette, who looked as if **he had been through some awful experiences**. He had such a bad cough that it sounded as if **he didn't have long to live**. With him was a little girl who looked so unhealthy that **I felt really worried for her**.

By the time my name was called I was feeling rather better – it seemed as if **I had completely recovered from my illness**. I stepped into the doctor's room.

"What seems to be the trouble?" asked the doctor in a such a **stern,** abrupt voice that I **started to panic**. I described my symptoms to her, feeling a bit like **a naughty schoolchild who was wasting her time**.

"You've just got the flu," she said. "Go home, go to bed and don't waste my time." I felt so foolish that **I left the room without another word and went straight home**.

D   Answers

drink too much alcohol – He drinks like a fish.
drive fast – She drove like the wind.
have a row – They fought like cat and dog.
forgetful – I have a memory like a sieve.
run fast – She ran like the wind.
sleep well – I slept like a log.
extravagant – He spends money like water.
swim well – She swims like a fish.
be good friends – We got on like a house on fire.
very quickly – The news spread like wildfire.

16.7 Synonyms   Vocabulary development

A   Students may need reassuring that *bored, unemotional* and *cross* sound very similar, and without seeing the speakers' faces it's difficult to tell which is which. Some answers may have to be worked out by a process of elimination.

Answers

1 furious	5 unemotional
2 cross	6 friendly
3 kind	7 sad
4 bored	8 amused

Transcript

Presenter: Listen to each speaker and select a suitable adjective to describe their mood or tone.

(The Presenter gives the number before each speaker.)

Speakers: Ah there you are. I was wondering where you'd got to. Luckily I had some work to get on with so I wasn't bored. Anyway, even if the film has started by the time we get there, I don't think it'll matter – do you?

(The exact words used vary slightly from speaker to speaker.)

(Time: 2 minutes 30 seconds)

➡ Suitable synonyms and phrases which could also describe the tone of the speaker:

1 furious – livid, vehement
2 cross – annoyed, indignant, upset
3 kind – sympathetic, amiable, affectionate
4 bored – jaded, weary, fed up
5 unemotional – phlegmatic, matter-of-fact
6 friendly – cheerful, reassuring, welcoming, pleased, glad, positive
7 sad – depressed, despondent, upset
8 amused – delighted, enchanted, taking it as a big joke, finding the situation hilarious

B   Answers

amazed – astonished   *annoyed* – indignant   *clever* – talented   *confused* – bewildered   *cured* – better   *depressed* – despondent
determined – persistent   *different* – diverse   *disappointed* – disillusioned
dull – dreary   *encouraged* – heartened   *exciting* – thrilling   *frightened* – scared   *glad* – delighted   *respected* – admired   *revolting* – disgusting
shocked – horrified   *upset* – distressed   *worried* – anxious   *worrying* – disturbing

⚠ Note that the contexts and collocations of the words in the lists may not be the same and this should be discussed with the class. There are few exact equivalents when it comes to synonyms. Ask the class to suggest phrases incorporating the adjectives and participles with suitable collocations.

C   Suggested answers

1 Surfing can be **risky**, but hang-gliding is **a far more hazardous pastime**.
2 There are many **effective** ways of keeping fit **and jogging is a particularly effective way of keeping in shape**.
3 I was **delighted** to meet my old friends again. It was **wonderful to have the chance to talk** about old times.
4 I'm sorry that you were **under the weather** yesterday. You look **as fit as a fiddle** today.
5 It was **very generous** of you to offer to help, but the work wasn't **particularly demanding**.
6 We went for **an invigorating** walk at the weekend, ending up at a **delightful** restaurant.
7 The original novel was **entertaining**, but the film they made of it was **dreary**.
8 The meal we had last night was **delicious**, but the wine was **disappointing**.

9 Keeping in shape is **essential** and keeping your weight down is **equally vital**.

10 I **enjoy a visit to** the cinema, but I **appreciate an evening at the theatre even more**.

D Answers

1 take back
2 put up with
3 put you out
4 held up
5 made up   took us all in
6 came apart
7 came up with
8 go along with
9 brings on
10 get (it) through/across to them   got me down

16.8 Was Freud a fraud?   Listening

A 🔲 Answers

TRUE: 2 6 8 9 10 11 14 15 16 17
FALSE: 1 3 4 5 7 12 13 18

B Suggested answers

Suitable words to describe Prof. Abrahams:

> *vehement sarcastic scathing brusque urbane malicious energetic erudite quick-witted*

A psychologist studies human behaviour, a psychiatrist treats people who have mental or emotional problems.

Transcript

Presenter: In most people's estimation the Viennese psychoanalyst Sigmund Freud ranks with Copernicus, Galileo, Darwin and Einstein as one of the greatest scientists of all time, in fact a true genius. Well, how true is this? Professor Carl Abrahams says we've all been fooled too long. Is that right, Professor Abrahams?

Abrahams: Yes, the truth is that Freud is one of the most successful charlatans who ever lived. He pulled the wool over his contemporaries' eyes and his followers continue to pull the wool over people's eyes today. Now, just for a start: there's no evidence whatsoever that psychoanalysis has ever cured anyone of anything. It's become clear that Freudian psychoanalysis is pure hokum according to over 500 empirical studies of patients. Now, those who supposedly benefited from psychiatrists' treatment fared no better than those who were left to their own devices, indeed there's good evidence that it made some patients worse. Now, most professional psychiatrists know this very well, but the world is full of amateur psychiatrists like teachers, social workers, probation officers, and even parents, who attempt to apply misunderstood and speculative Freudian ideas.

Presenter: Speculative?

Abrahams: Yes, yes. Freud's so-called apparatus for explaining human behaviour is pure speculation. Also there... there's no concrete evidence that his methods even worked for him. For example, the so-called 'wolf-man', this man who had dreams of wolves sitting in a tree outside of his house: now, he had exactly the same symptoms and the same problems for the rest of his life after supposedly being cured by Freud successfully. Freud concocted a beautifully literary story but he omitted certain factual details and he actually added his own imaginative content. Now, this has been proved by detective work in other patients he treated. Very often he clearly made an erroneous diagnosis and his treatment was unsuccessful but he chose to ignore these cases. In other words, Freud appears to have been a brilliant novelist but a lousy doctor.

Presenter: Now, Carl Jung's main criticism of Freud's work was that he placed excessive emphasis on sexuality and on childhood experiences as being the origins of neurotic disorders, wasn't it?

Abrahams: Absolutely, his equation of pleasure with sexuality was unjustified. Now, it's caught the public's imagination and kept it for the whole of this century. Take the Freudian slip that people refer to when they make a slip of the tongue... er... for instance: 'the breast thing to do' instead of 'the best thing to do', you see. Now this is popularly supposed to be due to a man's desire to return to his mother's body, like Oedipus, but it's... it's all absolute rubbish of course.

Presenter: But how did Freud manage to fool people in the way you say he did?

Abrahams: Ah well, it's very interesting. Firstly, he consciously set out to create a myth of himself as the misunderstood and persecuted hero, whose books were disregarded and poorly reviewed. Well, nothing could be further from the truth. Now, just look at the medical journals of the time and you will find long and enthusiastic reviews of every one of his publications. Some were even commenting back then on his genius. Indeed, the greatest myth of all is that Freud was a genius, that... that his was a truly original mind at work. He is popularly supposed to have invented the unconscious. Well... again this is utter nonsense. People had been writing about the unconscious mind for 2,000 years before Freud, indeed it was being widely discussed by educated people long before Freud claimed it for his own.

For example, his so-called Freudian symbolism was common knowledge in Greek and Roman times and his supposedly new method of free association had been publicised by Sir Francis Galton years before Freud claims to have invented it. Now, other theories he claimed as original had been proposed by... er... Pierre Janet, for instance, and so on and so on.

Presenter: Well, all right, so Freud may have been a fraud, but how has his influence been harmful?

Abrahams: Well... er... three instances. Number one: by encouraging speculation instead of experimental studies. Er... number two: by encouraging... er... nebulous philosophising and so on. And number three: by discouraging rigorous clinical trials. Now, although Freud is not taken seriously by any self-respecting

professional any more, the psychoanalysts of the world are making a very good living from the gullibility of... er... the public, who still believe that Freud can not only explain their problems but even that he... that he knows how to cure them. In short, it'll be a long time before the myths, the utter myths, that Freud himself so... so artfully created can finally be expunged.
Presenter: Professor Abrahams, thank you.
Abrahams: You're welcome.

(Time: 4 minutes 30 seconds)

16.9   Exam techniques   Use of English

Discuss the annotated answers with the class before they attempt the remaining questions in A and B.

A   Suggested answers

4 If she had been less determined she wouldn't have been able to get better so quickly.
   If she hadn't been so determined . . .
   If she weren't so determined . . .
5 It is not very likely that he will qualify as a doctor.
6 Only after a long time did the patient recover completely from his illness.
7 Jane's unfitness is due to the fact that she doesn't take any exercise.
8 Contrary to his preconceptions, not all nurses are women.
   Contrary to what he thinks . . .

B   Suggested answers

3 you had
4 rather than having
5 time you
6 didn't matter/doesn't matter
7 must have been
8 we were missing/was going to happen/a terrible shock was in store for us, *etc.*

16.10   Dreams   Reading

This is an exam-style comprehension exercise – but with an opportunity for follow-up discussion.

A   Answers

1 d   2 b   3 c   4 b   5 d

B Follow-up discussion   If this arouses a lot of interest, the last question could be the basis for some written work with students showing the completed narrative to each other and challenging them to guess if it's true or invented.

16.11   A healthy life   Composition

A & B Encourage students to add to the ideas given in the Student's Book, and make it clear that they will have to leave quite a lot of ideas out to keep to the 350–word limit.

16.12   Mind, brain & word   Idioms

A   Suggested answers

1 promised
2 freedom from anxiety
3 telling him off
4 says frankly what he thinks
5 decide
6 couldn't decide
7 get a chance to speak
8 believe me
9 in my imagination
10 I forgot to do it
11 the ultimate in
12 your final decision

B   Answers

1 brainwave
2 picked your brains
3 go back on her word
4 word perfect
5 take your mind off
6 have a good mind to
7 word for word
8 it's their/his/her word against ours/mine
9 have/had something on your mind
10 play on words
11 change your mind
12 racking my brains   ≫→

➡ Here are some more related idioms for you to have up your sleeve:

She has *a good head for figures*   I can't *make head or tail* of this
Let's *put our heads together*   He is *off his head*
They found it hard to *keep their heads above water*
Success *went to her head*
In a crisis, try to *keep a cool head*   You've *hit the nail on the head*

You must be *out of your mind*   I've *half a mind to* . . .
Bear it in mind that . . .   *To my mind*, . . .

She was *as good as her word*   Could I *have a word with* you
You'll have to *take my word for it*

17 The past

A If your students are quite young and/or can't remember any of these events, the warm–up discussion should be done as a class.

B 📼 **Answers**

IN THE WORLD:
  Emperor Haile Selassie was **overthrown** in Ethiopia **1974**
  Gerald Ford became US President **1974**
  Greece became a **republic** and the monarchy was abolished **1974**
  Isabel Peron ousted in **bloodless** coup in Argentina **1976**
  Jimmy Carter elected President of the USA **1976**
  Presidents Sadat and Begin shared Nobel Peace Prize (1978)
  US President Nixon **resigned** after Watergate tapes scandal **1974**
  Pope John Paul II became first non-Italian pope since 1542 (1978)
DEATHS:
  Agatha Christie, age 85 **1976**   Aldo Moro murdered, age 62 (1978)
  Duke Ellington, age 75 **1974**   Juan Peron, age 78 **1974**
  Mao Tse-tung, age 82 **1976**   Georges Pompidou, age 62 **1974**
SPORT:
  Austrian driver Niki Lauda crashed in German Grand Prix **1976**
  Olympic Games in Montreal **1976** Winter Olympics in Innsbruck **1976**
  West Germany beat **Holland** 2–1 in Soccer World Cup **1974**
  Argentina beat Holland 3–1 in Soccer World Cup (1978)
OSCARS FOR BEST FILM OF THE YEAR:
  The Deer Hunter (1978)   *Rocky* **1976**
  The Godfather Part 2 **1974**
TECHNOLOGY & MEDICINE:
  First commercial flight of Concorde **1976**
  First **heart transplant** operation **1974**
  Many killed when poisonous gas escaped at Seveso, N. Italy **1976**
IN BRITAIN:
  First **McDonald's restaurant** opened in London **1974**
  The musical *Evita* opened in London (1978)
  Very hot summer: Minister for **Drought** appointed **1976**

⚠️ The events that happened in 1978 are not mentioned by the speakers, they are all 'distractors'.

C   In order to prepare short talks students will have to do some research. The ideal book to consult would be *Chronicle of the 20th Century* which is published in several languages. If the members of the class are all the same age, they should talk about the month they were born in, to give some variation.

The talks should last 2 to 3 minutes.

D & E   Follow-up discussion   These answers are for discussion, not 'correct answers'.

1 themselves   2 misfortunes   3 a guide   4 learnt anything from
5 differently   6 biography

Transcript

Lecturer: Right, now I asked you all to do some research and find out what happened in the year you were born. Yes? Has everyone done that? Fine. Right, Tony, would you like to start? What year were you born?

Tony: Um... the year was 1974. And... er... on the political scene in 1974 I suppose the most notable event, well the one that received most publicity, was the fact that President Nixon resigned and was forced to hand over the infamous Watergate tapes. Um... Vice-president Gerald Ford became President, he'd become vice-president when Spiro Agnew resigned after pleading guilty to tax evasion charges. And... er... Emperor Haile Selassie, 'Lion of Judah', was overthrown in Ethiopia. And... er... in Europe, Mr Karamanlis won the first free elections in Greece since before the Colonels siezed power, and Greece became a republic and the monarchy was abolished.

A few notable people died in 1974, among them Duke Ellington, famous jazz musician, and he was 75 when he died. And the President of France, Georges Pompidou died at the age of 62. Juan Peron died in Argentina, and his wife Isabel became the first woman president of the country.

Um... on the sports scene, er... West Germany won the World Cup, beating Holland 2-1, and... er... the captain of Germany at the time was Franz Beckenbauer.

Um... entertainment: *The Godfather Part 2* won the Oscar for the best film.

And... er... there was a breakthrough in the medical world... er... with the first heart transplant operation being carried out by Dr Christian Barnard in South Africa.

Oh, and... er... another of the major events of 1974 was... er... the first McDonald's restaurant opening in London!

Lecturer: Hm, great gastronomic moment in history! Thank you, Tony. Now who's next? Er... Jane, you were born in . . .?

Jane: In 1976. Um... political events in that year: Jimmy Carter was elected President of the USA, he beat Gerald Ford. And Isabel Peron was ousted in a bloodless coup in Argentina.

Um... famous deaths: there was Agatha Christie, who died at the age of 85, and Mao Tse-tung died in China, aged 82.

1976 was a leap year, and therefore an Olympic year and the Winter Olympics were held in Innsbruck, and the main... main Olympic Games were held in Montreal: a 14-year-old Romanian girl Nadia Comaneci won three gold medals for gymnastics. And Austrian racing driver Niki Lauda was seriously injured and very badly burned after a crash in the German Grand Prix.

Um... in the world of entertainment: er... the film *Rocky* got the Oscar for the best film, it's about Rocky Marciano the boxer.

Um... under the heading of technology . . . – it wasn't about Rocky Marciano . . .

Lecturer: Never mind, Jane, carry on!

Jane: Oh, I thought it was about him. But anyway, tech... in technology, there was a very bad accident at Seveso in Northern Italy, a cloud of poisonous gas escaped into the atmosphere and a... a great number of people were killed. Um... on a more positive side, there was the first commercial flight of Concorde – a British and a French Concorde took off simultaneously bound for Bahrain and Rio de Janeiro, um... part of the way they both flew at twice the speed of sound.

Oh, and then it was a very very hot summer in the UK, and a Minister for Drought was appointed!

Lecturer: And very soon sacked! Thank you very much, Jane. Er... now, who's next?

(Time: 4 minutes 20 seconds)

17.2 War poetry   Reading & discussion

Background information about the three poets can be found in Activities 10, 37 and 43, which the students will be looking at in C later.

A   The poems are recorded on the cassette. (Time: 2 minutes 20 seconds)

B Suggested answers (These are intended for discussion and should not be considered as a 'test of understanding'.)

1 England's scenery and people
2 in spring or summer   (or 'during peacetime'?)
3 his Englishness is immortal
4 the poem would still mean the same   (though it is arguable that all three answers are true here)
5 optimistic   (again a case could be made for the other answers)
6 has only just died
7 a man should grow up to die in this way
8 sardonic   (or 'resigned'?)
9 incompetent
10 two typical private soldiers
11 liked him   (or 'respected him'?)
12 sarcastic   (or 'serious' ?)

⟫➔

C ⬛ Students find out more about the three poets by looking at Activities 10, 37 and 43. Then there are questions for discussion.

17.3 The end of the war

Background

Robert Graves (1895-1985) served in the First World War as an officer. *Goodbye to All That* (1929) is an autobiography describing his war experiences. Graves was nineteen when the war began, and many of his friends and fellow officers died in the fighting. His prose works include *I, Claudius* and *The Greek Myths*, and his poems are to be found in any anthology of modern poetry.

Answers

1 b   2 b   3 b   4 c   5 d (the 'best' answer)   6 c

17.4 Adjectives + prepositions

A   Answers (with one suggested meaning for *it* or *them*)

1 Drink up: it's good for you. – *This medicine will have a good effect on you.*
   He was very good about it. – *He behaved in a kind, calm way in spite of the problem or difficulty he had been caused.*
   She is very good at it. – *She has a talent for a particular sport or activity.*
   She was very good to them. – *She was kind to the children.*

2 She was angry with them. – *Her anger was directed at the people who had done wrong.*
   He was angry about it. – *She found the situation (of being passed over for promotion?) annoying.*

3 I knew I was right about them. – *My intuitions about those people were correct.*
   The choice was right for them. – *The people who made the choice made the right one.*

4 We were pleased with them. – *We were delighted that the children had performed well, which made us feel proud.*
   He sounded pleased about it. – *He had been promoted and from his voice I gathered that he was glad.*
   We were pleased for them. – *The team had done very well, and we tried to share their pleasure (even though it had done us no good).*

5 She was sorry for them. – *She felt sympathetic towards the people who had suffered.*
He was sorry about it. – *He regretted what he had done (broken the window?).*

6 She was very popular with them. – *Her fans admired her.*
He became popular for it. – *He was admired for what he had done (had a hit record?).*

B Answers

ahead ashamed aware capable conscious critical devoid envious guilty intolerant proud scared short unworthy wary weary *of*

accustomed allergic comparable courteous cruel devoted equivalent hurtful identical impolite indifferent inferior irrelevant kind loyal preferable sensitive similar superior susceptible unfaithful *to*

⚠ Note that *different from, different to* and *different than* are all used in English, though some purists have strong feelings about the relative 'correctness' of some of these. As all are used, none would be considered incorrect by an examiner. Certainly no question would hinge on this in the Use of English paper.

C Answers

annoyed apprehensive bewildered curious dubious fussy guilty indignant sceptical vague *about*
famous responsible *for*
absent far free *from*
dependent intent keen *on*
annoyed comparable compatible consistent conversant familiar indignant level patient *with*

D Suggested answers

1 apprehensive sorry
2 kind proud annoyed impolite guilty good
3 critical accustomed responsible
4 indifferent sensitive sceptical aware hurtful
5 intent capable sorry wary

17.5   The emigrants

A   🎧 Answers

1 famine (failure of the potato crop)   religious persecution
  unemployment   harvest failure
2 nothing   lose
3 gold   New York   Kansas or Oklahoma
4

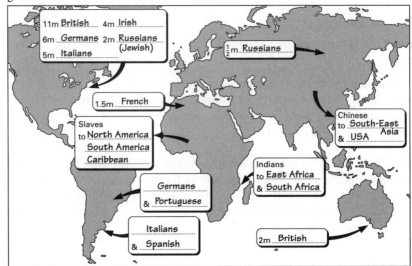

5 19th century
6 33 million
7 are the descendants of immigrants
8 looking through a telephone directory
9 form large, permanent communities in some countries
10 a rich mixture of different cultures (– though this answer may be open to
   discussion)

➡ Questions for discussion: if there are immigrants or members of ethnic
minorities in your class it may be circumspect not to use all these questions.

- What experiences do members of the class have of emigration?
- Have members of their family emigrated, or are they descended from
  immigrants?
- Would they consider emigrating themselves? If so, where to?
- What are the attitudes of people in their country to immigrants?
- Are there similarities between the position of immigrants, and of people
  who have newly arrived in a city from country areas?

Transcript

Lecturer: . . . so we can see from this that in the nineteenth century huge changes in
population took place which affected the entire world. The world population
grew from 900 million in 1810 to 1,600 million a hundred years later.
Throughout the century a pattern of voluntary and enforced emigration
developed. There were many reasons for people leaving their homes: the failure
of the potato crop in Ireland leading to famine on a massive scale, religious
persecution of the Jews in Russia, unemployment in industrial areas, harvest
failures in farming areas, and people forced off their farmland in Scotland by
landowners. But they all had one thing in common: the emigrants had nothing to
lose. Whatever happened to them at the end of their journey, it couldn't be worse
than what they were experiencing at home.

There were also the attractions of the New World, a place where according to
rumours cheap or even free agricultural land was on offer, where a penniless
immigrant could 'become a millionaire'. But of course the reality was different:
the streets were not paved with gold and reality for a poor immigrant could be
trying to farm a barren piece of land in Kansas or Oklahoma, or working for eight
cents an hour at a New York clothing factory. But still, there were opportunities,
and it was invariably better than the life they had left behind them.

First student: Um. . . can you tell us about the largest movement in the population,
where they came from and where they went to?

Lecturer: Yes, well the largest number of emigrants in the nineteenth century was
from Great Britain: eleven million went to the USA and Canada, two million to
Australia and New Zealand. Next came the Germans: six million to the USA and
many also to Southern Brazil.

Four million Irish people went to the USA, many as a result of the famine in
the 1840s – a million people died of starvation when the potato crop failed.

Um. . . five million Italians emigrated to the United States and many Italians
also went to Argentina.

Two million Russians, many of them Jewish, went to the United States – half
a million other Russians were forced to emigrate to Siberia, many to become
virtually slaves.

From Spain, people went to Argentina and other parts of South America, and
from Portugal especially to Brazil.

Large numbers of French people emigrated, mainly to North Africa,
particularly Algeria.

First student: Er. . . well, you've mentioned mainly only Europeans, but I take it it
wasn't just Europeans who emigrated?

Lecturer: Oh. . . no, by no means. Many people from India went to East Africa and
South Africa, many went to work temporarily as labourers on plantations and
never returned home.

And the Chinese went all over the Pacific: particularly to the various countries
of South-East Asia and also to the United States, where they helped to build the
railroads.

And we mustn't forget that the slave trade was still flourishing during the first
half of the 19th century: Africans were being shipped to North and South
America, and to the Caribbean.

Second student: And which country has received the largest amount of... of immigrants?

Lecturer: Well, as you can probably guess, it was the United States. Between 1821 and 1920 it accepted 33 million immigrants. Australia's population grew from a few thousand to five million by 1900.

Second student: And what... what are the effects of this mass exodus on the countries today? The implications today?

Lecturer: Well, that's an interesting question! Um... the numbers of second and subsequent generations grew and grew of course. There are said to be over 30 million Chinese people scattered around the world – in some Pacific countries, even where they are a minority, they effectively run much of the business and commerce of the nation.

If you go to Argentina, there are districts in Buenos Aires where you can still hear Italian being spoken. And there are German-speaking rural areas in Southern Brazil, where even second and third generation immigrants still speak German as well as Portuguese.

In the USA, the 'melting pot' effect has turned the descendants of all the 19th century immigrants into English-speaking Americans.

First student: Er... presumably lots of migrants will have been absorbed into the country that they have 'joined', as it were. Um... and it's not going to be obvious... for instance they will now speak the language perfectly. How can you find out, let's say, um... about these particular races... how... ?

Lecturer: Er... well, er... the way to find out... the best way to find out, if you go to a North or South American country, is to look in the local phone book. Even where people have been absorbed into the local population and intermarried, they've still kept their surnames. You see Swedish names in the Mid-West of the USA, Italian names and Jewish names in cities like New York, Ukrainian names in Pennsylvania, and in most cities you'll come across distinctive Polish names, Hispanic names and so on in the phone book.

In fact, very few countries have remained immune from the influence of immigration. Some of this has happened much more recently. Many Greeks, for instance, emigrated to Australia in the fifties and sixties: the third largest Greek community in the world (after Athens and Salonica) is in Melbourne.

Um... then of course huge numbers of people from Mexico and Central America have been emigrating to the USA since the 1940s. Um... furthermore, large numbers of Koreans emigrated to the USA in the seventies and eighties: the world's second largest Korean community lives in Los Angeles. And there are of course... Vietnamese people left their country in the seventies – you know, 'the boat people' – and they went all over the world . . .

(Time: 6 minutes 20 seconds)

17.6 Collocations   Exam practice

Suggested answers (The first word given is the one used in the original text – other variations are also possible.)

1 new/fresh   2 size/area   3 lead/example   4 domination/supremacy
5 race/ minority   6 destruction/downfall   7 war/slaughter/conflict   *etc.*
8 visible /stirring   9 uprising/ revolution   10 retrospect   11 phase
12 imprint/stamp   13 tempo/rate/ speed   14 spread
15 traditions/customs   16 process   17 ages   18 society   19 ill
20 wildfire

17.7 The life and achievements of . . .   Composition

This is the first of two composition exercises in this unit.

A   This task involves selecting which information to include and which to leave out, a problem which students often encounter when having to write about something they know a fair amount about.

B   It might be a good idea to decide in advance which national historical figure(s) everyone is going to write about, and discuss what kind of research might be necessary before writing.

17.8 Modifying adjectives & participles Vocabulary development

This section revises some of the points already covered in 6.5 Collocations: adverbs of degree.

A   **Answers** (*extremely pleased* and *extremely important* are OK. The others are wrong: it would be better to use *absolutely* instead.)

livid ✗ · indignant ✓   absurd ✗ · preposterous ✗ · improbable ✓
genuine ✗ · believable ✓   intelligent ✓ · sensible ✓ · brilliant ✗
happy ✓ · euphoric ✗   identical ✗ · similar ✓   priceless ✗ · valuable ✓
amazed ✗ · surprised ✓ · astounded ✗   interesting ✓ · fascinating ✗
worthless ✗ · futile ✗ · inexpensive ✓   delightful ✗ · pleasant ✓ ·
magnificent ✗ · enjoyable ✓   vital ✗ · essential ✗ · important ✓   fatal ✗ ·
hazardous ✓ · deadly ✗ · harmful ✓ · hurtful ✓   terrifying ✗ ·
frightening ✓

B   Suggested answers

1   He was **quite** determined to succeed, and he was **extraordinarily** disappointed when he didn't. We were **highly** amused, but pretended to be **really** sympathetic.
2   Many people were **seriously** injured in the accident, which was **widely** reported in the press.
3   The amount of work that is required is **considerably** greater than we expected, and we'll have to make a(n) **really** great effort to finish it on time.
4   We were **absolutely** delighted to hear he was getting married, especially to such a(n) **exceptionally** nice woman.
5   He was feeling **thoroughly** depressed after his illness, but he made a(n) **remarkably** quick recovery, and was **unexpectedly** cheerful after that.
6   We felt we had been **badly** let down when they told us the application had been rejected. We were **deeply** embarrassed because we'd told all our friends.
7   I'm sure her business will be **highly** successful, as she is a(n) **remarkably** capable person, even though it's **perfectly** true that most new businesses don't succeed.
8   It was a(n) **absolutely** wonderful film and I thought the performances were **deeply** moving. It was **totally** different from any other film I've ever seen.
9   They made a **thoroughly** good job of the report and we were **reasonably** pleased with it.
10   The role of women in history is not **fully** recognised by many historians, who tend to be **utterly** traditional in their attitudes.

C   Suggested answers

1   Some people find it is quite impossible to remember historical dates.
2   We should be absolutely delighted to accept your invitation.
3   It happened so long ago that it has been completely forgotten.
4   It's quite futile to ask him to be tactful.
5   She was absolutely livid when she found out.
6   It is totally improbable that he will succeed.
7   It is absolutely essential to remember to check your work through for mistakes.
8   We found the lecture quite fascinating.

17.9 Under exam conditions Composition

This is examination preparation: it could be done in class, but is best done 'under exam conditions' at home.

17.10 The interview Exam practice

➡ This section could be done earlier in the unit, if this would be more convenient.

A   Discuss what other questions might be asked about each photo and what issues might be raised about this topic.

B   Student A looks at Activity 13 where there is an extract from an editorial in *The Economist*, which appeared in the summer of 1989. Student B, looking at Activity 28, has an extract from a publicity handout on the history of coffee, published by Nescafé.

NOTE: In Activity 28 the phrase *to insure promptness* would be written as *to ensure promptness* in modern English.

C   This discussion activity does not involve an information gap. Both students look at the same information in Activity 20.

18 Modern life

→ If your students are doing the Listening and Interview some weeks before the written papers, make sure they are well-prepared for this by doing 18.5 and 18.6 in good time – before you reach this unit in the book, if necessary.

→ All of the sections in this unit can be done under exam conditions:

18.1 and 18.2 in 1 hour
18.3 in 2 hours
18.4 in 2 hours
18.5 in about 30 to 40 minutes
18.6 in about 15 to 20 minutes

18.1 Vocabulary and usage   Paper 1 Section A

A Answers

1 B   2 B   3 D   4 D   5 C   6 C   7 B   8 C   9 A   10 C   11 B   12 C
13 B   14 C   15 D   16 C   17 B   18 C   19 C   20 C   21 D   22 A   23 D
24 B   25 D

B   This discussion is about exam techniques. Further practice using *Cambridge Proficiency Examination Practice Books* is recommended, together with discussion of right and wrong answers.

18.2 Reading comprehension   Paper 1 Section B

Answers

A   FIRST PASSAGE   1 B   2 D   3 B   4 D   5 B

B   SECOND PASSAGE   1 A   2 D   3 D   4 B   5 A

C   THIRD PASSAGE   1 D   2 D   3 A   4 C   5 C

D & E   Some extra discussion questions:

- How do you feel in a crowd? Have you ever been in a tightly packed crowd, at a sports event or a demonstration, for example – what was it like? Do you feel vulnerable when alone in a house?
- What are the public transport facilities like in your city? How are people discouraged from driving their cars into the city? How should transport be improved for commuters in your city?
- Are vehicles clamped in your city? Is this done by the police or by private security firms? Can someone charm or bribe their way out of paying parking fines in your city?

18.3   Two compositions

These compositions could be written in class under exam conditions – or to save time in class, set for homework under self-imposed exam conditions.

In the case of Question 5, you should add a question that relates directly to the prescribed text your students have read.

More information on assessment – different criteria apply to Question 5:

1 A composition which is ambitious in scope and using high-quality language with a few native-speaker type mistakes would score 16 to 20.
2 A well-developed realisation of the task which is natural and appropriate in style but with a few errors would score 11 to 15.
3 A reasonably attempted realisation of the task using structures and vocabulary which communicate the writer's ideas in a clear but limited manner would score 8 to 10.

4 A composition which neither extends nor explores the topic area, and which shows a lack of control of language and numerous errors would score 5 to 7.
5 A composition which is grossly irrelevant or too short, containing errors and narrow vocabulary which prevent communication, would score 1 to 4.

➡ Refer to *Cambridge Proficiency Examination Practice* TEACHER'S BOOKS for a more detailed marking scheme together with sample compositions and Examiner's comments.

1   Cloze test   Suggested answers (The first word is the one that appeared in the original article.)

1   subjects/topics
2   state/condition
3   become
4   designed
5   problem
6   infuriating/annoying
7   few
8   way
9   endless/continuous
10 working/effective
11 systems/streets
12 generates/creates
13 merely/only
14 zones/streets/precincts
15 banned
16 closely/carefully
17 date
18 suffice/work
19 suburbs
20 help

2   Transformations   Suggested answers

1   Whenever we meet again, we'll remember these days together.
2   Much as I admire her achievements a great deal, I loathe her as a person.
3   If he hadn't been reprimanded he wouldn't be feeling so upset.
4   I'd rather you admitted that you're to blame, and didn't try to conceal it.
5   Only later did I realise that I had been swindled.
6   Due to an increase in the number of robberies, the police are advising vigilance.
7   There is little likelihood of his being convicted of the offence.
8   I wish my story had sounded more convincing.

3   Fill the gaps   Answers

1   though they were   4   have I heard of/have I read about
2   must have been   5   Nevertheless/But   in escaping
3   however small   6   to living/working   neither/nor did

4   Use the word given   Suggested answers

1 The work of the police depends on the cooperation of the public.
2 She was afraid to scream/She didn't scream for fear of waking up the neighbours.
3 The accident was no one's fault.
4 They have had their flat broken into twice this year.
5 Her journey to work every day takes an hour.
6 It is doubtful/I am doubtful whether they will arrive on time because of the heavy traffic.
7 You may not be able to rely on him as much as you think.
8 What I hate is the stresses and the pressures of modern life.
  The stresses and pressures of modern life are what I hate.

5   Questions and summary   Suggested answers

1 They are expected to give their provisional approval to the scheme.
2 Because of its small size and lack of sprawling suburbs, and because large numbers of residents use their cars to get to work.
3 Because its traffic is already as bad as London's and is likely to get even worse as more and more people work in the city – the traffic might prevent the city's expansion.
4 They might change the character of the city and discourage tourists.
5 His own idea
6 By charging motorists for being in stop-start traffic, it would encourage them to travel at less busy times.
7 Nothing, the meters will be fitted free (they'll only have to pay for their 'smart card').
8 When the units on the card have run out, the petrol supply is cut off next time you start your car. So, if you stall in traffic, you wouldn't be able to restart your car and this would hold everyone else up.
9 After the council has approved the scheme, there has to be further research followed by a pilot scheme. Finally, before the scheme could be implemented, it would have to be approved by Parliament.
10 There is no mention of this in the article, we can only assume that they would be exempt from the charges, or have to use park and ride car parks.
11 **Model summary**

> Every car would be fitted with a meter into which the driver would insert a card containing pre-paid units. The meter would be turned on by a beacon when the motorist entered the city limits. Motorists would pay according to how much stopping and starting they were involved in. When all the units had been used up, the

motorist would insert a new card, otherwise the petrol
supply to the car would be cut off next time he or she
tried to start the car. The proceeds of the scheme
would help to finance a super-tram line across the city.

➡ Remind everyone how important it is to rephrase information in the
Questions and summary section, using your own words. But don't waste too
much time searching for a synonym for every word. If time is running out,
answers in note form are better than blanks. Marks are lost for irrelevancies
and incoherence.

18.5 Listening comprehension   Paper 4

🔲 🔲 Play each part TWICE, allowing students time to read the
questions through before each playing. Set the counter to zero between
sections, so that you can find the beginning again easily.

A   Rules and values   Answers
1 D   2 B   3 C   4 A   5 D   6 C   7 B   8 A

B   A New York cop   Answers
1 disturbed   2 problem   3 negative   4 rewarding
5 delivered   enriched   6 take   7 society   anarchy   8   grey

C   A British police officer   Answers
4   5   8   9   11 & 12   are true
1   2   3   6   7 & 10   are false

Transcript

A

Presenter: Part A. Rules and values. You'll hear an interview with Dr James White,
who is a sociologist.

Interviewer: Dr White, as a sociologist, you're an expert on the patterns of behaviour
that exist in different societies and on the rules that are followed. What is meant
by a 'rule' in this case?

Dr White: Now, that's an interesting question. Well, we must make a distinction
between a rule and a law. Both may have equal power but a law is a written-down
version of a rule of behaviour. Now, to understand the power of rules, I'll give
you an example, let's take chess. To understand what's going on in a game of
chess you have to know the rules that are being followed and to play you have to

follow the same rules. You have a choice of moves to make but they must all obey the appropriate rules, and so likewise in society. The trouble is that these rules may be mostly internalised, we don't realise that we're following them. For example, the rules of our mother tongue, the way we speak. Now, we don't have to obey the rules – if we're losing a game we can spoil it by cheating or by refusing to continue playing.

Interviewer: Yes, but to take up your chess analogy, we know that our aim is to win so that's the purpose of the game.

Dr White: Well, don't ask me what the purpose of life is, but playing chess is also a way of organising time and interaction... er... the rules of society have the same purpose. If we act in ways that other people approve of, then they reward or praise us; and if we act in ways they disapprove of then they can show their disapproval or punish us by taking away our life or our freedom or our physical comfort or our goods. In Western society these punishments are all controlled by written-down laws and people who are punished are called 'criminals'. But parents or teachers may in some cases have their own rules that entitle them to punish the children that they're responsible for.

Interviewer: But surely the majority of adults conform to the rules and laws because they want to, not because they fear punishment if they don't?

Dr White: Absolutely, the strongest motive is the desire to conform. Also we're very sensitive to approval, for example, we suffer an agony of embarrassment if we do something supposedly wrong in public. It's the existence of a shared set of rules that makes it possible for there to be stable patterns of social interaction. We play roles which have different er... role expectations. For example, a teacher gives lessons and instructions and a pupil attends and follows. If everyone accepts the rules then any deviance is inhibited by this.

Interviewer: Another factor is the sharing of values within a society, isn't it?

Dr White: Yes, absolutely, for a complex society to operate, its members all have to subscribe to the same set of values. Values represent a consensus of what is good or right. Now, they may be part of a... say a religious or a political system: Protestantism, socialism, capitalism, etc. For example... um... in the USA success is sometimes said to be the controlling value of all social endeavour... er... whether in work, in sport and school, whatever. Acceptance of the same values creates solidarity and unity among all the people. We associate with people who share the same values as us, well, we like them more than those who have different values.

Interviewer: Of course. No society's perfect and there are likely to be many contradictory and ambiguous rules.

Dr White: Oh sure, and no society could ever eliminate these but the fact that there is social harmony to a great extent suggests that there are many more rules and values that are shared in common. But in any society there's likely to be deviance from the rules and values. There are two ways that this deviance can manifest itself: er... there's dropping out for example in... in the US, where... er... financial success may be hard to obtain by someone who is... is poor or illiterate or has no skills. Then... er... dishonesty or taking drugs or getting drunk, becoming a tramp or a hobo all these things may be ways of dropping out. Alternatively, a reaction may be to rebel, to rebel against society... er... substituting new values and rules. This can be considered as... as positive, it

leads to finding ways of altering values for the benefit of a changing society, or it
can. But more often it's considered anti-social, for instance it manifests itself in...
er... in street gangs and... er... the criminal sub-culture, etc.
Interviewer: Mm, though the terms positive and anti-social would be the ones used
by the members of the society in question?
Dr White: Oh yes, that's right. Well, they're not objective terms.
Interviewer: Dr White, thank you.

(Time: 4 minutes 30 seconds)

B

Presenter: Part B. A New York cop. You'll hear an interview with a New York cop.
We asked him to talk about his job. This interview was recorded on location.
New York Cop: I'm a New York City police officer. Yeah, I spent sixteen years on
patrol, that's twenty-two years in the police department... er... the last six years I
spent in an investigatory capacity. Er... I work with youth now... er... what I
mean by youth is children under sixteen. All right, I'm talking about a patrol
officer, right, these are the guys that you see out in the radio cars or on foot...
er... walk... patrolling the streets of the city of New York. They... er... they're
out there twenty-four hours a day, seven days a week, all weather, all the time.

Er... all right... hm... stressful, like I always thought it was stressful. Er...
number one: you're dealing with people, large amounts of people, specially in a
city this size, seven-eight million people... er... you're dealing with all kinds of
people. Many... many of these people are mentally **disturbed** – quite a few of
them are – I mean, let's face it, who... who calls a cop? What do you call a cop
for? Only when it... there's a **problem**. I mean, nobody... nobody ever calls a
cop over to say, 'Hey, how are you doing, officer? Have a nice day,' you know.
Really, at least not in my experience. Usually when people have been mugged,
robbed, got a... assaulted, er... somebody's dead, somebody's dying, and you see
the **negative** side of society.

Er... you do become jaded after a while. Er... you try not to, but it does, it
does jade you, you become cynical. Er... huh... it... it's a tough job. I guess that
the stress is always there, you never know what you're dealing with, you never
know what kind of situations you're going into. You... some of them are very
rewarding: I've **delivered** two babies myself in twenty-two years, that was a
very very per... personally I think it **enriched** me so much... er... just the
experience alone. Er... I've saved a few lives. I've... er... I've never had to **take** a
life, thank goodness, in twenty-two years. I've been in a few serious situations, a
couple of combat situations, er... I've been shot at, stabbed, er... kicked, spit at.

I mean, let's face it, er... cops represent **society**, you know, without law you
have **anarchy**, so you have to have law, you have to have police, the police
enforce the law. Er... the one thing I really don't care about, it's black and white,
you know and we have to enforce that, there are no grey areas in the law, but
when you're dealing with people, there are **grey** areas, let's face it. So a police
officer has a lot of responsibility on him, and I guess that's about it for the job.

(Time: 3 minutes 20 seconds)

C

Presenter: Part C. A British police officer. You'll hear an interview with a senior police officer. She begins by introducing herself...

Kate Gooch: I'm Chief Inspector Kate Gooch. Er... my office is situated in the middle of Cambridge... er... which is obviously one of England's most famous cities, but the area I actually work is the rural area which surrounds Cambridge. The city itself is not my responsibility. Cambridgeshire Constabulary... er... I mean, in this country the constabularies are divided up into counties. Each county has its own constabulary, which covers a territorial area, unlike some countries where you have a national traffic police or a national security police. So... er... we police in geographical areas. Now, Cambridgeshire itself is sub-divided into six geographical or territorial areas... um... and I am the deputy commander for one of those six areas. And in that area we have total responsibility for policing... all the aspects of policing.

Presenter: Are the problems different in a rural area?

Kate Gooch: In some ways, yes, the problems are different. In other ways the problems are exactly the same. I think for as long as you're dealing with human beings the problems are going to be very similar. But we don't have the kind of inner city problems which the bigger city conurbations have.

Presenter: What kinds of police work has she been involved with?

Kate Gooch: I've turned my hand to just about everything over the years... er... I've been out on... as a constable. I started off in a policewomen's department because in those days the policewomen worked separately from the men, very much as the armed forces do. But i... in the mid-70s we were integrated so that men and women were doing exactly the same job. And after that I've done foot patrol, and I've done patrol in the cars, and I've also done various specialist jobs, in for example, recruiting, in charge of the force control room and... um... well, quite a wide range.

Interviewer: Why did she decide to join the police force?

Kate Gooch: Er... I was originally a customs officer and when I got married I was unable to get a posting in this part of the country, which is where my husband was stationed, and therefore I was looking about for some other job. Having worked in a uniformed job, in a job where I was in a position of some... er... authority over members of the public really, I felt that perhaps I could transfer the kind of knowledge that I'd learnt there, dealing with the law, dealing with the public, er... dealing with all sorts of people internationally, perhaps I could transfer that into something like the police force, and so that's what I did.

Presenter: To what extent does police work involve dealing with people?

Kate Gooch: Well, without people we wouldn't have a job! The police force is all about dealing with people, whether you're dealing with somebody who's lost their keys or found a stray dog or wants to cross the road and is... er... blind or... or handicapped in some way. From the very elementary things like that up to dealing with people who perhaps have lost a relative in a road accident and you have to break the news to them, or whose house has been burgled and is very very distressed and... er... needs some kind of support as well as needing the practicalities of being advised on locks and bolts and needs somebody to go out and try and solve the crime. Er... right up to dealing with the murderer or the...

the person who's been assaulting a small child – um... this job is all about people.

I think probably the majority of our time our interaction with the public is on what might almost be called a social level, although that's perhaps... um... exaggerating it a little bit. The number of times that you... or the number of hours that you spend arresting murderers and rapists is absolutely minimal. The number of hours that you spend in public... in situations of public disorder is minimal. The number of times that you are... er... dealing with members of the public who've had some crime committed against them, who've lost their bike, who want directions to somewhere is very great indeed.

Presenter: Do police officers sometimes get affected emotionally by what they have to do?

Kate Gooch: I think it's inevitable, yes. For as long as we're recruiting from the human race, you can try to be professional, you can try to be detached, but in some ways if you're not treating people with sympathy and empathy and understanding you're almost not doing your job very well. But I think this is something that's only been recognised in recent years, I think until even just a few years ago it was assumed that police officers were almost robots and could handle anything and deal with anything without feeling involved at all in any way. Um... I think this was a mistake and I'm sure it created problems for a lot of people, trying to present this sort of very macho image whether you're male or female, that you really could take anything and didn't need any help at all.

We now understand that it puts additional stresses on officers if they're not able to talk about experiences, or if they feel they have to conceal them. Um... I used to find when I was a sergeant many years ago that a probationer, that's a very young constable in the first two years of service, er... would be sent to deal with something fairly horrific and if I could either go with them and say to them, 'Look, this is going to upset you if you're a normal person. Don't worry about it, you'll come out the other side. Er... better accept that you may have nightmares about it, or you may feel very stressed about it, or you may feel unable to talk about it. Because not everyone wants to go home to wife and family or husband and family and talk about some of the horrendous things they've dealt with. If you can accept that now before you go and realise it's a normal process, then you'll be better off than if you think, " I'm the only one who feels bad about this issue and... and I can't talk about it in case someone thinks I'm weak and incompetent." '

Presenter: What is the attitude of the public to the police?

Kate Gooch: I think... er... most members of the public are very supportive of what we try to do, but quite rightly they feel entitled to criticise us if we don't do things in the way that they want us to do or expect us to do. Nevertheless I feel there is a little... um... a little wariness about the police. You know, if... if you realise by looking in your rear-view mirror that you are driving right in front of a marked police car, your behaviour probably does change: you have a quick glance at the speedometer and realise you really must slow down because you are in a built-up area. Um... if you see a police officer approaching your house coming to knock on your front door, your first thoughts are probably, 'What have I done wrong?' or 'What is this bad news that this officer's coming to tell me?' rather than 'Oh, how pleasant, a social call from the police!' – and I think that's understandable.

Presenter: What's it like to be a police officer?

Kate Gooch: There is a sense of belonging, of camaraderie – one doesn't necessarily like or wish to be personal friends with other individuals in the police force but there is a sense of mutual support in the organisation... um... which is... is quite a good feeling.

(Time: 7 minutes 10 seconds)

18.6 Interview: law and order — Paper 5

A, B, C & D If at all possible, arrange for a colleague to play the part of Examiner in mock interviews for each member of your class. Doing this will enable everyone to feel much more relaxed when they come to do the real thing.

Some of these could be done in front of the class and helpful advice offered afterwards in follow-up discussion.

➡ See *Cambridge Proficiency Examination Practice* TEACHER'S BOOKS for detailed marking schemes for the Interview.

Finally, twelve more tips for the exam:

1 If you're taking part in a one-to-one interview with the examiner, don't feel you have to keep talking if there is an embarrassing silence. Give the examiner time to introduce the next task or topic.

2 If you're taking part in a 'paired' interview with another candidate, don't keep interrupting each other: wait until the other candidate has finished his/her sentence. The examiner will make sure you both get a chance to have your say.

3 Read the rubrics carefully and make sure you follow the instructions exactly – especially in Paper 2.

4 Use a highlighter or pencil on the exam paper itself – you *are* allowed to make notes on it.

5 Check through everything you have written for mistakes: grammar, spellling, punctuation and vocabulary.

6 Don't skimp on paper in the exam: leave plenty of space for amendments and corrections. Leave a wide margin, a couple of blank lines between paragraphs and even a couple of blank lines at the end of each page. Write clearly.   ≫→

7 Stay calm – use your time wisely. If there's time to spare, re-read and re-re-read your work, looking for places where it can be improved.

8 Don't spend too long on the hardest questions to the detriment of the rest of a paper. Do the easier questions first and come back to the trickier ones later. Make a pencil mark beside any that you're missing out so that you can spot them again quickly later.

9 Although the exam tends to follow a predictable pattern, don't panic if there is a 'new' item. Expect the unexpected. And don't worry if parts of the exam are unexpectedly difficult – they're probably equally difficult for everyone else.

10 Don't leave any blanks – if you don't know an answer, first eliminate any obviously wrong answers and then guess!

11 Go to the exam armed with all the equipment you'll need: several pens, pencils, highlighters, rubbers, rulers – at least TWO of each!

12 Read the rubrics carefully *again*. Make sure you follow the instructions exactly!

PLUS . . .

Your own tips, based on the foibles and proclivities of your students:

➡ Remind everyone to look again at the ★ ★ Exam tips in the Student's Book before they do each paper in the exam. Perhaps insist that each student writes down the six main points he or she must remember in the exam.

Acknowledgements

The author and the publishers are grateful to the authors, publishers and others who have given permission for the use of copyright material identified in the text.

p.97 Jonathon Porritt and Dorling Kindersley for the extract from *Save the Earth* by Jonathon Porritt; p.195 Jonathan Cape Ltd for the extract from *Pilgrim's Way* by Abdulrazak Gurnah; p.227 'Nighthawks' by Edward Hopper, American, 1882–1967, oil on canvas, 1942, 76.2 × 144 cm, Friends of American Art Collection, 1942.51, photograph © 1991 The Art Institute of Chicago. All Rights Reserved.

Notes

Notes

Notes

Notes

Index